# THE
# FISHING
# CLUB

## BROTHERS AND SISTERS
## OF THE ANGLE

*For Peter*
*A Second Creek Legend*

### BOB RICH

*Tight lines!*

*Bob Rich*
*6-10-06*

THE LYONS PRESS
Guilford, Connecticut
An imprint of The Globe Pequot Press

Copyright © 2006 by Robert E. Rich, Jr.

The Lyons Press is an imprint of The Globe Pequot Press.

10 9 8 7 6 5 4 3 2 1

Printed in the United States of America

Designed by Maggie Peterson

ISBN-13: 978-1-59228-929-5
ISBN-10: 1-59228-929-0

Library of Congress Cataloging-in-Publication Data is available on file.

# CONTENTS

THE MOST HUMBLE FISHERMAN has this in common with fishermen of all degrees. Even the thousandth trip to the same old familiar fished-out stream begins with renewed hope, with unfailing faith, *Quien sabe?* as the Spaniards say. You cannot tell what you might catch. And even if you do not catch anything the joy somehow is there. The child is father to the man. Saturdays and vacation times call everlastingly. The pond, the stream, the river, the lake and the sea! Something evermore is about to happen. Every fishing trip is a composite of all other trips; and it holds irresistible promise for the future. The cup cannot be drained. There are always greater fish than you have caught, always the lure of greater task and achievement, always the inspiration to seek, to endure, to find, always the beauty of the lonely stream and open sea; always the glory and dream of nature.

—Zane Grey,
Introduction to *Tales of the Angler's Eldorado,*
New Zealand

To Jenna, Nate, Nico, Amelia, Connor, Eric, Ali

Just as it is the obligation of grandparents
to spoil "the kids," so too is it our responsibility
to teach them to fish

# ACKNOWLEDGMENTS

Every writer needs a good editor—whether he or she admits it or not—and I had the best. Holly Rubino helped me refine my thinking and writing. I owe her my thanks. I'd hate to have tried to finish this book without her. I also want to thank my copyeditor Melissa Hayes.

Speaking of editors, my friend Jay Cassell from *Field & Stream* magazine has honored me by writing the foreword. Thank you, Jay.

Thanks also to my agent Lisa Queen, who represented me, and to my longtime assistant Elaine Gallagher, for not losing her sense of humor with me and my never-ending rewrites as well as my publicist C. J. Purdy.

Finally, I want to thank my wife Mindy for inspiring me with innovative and thoughtful suggestions for improving my text.

# FOREWORD

I FIRST MET Bob ("Bubba") Rich in 1999, when I was working as the senior editor of The Lyons Press. Back then, the press was independently owned, a small publishing house that specialized in fly-fishing books. We were located on the sixth floor of an older building on West 18th Street, in a part of New York known as Chelsea. Our offices were a wreck—manuscripts, page proofs, and books were piled everywhere; duct tape held the carpeting together; and all the walls were dreadfully in need of a new coat of paint. There was no time for that, though. We were a publishing house, a beehive of frantic activity: Everyone was either on the computer, on the phone, reading manuscripts, or scurrying about the office, working with ad salesmen, publicists, designers, and proofreaders. There wasn't much time for anything other than the books.

Into the middle of all this hustle and bustle came Bob and Mindy Rich, looking somewhat bewildered at all that was going on in this maze of offices, cubicles, tables, and bookshelves.

"Jay," our head sales rep said, sticking his head into my doorway, "I've got this guy out here who wants to write a fishing book. He's never written a book before. Can you just talk with him for a minute?"

Hard in the middle of working on a new book by Dave Whitlock, I remember thinking to myself that this was the last thing I needed right now. But, you never know what could happen, so I looked up and said sure, bring him in.

Bob and Mindy were in my office in a minute. After introductions, Bob sat down and launched right into a description of his book.

"It's called *Fish Fights,*" Bob said, "and it's about my quest to catch ten species of gamefish on specific types of tackle." Bob—his friends call him Bubba—went on to explain that by so doing, he qualified for the Metropolitan South Florida Fishing Tournament Hall of Fame.

"There's a lot of good fishing in the book," he continued. "Plus, I've written about all the people who helped me do it, and all the crazy stuff that goes on in the Florida Keys. You're gonna like it, I just know."

There was something about Bob's boyish enthusiasm that was contagious. Before I knew it, I was agreeing to take a look at the manuscript. And you know what? I'm glad I did. *Fish Fights* turned out to be exactly what Bob and Mindy said it would be—a fun-to-read book about fishing and real people. Bob's passion leaps off the pages, and you wish you could be down in the Keys with him, fishing for bonefish, permit, or any of the other ten fish he caught to achieve his goal.

Now Bob has done it again, with *The Fishing Club.* Bob told me about his second book project a few years ago, while we were dolphin fishing in a tournament out of Islamorada. (Don't ask me how we did— we had lots of fun, with Rusty Albury at the helm, but the results were pretty unimpressive.) I was still with The Lyons Press at the time, and I had to admit, I had my doubts about this new venture. A book about random people who fish? Who cares? Bubba disagreed with me, and said he'd send me a few chapters once he finished his research. Having been down this road with him on *Fish Fights,* I agreed, and damn, he was right again. I liked what I saw. His quest to find out exactly *why* people fish really intrigued me. I've always wondered why I like to fish so much, and it was fun to see what other people had to say. Bob has a way of making people feel at ease; his one-on-one, down-homey interviewing style encourages people to reveal their true feelings, no matter if they are the former President of the United States (George H. W. Bush) or a retired steelworker who has been fishing from the same spot on the same pier in the Niagara River every day for forty-one years.

Ultimately, everyone in this book is a member of the angling fraternity; Bob's a member of that fraternity, and I am too. If you bought this book, chances are that you're a member as well. And, as Bob discovers, we all fish for different reasons, and the same reasons. At first, Bob thought he would find that optimism and patience were the two common traits of all fishermen. But he discovered it's a lot deeper than that, as you'll find out when you read *The Fishing Club*.

Jay Cassell
Deputy Editor, *Field & Stream*
February 2006
New York City

# INTRODUCTION

*Man never stands on more common ground than when he's fishing.*

—Forrest L. Wood

I LIKE PEOPLE WHO FISH. They are categorically the most positive, optimistic people in the world. It's never a question for them of whether the glass is half empty or half full. Most anglers see the glass as full and running over. Maybe that's because they actually see it as half full and then lie about the other half.

I have been blessed with some great friendships made through fishing and have written this book about some of those friends. They come from all walks of life and fish with different kinds of tackle in different waters across the country. One of these friends, in fact, travels around the world in search of fish while another never budges from his spot on a hometown pier, preferring to let the fish come to him. One friend kills everything he catches while another is content to just observe fish in their natural environment. One friend loves Alaska; another stays in salt water and is scared to death of bears, while yet another once stared down a tiger on his way to a river in India.

Being "rich and famous" was not part of the criteria for their selection, but some are one or both. "Interesting" was a prerequisite, and I believe all of these friends are—but I'll let you be the judge of that.

I set out not only to celebrate their differences but also to discover if there was a common interest that drew them, like all of us anglers, to the water and the pursuit of fish. What I found out was somewhat unexpected, but I hope you'll agree, very interesting.

I hate long introductions, so let's get started. My methodology was simple: I asked each angler to tell me his or her favorite fishing story. Then I set out to profile them as individuals and anglers, being as objective as possible, notwithstanding the fact that they are all my friends. I hope that you too will enjoy spending time with them, in these pages.

One of the first things I learned about all of the anglers I chose to profile is that regardless of their means, they are all humanitarians who have made significant commitments of their time or money to one or more charities. In appreciation of their patience with me during the research and writing process, I am donating the proceeds of this book in their names to their favorite charities, listed with their e-mail addresses later in the Epilogue.

# THE
# FISHING
# CLUB

The wildness and adventure that are in fishing still recommend it to me.

—Henry David Thoreau, *Walden* (1854)

1

# JOHN BAILEY:
# ENGLISH ADVENTURER

———◆◆◆———

*I grew up in the north of England where the fishing is, as char-*
*itably as I can say it, difficult. In fact, when I was a child start-*
*ing out, I fished for two and a half years and never even caught*
*a fish, but I kept at it.*

*Then one day, my grandmother took me to a beautiful lake*
*to fish. Hope was running high. We baited the hook, attached a*
*bobber to the line, and cast out as far as we could. About half an*
*hour later, the bobber started going up and down. I'd never*
*fished with a bobber before. I had no idea of what to do and my*
*grandmother didn't either, but I set the hook and reeled in the*
*line. It was a big green frog.*

—John Bailey

CAN YOU BELIEVE IT? After a lifetime of loving waters, compelled, as
he says, "almost since crawling to learn how water works, how it curls and
creates its own world"; after a lifetime of passion for seeing and understanding fish, "more and more fish, always seeking to complete a cosmic
vision," and with more than thirty fishing books to his credit—not to

mention several television and radio shows on the subject, plus leading several expeditions to some of the most remote fisheries on the planet; and even after pondering the question for three days—internationally renowned author and photographer John Bailey's favorite fishing story is about catching a frog with his grandmother. I believe that for John, like many of the others I chose to profile here, the love of fishing is deeply rooted in their earliest family memories. To these people, the largest fish ever caught may not be as important as a first catch made with a loved one. I found John to be one of the most interesting and unusual people I've ever fished with. As prolific a writer and articulate a storyteller as he is, John seems to be painfully shy, proficient at deflecting questions about himself and turning them into discussions about rivers and fishing—two-way conversations where he can learn as well as teach.

My wife Mindy and I got to know John and his wife Joy on a fishing trip they set up and shared with us in 2002 on the beautifully historic Test River in England—the Mecca or birthplace of fly fishing. While we hadn't previously met, I had become a fan of John's many books. Never had I read anyone who articulated the sport of fishing as he did in books like *Trout at Ten Thousand Feet* where he penned this sentence, "I yearned to become part of that world, to be with those fish, those great olive-backed tench as they sauntered down the avenues amidst the weed across floors of polished sand, into their darkened rooms beneath the drapes of lilies."

So meeting John Bailey was a long-anticipated thrill for me. When we shook hands in the lobby of the Lainston House, a beautiful seven-hundred-year-old inn (or as they call it, "country residence") located between Stockbridge and Winchester in southwest England, I was surprised. I'd expected him to be much older, based on his prodigious number of works—everything from how-to/where-to books on fishing, virtual encyclopedias on tackle, fishing travel adventures, and even a love story. All in all, John has written more than thirty books on all aspects of fishing and people who fish, as well as numerous magazine articles, supplemented by an entertaining variety of radio and television shows designed for anglers who may be literarily challenged.

I was attracted to John's books not because of his technical skills or even his extensive travel to find big fish, but rather, by the humanity of his stories. Ironically, I read his last book, *Trout at Ten Thousand Feet*, first. In the first chapter, called "John the Fish," he tells a story about how as a young boy, he was so intrigued by water that his mother used to tease him about watching it in a sink. One day John was out walking with his parents when they came upon a woman who was stricken with panic and fear because her daughter had fallen into the river. John's father dove into a deep pool where the girl had gone under. Knowing "how water works," young John "slipped unnoticed through the reed beds and there, at the first bend, a golden-haired girl lay in the margins, dress rippling, face as though in sleep." He shouted for the adults while pulling the girl to shore.

*John, "the little fish" shows off some early fishing awards.* PHOTO CREDIT: JOY@ANGLING-TRAVEL.COM.

The little girl lived, and John, eschewing the title of hero, says merely, "What was important to me though was that never again did my mother laugh when she saw me on the stool by that sink. No longer was I 'an odd little fish.' Henceforth, I was her 'little fish' only, as though my strangeness was now accepted."

To my surprise, in spite of his long list of accomplishments, John was a youngish man in his forties, thin and fit, who could double for Roger Daltrey of the legendary British rock group, The Who. His wife Joy—petite, with shoulder-length blonde hair—looks to be about the same age as the girlfriends of the high school boys she and John taught ten years ago in northern England. Today she expertly handles the logistics for the far-flung trips John leads for their company, Angling Travel, which specializes in offering the ultimate in fishing adventures. On this particular day, however, we were just four weekend anglers—two of whom had journeyed from the United States and two from northern England—here to enjoy one of Great Britain's most beautiful countryside inns radiating in absolutely picture-perfect fall weather under cloudless skies.

*John's wife Joy shows off*
*a nice Indian mahseer.*
PHOTO CREDIT:
JOY@ANGLINGTRAVEL.COM.

Nestled into a corner table adorned with fresh-cut flowers and candles, we shared stories of fishing in both salt water and fresh. Like me, John feels most at home with a fly rod, but he loves to hunt all types of species with any kind of tackle—what the British call "course fishing." Like many other good anglers I've met, John likes to match up fish and tackle, not trying to underweight all his gear in pursuit of records. "A fair fight for the angler and the fish," I believe is how he describes it. Over dinner John told us about how he and Joy had met while teaching school in Norfolk. After they were married, they left teaching for a happier life out of doors.

John says, "The trips that I lead are very special to me and my client friends as well. For me it's not just about fishing. It's about being there and experiencing adventures of life. It's a thrill for me to see others catch fish. My greatest happiness in life is making people happy. I think my overwhelming desire to please others goes back to the illnesses and early deaths of my parents when I wanted so desperately to make them feel better. As long as I can remember I've combined my fascination with water with wanting to help others enjoy themselves. That may sound strange to you, but it's the way I feel."

Over coffee, John explained the drill that would define our fishing lives for the next three days. The River Test where we would be fishing runs for thirty miles through the adjoining countryside, past many old estates that had been in families for centuries.

Being conservation minded and anxious to ensure the long-term sustainability of the river, local landowners instituted a simple yet ingenious way to guard against overfishing. They started by identifying stretches of river (called *beats*) and then determined how many anglers (*rods*) they would allow to fish there. For example, an estate with five miles of riverbank might divide the river into five one-mile beats, each one available to two rods, thus allowing a total of ten anglers to fish their property on any given day. This system is overseen by a riverkeeper whose main duties include the care and upkeep of the riverbank as well as enforcement of the estate's fishing rules.

Some of the estates keep their fishing rights for the owners, while others sell them outright; others rent them through *ghillies*, local anglers who serve as guides. This is the way we acquired access to these storied waters, and where John told us we would meet the next morning.

"No need to get up early," John said. "This fishing is very civilized. These fish will bite just as well at mid-morning. I suggest we have breakfast at eight-thirty A.M., meet our ghillies at nine-thirty, and be fishing by ten."

Very civilized indeed. After a day of traveling, who were we to argue? John said we would stop by mid-afternoon for lunch, and then fish as late as we liked, until after dark even, if the fish were biting. After saying our good-nights at the table, I fell asleep and dreamt of other fishing trips with spartan accommodations and wake-up calls before the sun even thought about rising.

At breakfast the next morning, John filled us in on the local rules. As in the U.S., fishing licenses were required. Wading was prohibited—all fishing was from the riverbank—and fly fishing only. At some of the estates (where they were opposed to catch-and-release), you were allowed to catch four fish, all of which were to be killed, at which point your fishing day was over. All catches were to be reported in a log usually kept at a riverside fishing hut.

I couldn't believe this news! Here we were at arguably the oldest, most revered and well-maintained fishery in the world, and we were expected—no, *required*—to kill fish! After all that enlightened, modern-day anglers have been doing to save the resource, this seemed almost blasphemous. I asked John the question.

"It's all part of river management," John said. "These waters are stocked throughout the summer, supplementing the 'wild' fish that live here. Then specific records are kept to assist in the stocking plan for the next season. It's also a benefit to the anglers in that no one is catching a fish that has been caught before." In other words, every fish you engage has never been bested and may never have been hooked or fought before.

As keen as I am on catch and release, these rules seemed to make sense as a means of ensuring stream management and they also explained why the maitre d' told me that many anglers brought their day's catch to the restaurant.

"And what kinds of fish will we be catching?" I asked John.

"Rainbow and brown trout," he said, "and grayling as well. A lot of people don't like grayling, but I think they're great fighters—a worthwhile adversary."

After breakfast we met Stan Conway and John McCormick, our two ghillies, in the sun-drenched courtyard of the Lainston. Stan holds and sublets the fishing beats. He and his friend John were ready to go. Both in their fifties, they are passionate anglers equally interested in introducing us to "their river" and in finding out what is happening with fishing in the States. I liked them both right away. The fact that they were wearing brown felt hats just like the one I'd bought for the expedition (at Farlow's, the famous London outfitters) made me feel right at home.

En route to our first estate in John's Jeep Cherokee—with the steering wheel on the right, of course—Stan told us that they had recently fished with dry flies and nymphs, but he expected we'd have better luck with the latter, as this was the last weekend of trout season. He anticipated that the fish would be down deep and rather sluggish. He explained that their season extends from May until the last week in September. The fish spawn in March. "The best time for fishing dry flies is the first two weeks of the season when the mayflies are hatching. It's so easy to catch big trout then, we call it Duffers' Fortnight."

As we drove through the beautiful English countryside, I started to get excited for the adventure ahead and the chance to meet a new river. I thought of a passage from one of John's books, *In Wild Water*, that I particularly loved:

> It is easily possible to love rivers, just as easily in fact as human
> beings themselves. Both have beauty, character and both have
> good and bad moods. You can feel at ease in the company of

rivers. They can soothe like a mother, interest like a teacher or even excite at times like a lover. Rivers roll on through history and make their own marvelous legends. They give off a charisma. They can, simply, be magical.

Arriving at the first estate was exciting. We checked in with the riverkeeper, a nice young man by the name of Howard Taylor, who had worked as a ranger and specialized in forestry. As anxious as we were to get to the stream, it was fun to chat with this young conservationist about fishing. Halfway through our conversation two birds flew by overhead and I asked Howard what kind they were.

*Howard Cooper with Stan Conway. Howard is a young Renaissance man who has worked as a ranger, a river keeper, and a guide.*

"Those are magpies," he said, then added, "one is for sorrow, two is for joy, three for a girl, four for a boy. Five is for silver, six is for gold, seven for a secret never to be told."

*Wow,* I thought to myself. *This really is a "civilized outing," with poetry and all!*

Howard opened a few gates for us and we drove across some fields, walked about five hundred yards through a sheep pasture, and all of a sudden, there we were on the banks of the River Test. It was beautiful, just like the many pictures I've seen—a blue ribbon of gently flowing clear water just wide enough at its widest place that a good cast could deliver a fly to the opposite bank. The river depth seemed to vary from one foot to six feet, with some pools that might have even been ten feet deep. The bottom was covered with thick greenery that undulated gently in the steady current. Large patches of gravel provided the fish with great resting points where, with heads turned into the flow, they ambushed the insects that hatched there throughout the season. And the visibility—unlimited.

The grassy riverbanks were mowed, and much of the background bushes had been cut down to make backcasting possible. On many of the opposite banks a variety of trees were starting to show the early colors of fall foliage while providing great cover and falling food for the resident fish.

Flocks of large white swans live on the river and their leisurely swimming as they forage for underwater vegetation seems to set the pace for life on the Test. The swans "all belong to the Queen" and are protected. They have tags attached to their legs for identification and every year they are counted as part of an environmental control program. Can you imagine listing the job "Royal Swan Counter" on your résumé?

Our group split up as we reached our respective beats. John Bailey and I started with an inspection of the flies that Stan had told me to bring. My fly case was packed with some flies I knew and some that were unique to the Test. My dry flies included Emerging Parachute Duns, Adams Parachutes, Black Gnats, Parachute Pheasant Tails, olive and orange Klinkhammers, CDC Comparaduns, Humpy Yellows, Cinnamon Travis Parachute Ants, CDC Emerging Caddis, and olive CDC Adult Caddis all tied on #14, 16, and 18 hooks. My nymphs included American PTs, English PTs, Tunghead PTs, Gold Headed Ribbed Hare's Ears, Weighted Caddis, Bead Headed Princes, Flashback Scuds, and Bead Body Scuds tied on hooks from 10 to 18.

I had brought a five-weight Loomis rod that I fished with a 4/5 Abel reel. John and I chose an Adams Parachute which I tied on to a nine-foot, four-pound test leader, while John told me a little more about the river.

"The Test is one of several chalk streams in this area," he said. "The surrounding land is high in chalk that filters the water, which is why it is so gin-clear and gives us such good visibility," he explained. The local farmers have banned the use of chemical-laden fertilizers on the surrounding land, thus adding to the clarity of the water and the health of the fish. With no chemical runoff, the trout and grayling have a great environment in which to survive and prosper. "Of course," John added, "with this clean water and cloudless blue sky, these fish will be able to see us better too, but that shouldn't bother us."

With one rod on our first assigned beat, I asked John to go first and show me how it was done. He protested at first, but finally agreed, and proceeded to crouch down and literally slither his way to the river-bank. Across the river, he spotted a nice brown trout on a gravel patch near the far bank. He stripped out about forty feet of line and from his knees, false-casting once, laid the Adams Parachute three feet upstream of the unsuspecting trout. The current carried the fly directly over the fish's nose and it reacted with an instantaneous take, attacking the fly with incredible ferocity. The brown trout jumped twice and was gone, leaving John the teacher smiling, and me the student wondering out loud if I was going to have to crawl around like John had just done for the next three days.

"Probably not," John said with a laugh. "I just like to get really close so I can see them well and not spook them. It also helps me photograph them."

I took my rod back from John, noticing that the river was literally teeming with trout and grayling of all sizes. It was clear that an angler could spend an entire day sight-casting these marvelous fish. No blind-casting would be required.

In the Florida Keys many of the target species literally hook themselves, rendering a hook-set almost unnecessary. This is not the case with fish in the chalk streams, where most of the bites could be characterized as little nips. In response to a bite, the trick is to keep firm control of the line and lift the rod as fast as possible with one hand, keeping your line tight in the other hand. It sounds really simple, but believe me, it's not. I blew a lot of strikes in the morning until I got the hang of it and landed two grayling and a twenty-two-inch brown before we broke for lunch.

*A typical rainbow trout from the River Test.*

We drove for fifteen minutes to a popular pub named The Mayfly, after the trout's favorite springtime food. Located on the riverbank of the Test, this wonderful pub dates back a few centuries, and features both indoor and outdoor terraced seating overlooking the river. Nearby, feeding trout and a variety of swans and ducks look for a handout from the countryside diners.

Our party squeezed around a picnic table next to the stream, so we could get a close-up view of the relatives of the fish that we had been trying to catch that morning. We feasted on bangers and mash, fish and chips, and steak and kidney pie.

From the many glances we got from neighboring tables, it was easy to see that John Bailey was readily recognized by several of the other diners. If he noticed, which I'm sure he did, he never let on. John, in his very quiet yet enthusiastic voice, asked everyone at our table how their fishing had been. We then settled into a discussion of local environment management and stream welfare. John was an active participant in our conversation, and yet a courteous listener. He is so humble, it's hard to believe that he is one of the most knowledgeable and accomplished anglers in the world. He is a soft-spoken gentleman whose passion for his sport is omnipresent.

Returning to the stream after our lunch, and no doubt fortified by the beer, it all came together for me, and I started catching fish with ease. One of the things our ghillie John told me really made sense. He instructed me to collect slack quicker after each cast and to be ready to strike faster. "Get in contact with your fly and you'll be better able to anticipate the bite," he said. It worked. At the end of the day, I'd caught twelve nice fish, eight rainbows and four brown trout.

The fishing was great, matched by the incredible countryside scenery. Around every corner was a stone bridge or a picturesque farmhouse or a barn or some other timeworn landmark of this historically rich landscape. I fully expected Izaak Walton, William Shakespeare, or Geoffrey Chaucer—all of whom frequented this river—to walk by and tip their cap, but the only others we saw on the banks were herds of cows or flocks of curious sheep that wandered by as if to see how the fishing was going.

Ghillie John McCormick won the livestock storytelling contest that day with a whopper, about fishing one beat a few years ago when his backcast lassoed the horns of a cow grazing behind him. He said that when he tugged on the line, the cow was so shocked that he fell down the bank, still attached, taking John with him into the river, fly rod and all.

"We were quite a sight," he said. "Floating down the river next to each other, still connected by my fly line."

"Did you measure him before the release?" I asked him.

"Actually," John said, "I think he released me."

*John McCormick shows off a nice rainbow.*

John's story reminded me of a Rudyard Kipling tale of hooking a
cow in the nose on his backcast in a piece entitled "On Dry-Cow Fishing as a Fine Art." After the hookup Kipling said, "I reeled in very
swiftly and cautiously, but she would not wait. She put her tail in the air
and ran away. It was a purely voluntary motion on my part. I struck.
Other anglers may contradict me, but I firmly believe that if a man had
foul-hooked his best friend through the nose, and that friend ran, the
man would strike by instinct. I struck, therefore, and the reel began to
sing just as merrily as though I had caught my jack."

Between the people and their stories and the river and its rich history, I found myself enjoying my experience immensely. Solitude was a
wonderful side benefit of our trip. While we barely ran into any other
anglers, let alone any classic authors of antiquity, we did have a chance
meeting with an incomparable international artist of the music world.

One morning we were walking back to a riverbank fishing hut for a
picnic lunch. As I was crossing a bridge, I met a crusty-looking angler who
was heading the other way. Dressed in typical countryside fishing gear and
sporting a scruffy salt-and-pepper beard, this British angler stopped to chat
and find out how our fishing was going. I didn't recognize him until I heard
his voice. It was Eric Clapton—unplugged, up close and personal—perhaps

the world's greatest blues guitarist and singer/songwriter. I couldn't believe it. Here he was, a friendly stranger talking about trout fishing, while chords of "Layla," "Tears in Heaven," and "Change the World" swam into my head.

Actually, I shouldn't really have been surprised. I remember reading in a magazine how EC, as he's known, credits fishing with saving his life when he was going through a battle with alcoholism. Now he fishes whenever he can on tour and, of course, at home in England. We chatted for a few minutes and I invited him to join us for lunch. He declined. Like all intense anglers, I'm sure he was anxious to get back to the river, and, I'm equally sure, not interested in breaking bread with a stranger from the colonies like myself. Nonetheless, he was gracious, and I'll always remember our brief meeting when I hear any of his wonderful songs. Who knows? A few years from now as age dims my memory, I'll no doubt recount him as being a longtime close fishing buddy—you know how fishermen embellish stories, especially over time. In the meantime, I thought a lot about how fishing appeals to a wide range of people, celebrities and unknowns, young and old, princes and paupers. Fishing clearly had more meaning in people's lives than prevailing against a fish. I felt more and more committed to discovering what it is that motivates people to take up the sport.

*Stan and my wife Mindy hold the estate log book, after recording the largest catch of the day (note the celebratory bottle of wine).*

Time went by pleasantly on the rest of the trip as we got to know Joy and John Bailey, who took some wonderful photographs of the countryside during our trip. While John shares personal information sparingly, his fishing stories are without parallel. As we fished together on the Test, John shared with me several spellbinding tales from his books which have set new standards in extreme angling. In *Trout at Ten Thousand Feet*, John recounts how he was confronted by a Russian mafioso, chased by a musk ox, and nearly killed in a small plane crash. Together with Joy, he stared down a tiger in the wilds of India. Then Joy took the spotlight herself when she nearly drowned in the rapids of an Indian river before being pulled to shore by members of her party.

When they're not traveling, John and Joy live in a cottage in Norfolk, England. John maintains a full plate of literary and photographic projects, like his current work for the Irish tourism board, identifying, photographing, and writing up the best fishing spots in Ireland. His pens and cameras always accompany him on some of the most spectacular fishing trips you can imagine. With Joy taking care of logistics, John leads fishing expeditions literally to the four corners of the earth. Mongolia, India, Russia, the Arctic Circle, Tierra del Fuego, Greenland, and the northern reaches of Scotland, where he and Joy were married, have provided exciting settings for his guests over the years. His destinations are the dream fishing locations for anglers around the world. Some of his adventures took place years ago in locations like Kashmir; deadly politics have probably omitted this place from any sane person's itinerary, making John Bailey's published memories one of the best sources of information about this exotic destination.

*John teaches a Mongolian friend the newest English dance step.*
PHOTO CREDIT: JOY@ANGLINGTRAVEL.COM.

John has always been capable of shrugging off the danger of his trips and concentrating on the beauty and remoteness of the faraway venues—and of course, the ever-present, if always elusive, fish. Giant *mahseer* (a tarponlike fish) in India hold center stage.

Protected by royalty and deemed mystical by many who make their living fishing for them, John speaks of them in reverent terms. Listen to his description of them in *Trout at Ten Thousand Feet*: "Mahseer, you must understand, are not like any other fish. Everything about them is so intense that they bring out the heaven and the hell lurking in each day you live."

"Why would you put yourself through all of those travails to get to fish that will absolutely kick your butt?" I asked him one night over dinner.

"Because that's what life's all about," he answered thoughtfully. "These fish live in beautiful houses, breathtaking bodies of water that many people have never or will never see. It's a thrill to visit them that I'll never forget." As usual, I think, John Bailey was much more expansive on this subject in his writings than in conversation, this time in an English magazine called *The Field*. In his article called "Mahseer Madness," Bailey concludes, "[I]t is the ultimate test in the fishing world. I have never experienced any other situation where the battle between man and fish is so direct, personal, raw and brutal. Deep down we all want to know how good we really are, how we will react in the face of something that's all but beyond us. I know that I'll only really be able to call myself an angler when I've finally landed that monster mahseer . . . that is the test. Everything else in my fishing life has simply been preparation."

John Bailey, a soft-spoken man, is a talented angler, totally involved in his chosen sport. Fishing and the water itself had early on become drivers in his life. Through his perseverance in guiding others to find happiness in fishing as well, he seems to have found the satisfaction that he started searching for in his youth.

I hope to wander out again with John Bailey, this I know for sure. But whether or not I'm ready for his "Mahseer Madness"—only time will tell.

---

*I immersed myself in the watery world of fish and fishing: drinking in mystery and magic, sensing that the objects of my desires were infinitely noble, constantly intriguing, eternally amazing and always beautiful.*

—JOHN BAILEY, *TALES FROM THE RIVERBANK*

Perhaps nothing compares in angling to seeing a thousand-pound fish leap fifteen feet in the air, shaking its head violently to dislodge the hook as its ten-foot body cartwheels in the air to crash against the water. Nothing in angling is as physically challenging as bringing such a fish to the gaff. And nothing in angling takes as much moral courage as releasing that extraordinary predator to live and fight again.

—Herbert A. Schaffner, *Saltwater Game Fish in North America*

# 2

# DON TYSON: CHICKEN KING, MARLIN TAMER

*I'd never fished before. I was watchin' TV at my home in Springdale, Arkansas, in 1962 and there was a fishing show on catching 1,000-pound black marlin in Australia, and I thought, Boy, it'd be fun to go and do that. So I called down to Florida to a guy who was on that show named Jo Jo Del Greco and I got his captain's name, Peter Bristow, and called over there and booked him for a trip the next year.*

*I took my son with me and my brother and we went out, and my brother caught a 1,000-pounder, and we turned it loose. I didn't catch anything close to that.*

*So I go back the next year and just took my son and he caught a 1,000-pounder, and once again I didn't get one.*

*The third year, I didn't take anybody but me and I got my 1,000-pounder. He weighed 1,123 pounds. The reason I know is 'cause he died on me. We towed it, turned it loose, and it floated. We tried everything we knew but nothing worked.*

*We had a "Request for Marlin Data" form on board from New South Wales University, so we dissected it and did all of the research work we could. That's the only black marlin I've weighed in forty years, and I've only fished for big marlin ever since.*

—Don Tyson

THE HISTORY OF AMERICAN BUSINESS is punctuated with unforgettable stories of daring and successful visionaries with the courage of their convictions, but few of them are as colorful and compelling as the story of Don Tyson, the man from northwest Arkansas who says with a twinkle in his eye, "I'm just a chicken farmer," while he turned his small family business into one of the top-ten food companies in the country. I first met him in the mid-1960s and asked him a simple question about bringing chickens to market. He defined the entire process and its costs down to the penny. To this date, I've never met anyone who had a better knowledge of costs than Don Tyson.

Pursuing his passion for catching large marlin with the same commitment and energy he used in building his business, he has also become one of the best-known and most well-respected anglers in the world. His disarming "Aw shucks," good-ol'-boy demeanor barely disguises his devotion to conservation and the practice of catch-and-release fishing which he has helped popularize through his unparalleled generosity to the Billfish Association and the International Game Fish Association.

Like any successful entrepreneur, Don Tyson has more than his share of critics, but he also has a legion of friends and supporters whose lives have been touched by his expertise and generosity. His inclusion in any book on interesting anglers is a must, and I feel honored to present his story.

Don's dad, John, moved his wife and young son to Springdale, Arkansas, in 1931, the year after Don was born. John made a living hauling hay, fruit, and chickens for local farmers. He'd buy live chickens, which they would butcher and dress, box in ice, and deliver to market in a battered old truck. Thus Tyson Foods was born, though it was first known as Tyson's Poultry. John Tyson expanded his geographical

*Young Don with his family in Arkansas.* PHOTO CREDIT: TYSON FOODS.

distribution, went into the feed business, and started raising his own chickens. As the senior Tyson worked, young Don got an education in agriculture studies at the University of Arkansas before joining his father in the business in 1952.

In 1966 at the age of thirty-six, Don Tyson became president of the company. Then a year later, tragedy struck. Don's mom and dad, who had just completed building their "dream home" on Beaver Lake, twenty minutes from their office, were driving home one rainy foggy night when their car was hit by a train at an unprotected railroad crossing. They were both killed instantly. To this day, John Tyson's office at the company has been left intact, complete with family photographs and the very papers that were on his desk at the time of the accident. It was renamed the Founders Room by Don Tyson, as a tribute to his father.

*Don with his father John before his untimely death.* PHOTO CREDIT: TYSON FOODS.

"What a loss," I said to Don. "Did you ever get a chance to go fishing with your dad?"

"No," Don said matter-of-factly. "I never did. He was too busy working, although I think he was just beginning to relax and enjoy life a little."

"So did you ever fish as a child?"

"Never," he said. "Not until eleven years after joining the company. The first time I ever fished was that trip to Australia in 1963. My father always said that those first years of my career were the most important and I took his advice seriously and never even took one day off for the first eleven years with the company."

"So your third fishing trip to Australia, you caught a black marlin?"

"Yeah, not a bad start."

"How about freshwater fishing, Don?" I asked. "Are you into it?"

"No, not really," he said, "although I do try to go once a year to some interesting freshwater fishing place with friends. I've caught a twenty-pound peacock bass in Brazil and salmon in Alaska, even fished in Lake Victoria, but freshwater fishing is not my thing. Beaver Lake is supposed to be full of big bass. They even have a million-dollar tournament there. Somebody told me our company sponsored a boat in the tournament this year but I've never fished it," he said almost wistfully.

After his mom and dad died, young Don Tyson threw himself into the business with a vengeance. His ambition reached way beyond "iced chicken," and he set out to reengineer the company.

Dressed in his trademark khaki shirt and pants, Don led his company through a diversification that featured frozen application of his chicken products to everything from boneless chicken breasts to hot wings, and even McDonald's Chicken McNuggets.

Don Tyson proved to be a brilliant strategist and his company grew exponentially. Tyson Foods became the largest chicken company in the world, but the "Chicken King" wasn't done yet; he invested in other new product platforms for growth like seafood, pork, and ultimately, beef. A business consultant friend of mine, Bill Hale, succinctly sums up Don's success when he says, "Don Tyson is a risk taker. He looks beyond the existing business. He sees the future and makes it happen."

As his business expanded over time, Don Tyson started getting away more often to hone his skills as an offshore fisherman. He remembers his first fishing trip to Bimini several years ago. "A friend of mine called and invited me and I went; I didn't catch anything the first

*Pride has always played a large part in the success of Tyson's, as indicated on their packaging.* Photo credit: Tyson foods.

trip, but I found out there weren't any telephones and chicken feathers out there."

"So it was a good getaway?" I asked.

"Yeah, and as our business grew I used fishing as relaxation and to get a break. The Bahamas is where I first started fishing regularly, and I kept a boat down there," Don said. "You know, my dad was just starting to take some time off a little bit when he was killed in that train accident. After that happened, I looked at myself and said, When I get this thing organized when I'm forty, I'm going to take off a week a month, and when I'm forty-five, I'm going to take off *two* weeks a month, and when I'm sixty-five, I'm going to take off whenever I want to."

"Isn't that what you've called progressive retirement?" I asked, remembering a newspaper article I'd seen on Don.

"Yeah," he said, "and you know the darnedest thing—my business got better. The guys who were left here had to stand on their own two feet and not look around or ask me how to handle things."

People who know him, know that he loves to do deals and has a high tolerance for risk. In 1992, or almost thirty years after that first fishing trip to Australia, he went on his "biggest fishing trip ever" when he bought two companies called Arctic Alaska and Louis Kemp Seafood, making his company a huge player in Alaska fishing.

"As a sportfisherman," I said, "that must have been pretty exciting!"

"Yeah, it was," he replied. "We had thirty-six boats up there, making ours the largest fishing fleet in Alaska."

"You've always been a catch-and-release sportfisherman. How did you square that with becoming a commercial fisherman?" I asked.

"Well, you see, we're all on quotas up there in Alaska. They open up that fishery and when they get so many pounds—whether it's crab or salmon or whatever it is—they close the fishery. I wouldn't have gotten in the commercial fishing business if we just went out and went fishing. And I sold that business, Arctic Alaska, a few years ago because quite frankly, I had other things that were making more money."

"So was it tough selling that business with your being such an avid and knowledgeable fisherman?" I asked.

Don Tyson, the consummate businessman, said succinctly, "It's not hard when you're sitting at your desk looking at numbers." Know this about the man, all stories aside—Don Tyson understands his businesses, and they must perform. As he has often said to me, "You know what the eleventh commandment is?" Then, answering it himself, he says, "Thou shalt make a profit." Don't expect to see Don Tyson investing in any "hobby businesses."

While he's now out of the commercial fishing business, he has intensified his search for marlin—not just any marlin, but really big "blue marlin." He fishes often with a friend named Shelby Rogers, who has herself established an excellent reputation as a bill fisher, catching a 1,059-pound world-record blue marlin in Madeira in 1995.

Of the five marlin identified—white, striped, blue, black, and the uncommon hatchet—blue and black females grow to be the largest. Blue marlin range up to 1,800 pounds and are the fish of dreams. While other species like bluefin tuna may grow to be larger, blue marlin are the

*Don and Shelby with a 602-pound blue marlin in Puerto Rico.* PHOTO CREDIT: TYSON FOODS.

most spectacular sport fish in the world, fighting on the surface and in the air with razor-sharp bill and pronounced dorsal fin flaying, propelled at great speed through the water by a giant sickle-shaped tail. A fight against a blue marlin can take hours, and just when you've gathered in most of your line, sensing victory, they can sound, running for deep water and taking back all of the line you fought to return to your reel.

These are the fish of Zane Grey, Ernest Hemingway, and Don Tyson, and the greatest prize of all is "The Grander," that marlin who has prevailed in her environment and grown to 1,000 pounds or more. This is the ultimate experi-

*Blue marlin fight all the way to the boat and then some.* PHOTO CREDIT: TYSON FOODS.

ence, and only a handful of anglers have been fortunate enough to catch one. Don Tyson has caught six solid granders and released them all, all that is with the exception of that first black marlin that they couldn't revive in Australia.

"I only count them if they are over twelve hundred pounds, to be sure," says Don. These catches have never been verified, but knowing his memory for numbers, how he attacks his sport, and his experience in the quest, I'm guessing that his memory is pretty darn accurate. (On his most recent trip to Australia, Don caught and released eight big black marlin, two of which were over 1,000 pounds, the larger being well over 1,200!)

"I tell everybody that marlin fishing is like being on dope," Don says. "You catch one that's a hundred pounds, and then you want to catch one that's two hundred pounds; then you want to catch a bigger one and a bigger one and a bigger one. If I go fishing today, I'm looking for blue marlin. That's all I'm looking for."

"Why blue marlin?" I asked him, already anticipating his answer.

"I think they are the most exciting fish in the world. They're just so pretty when they jump out of the water, and they're so hard to find, and that's part of it too. Last year I had a boat in Mexico about halfway up the Baja and I was fishing with my friend Shelby. In two and a half days we got one hundred and forty-two striped marlin. And that was great fun, but it wasn't like going out there and working hard and going places and maybe getting a blue marlin.

"I pull away from other species. I've caught some big tuna, maybe a thousand-pounder, but blue marlin are what I'm after."

I asked Don a familiar question often put to longtime anglers in any fishery: "From the time you started, has fishing changed?"

"Sure," he said. "There were more fish around then, but I do believe that in the last five years in the places I go, I'm seeing almost as many fish, and I'm not totally sure why. Hopefully conservation is working."

"So, Don, where is your favorite place in the world to fish?" I asked him.

"That's easy," he said smiling. "My favorite place to fish in the world is the last place I caught a fish. Now, if I even hear about big fish being somewhere, I'll go there."

As far as the places Don Tyson goes to find big blue marlin, it would almost be easier to list where he *hasn't* been. Some of his favorite spots over time include the following venues, with his editorial comments included:

*On the Bahamas*—"That's where I started, and I kept a boat down there. The fishing went down, but now it's coming back some."

*On St. Thomas*—"It's famous for its blue marlin, but it's probably down about sixty percent from when I first started fishing there. The seas there are pretty big."

*On Cabo San Lucas*—"One of my favorite places. I have a house and keep a boat there, a forty-eight-foot Hatteras. A lot of variety—striped marlin and pacific sails and some blues—but not as many as before."

*On Costa Rica*—"Great fishing for sailfish, although I've been disappointed in marlin fishing there the last few years."

*On Australia*—"A great place for black marlin with some blues. I've fished all the way from Sydney up. Port Stevens has some small ones but mostly Cairns is where the big ones are."

*On the Ascension Islands*—"It's tough to get to. You've got to go to England and climb on an old RAF troop plane to get there, and it's rough, but last time there I caught some blue marlin and that's all I fish for."

*On the Azores*—"Well, I've got some eight- and nine-hundred-pounders there—but it's been kind of slow the last few years."

*On Madeira and the Canary Islands*—"Went down to almost nothing, no marlin."

*On Cape Verde*—"It's off the coast of northern Africa. It's really tough fishing. You need a mother ship, 'cause they have no food or supplies, especially in the outer islands. They've got some big blue marlin down there, but the seas are really rough, like St. Thomas."

*On Ghana*—"We stay in an old hotel in Accra called the Golden Tulip. It's pretty nice. We've caught some big blues in those waters."

*On Bom Bom Island*—"It's an island south of Ghana—pretty primitive. We think the marlin there are migrating south from the Azores past Madeira and Cape Verde."

In conversations with Don, fishing and conservation are totally interrelated, and it's easy to see how strongly he feels about the International Game Fish Association. He tells people who love fishing to support the IGFA because it will help protect their fishing.

"I feel special about the IGFA," he says. "When it started it was just for folks with big yachts who wanted to see if they had caught a record. I got down there to their offices in Pompano Beach and thought we needed a new headquarters, so they made me chairman of the building committee," he relates with a smile. "And now we've got a nice new museum and headquarters in Fort Lauderdale, and we're doing the right things.

"We're telling folks to protect fish by releasing them. We keep freshwater records as well as saltwater. We have a junior angler tournament, and we're teaching the kids that the fun is in catching 'em and not killing 'em.

"Of all our programs, I think our Washington efforts in conservation are the best things we've done. Ten years ago they had a hands-off attitude on conservation. We lacked a strong voice in Washington, and it's too important. It affects all fishermen's interests. Now I think we're headed in the right direction."

All of this would have been impossible without Don Tyson, who is uniquely qualified to help IGFA set their political agenda for conservation. Working out of his office in Springdale, Arkansas, whimsically designed to replicate the Oval Office, he understands the political process. He has also been a friend to many presidents, including George Herbert Walker Bush and Bill Clinton, and as a creator of jobs, he is well known in Washington and other state capitols as an action guy ready to fight for his beliefs.

The new IGFA museum and headquarters is a testament to many people, but most of all to Don Tyson and his friend Johnny Morris, the founder of Bass Pro Shops. Morris contributed money as well as sixteen acres of prime property on Interstate 95 where the new building now stands. Don oversaw the project with his customary energy and disdain for long meetings.

Twenty-year IGFA president Mike Leech says of Don, "He has been totally invaluable to us. He's never turned down any of our many requests and has contributed more time and money to the cause than anyone in the world. Whether it's advice and counsel, financing for our

*"Big fish" exhibit at the IGFA museum.* PHOTO CREDIT: INTERNATIONAL GAME FISH ASSOCIATION.

building, or contributions of money or auction items for our fund-raisers, he has always been there for us. It's appropriate that our new place is named the Don Tyson Building in his honor." (For more information on IGFA, see the Appendix.)

*The IGFA museum is an interactive learning experience for all ages.* PHOTO CREDIT: INTERNATIONAL GAME FISH ASSOCIATION.

Don Tyson has left an indelible mark on his sport, as well as on his company and American industry as a whole. Under his son John's direction, Tyson recently completed another major acquisition, making them a $26 billion giant.

Now as senior chairman, Don says, "When I'm in town I come in at eight-thirty A.M. and I'm gone by noon." Quite a change from the guy who worked for his first eleven years without taking a day off.

*Don stands proudly before a picture of his dad.* PHOTO CREDIT: TYSON FOODS.

Of his son, Don was quoted as saying in a company press release, "I am confident that my son John, and the leadership team he has put together, are fully prepared to take the company to the next level as the premier provider on the planet." He added, "I look forward to following their progress from my boat."

"So at the end of the day, Don," I said, "you get on the boat and see a challenge. Do you see similarities between business and fishing?"

"Well, you know when you stop and think about it," he replied, "fishing is just like running a business. You got to get the right people, the right equipment, and then you got to get information about where they are and then you just go."

"Don," I asked him, "do you think you'll do more or less fishing in the next year?"

"I've pretty well settled into two weeks a month," he said. "That kind of fits my schedule, but sometimes I might leave for a month, then maybe I'll be home for a month. I find any more than that and maybe the newness would wear off."

"You never fished with your dad. You never fished as a child. You picked up this sport later in your life. Have you had any teachers?" I asked Don. "Any mentors?"

"No, not really," he said. "I've learned from some of my captains and crew. It's been like a mutual learning situation. One of my first captains was a guy named Rick Difeo. I started fishing with Rick when we were chasing swordfish in Chile. I think I learned the most about fishing from him. He was a fine professional." Rick was a fishing legend who died of cancer a few years ago.

"And then, of course, Terry Robinson captains my boat, *Tyson's Pride*. He started off as a mate, as everyone does. He's a New Jersey guy. He fished with his dad and then started mating when he was in high school, and then he came with me and worked as a mate for Rick, and he's doing a heck of a job."

I had the chance to meet Terry and his crew when Don invited Johnny Morris, the founder of Bass Pro, and his family to fish on *Tyson's Pride* in Costa Rica this summer and stay on the *Horizons*, a 102-foot mother ship. Johnny invited me and my wife along for what turned out to be an unforgettable three-day fishing trip.

Well-positioned mother ships give anglers a chance to enjoy some of the greatest unpressured fisheries in the world while living in the lap of luxury. *Tyson's Pride* is a well-equipped sixty-five-foot Merritt sport-fishing boat, and *Horizons* is a 102-foot metal boat that Don Tyson found in a boatyard in Ensenada, Mexico. Originally designed as a tuna boat, he had it completely rebuilt at the American Boat Yard, plumbed it, and put in electricity to make it into a brand-new boat. In business or fishing, always with the consummate memory for facts, Don says, "It's really more of a supply ship than a mother ship. It holds thirty-three thousand gallons of fuel, food for sixty days, and makes five thousand gallons of fresh water a day. Just what we need to go wherever we want to go." It has nine staterooms—four for guests and five for crew—more amenities than the finest hotel, and under the direction of Captain Randall Moore and Chef Adrian, better food than a five-star restaurant.

It was late one night, and everyone else was asleep when I asked Johnny about his take on Don Tyson.

"Buddy," Johnny said, "Don is a character. I don't know of anybody else who has been more generous in supporting fisheries conservation. In addition to his extraordinary financial support, Don Tyson has donated lots of his time and marketing talents to the future of fishing. You know those bumper stickers that say 'Release Me'? Don helped foster this idea in conjunction with the Billfish Foundation. Don must have printed and given away hundreds of thousands of these decals to promote catch-and-release fishing. They show up everywhere, on cars, boats, briefcases, luggage, tackle boxes—and every time I see one, I think of Don Tyson. He's a great guy."

The next day, Johnny's ten-year-old daughter Megan and her friend, Liza, neither of whom had ever caught a sailfish, caught five to go along with the giant tuna that his son John Paul landed, and two Pacific sails that Johnny and I caught and released on fly—but alas, no marlin. It was a day of a lifetime for me, but merely a "no marlin day" for our host Don.

"So, Don," I asked him, "if you had just one day to fish, where would it be?"

"Cabo San Lucas," he said. "It's a great fishery."

"And what makes your fishing day if you don't catch another grander?" I asked.

"Hearing that my friends had a great day," he said without pause. "Like a pal of mine called me from Cabo and said that they'd just got in from catching a five-hundred-pound black marlin and just quit counting the striped marlin they'd caught. That was great!"

For a legend in the making, Don Tyson has been very generous with his time with me. As we wound up our discussion, I looked forward to asking what I believe is the seminal question of the man from northwest Arkansas: "At the end of the day, what's it all about? Is it about the water? Is it about the people? Is it about the fish?"

"It's the challenge," Don said, characteristically jumping in without hesitation. "It's the challenge when you step on that boat and you look at that ocean, and you say there's one out there with my name on it and I've got to go find it."

*Don Tyson on the business end of a 1,000-pound blue marlin.* PHOTO CREDIT: INTERNATIONAL GAME FISH ASSOCIATION.

Conservation is gaining momentum around the world and Don Tyson's role in the movement has been enormous. I hope that he's out there trying to find those big fish for many, many years to come, and I know that because of him and his efforts, there will be a lot of big ones out there in the future, not just for me but for my children and their children as well.

In the meantime, I have learned some interesting fishing lessons from Don Tyson. First, that fishing can be a great way to relax no matter how many chickens you have on your farm; and second, if you want to catch the really big ones, you'd better be ready to travel far on a moment's notice.

*Exultation is the going*
*Of an inland soul to sea—*
*Past the houses, past the headlands*
*Into deep Eternity!*

*Bred as we, among the mountains,*
*Can the sailor understand*
*The divine intoxication*
*Of the first league out from land?*

—EMILY DICKINSON, "SETTING SAIL,"
FROM *COMPLETE POEMS*, 1924

WANTED: ATTRACTIVE YOUNG WIDOW WITH HOUSE OR TRAILER, PICKUP TRUCK AND BASS BOAT. SEND PICTURES OF BASS BOAT.

—Popular Bumper Sticker

# 3

# BILL DANCE:
# BASS CATCHIN' LEGEND

*My granddaddy used to take me fishin' a lot in middle Tennessee. One day when I was about eight, we went to Cumberland Springs Lake, a beautiful spring-fed lake fifteen miles from his home in Lynchburg, Tennessee. I'd never caught a largemouth bass before—although I'd caught smallmouth bass with cray-fish—but wanted to give it a try. My granddaddy went one way on the bank, bottom-fishin' with live bait for redears. I had just used my chore money to buy my first two artificial lures, a hula dancer and a jitterbug from Motlow's Hardware Store, owned by Connor Motlow. He was the grandson of Lem Motlow, nephew of the founder of Jack Daniel's whiskey.*

*Well sir, I walked down the bank and looked out and saw this pair of bass swimmin' together side by side. My gosh, they looked huge at the time. Must have been eight- or ten-pounders. Now as I think about it, they were probably more like two-pounders. Boy was I nervous. My hands were shaking so badly I could hardly tie on that jitterbug.*

*I snuck up to about twenty feet from those fish, reared back, and made what I thought was a great cast that unfortunately landed about twenty-five feet from those fish. Think about it; that's hard to do. But you know what, when it hit the water, both of 'em stopped, then one tailed off and swam toward it and stopped about four feet away. Totally stopped. Then when I started reeling in that bait, he followed it. When I stopped it, he stopped too, this time one foot away. Then as soon as I started movin' it again,* kaboom, *he was all over it.*

*I was so excited I just threw my rod over my shoulder, grabbed the line, and, well,* roped *that fish in and drug it up on the bank. I've relived that moment umpteen-jillion times.*

*Eight-year-old Bill Dance and his first (of many, many) largemouth bass.*

*Of course I didn't know what I was doin' at the time, but I learned two things that day. First, how far away a fish can hear or see a bait hit the water, and second, how changin' the action of the bait can entice the bite.*

*The most amazin' thing to me is that you could take somethin' made out of wood, plastic, hair, or rubber and create life and entice another living creature like a bass to think that it's real food and come up and eat.*

*From that day on I never again fished real bait—only artificials. To this day I love to pick the right color, make the proper presentation, and lure that fish out of his world into mine.*

—Bill Dance

WHO CAN DENY THE ENORMOUS IMPACT that rural culture, deemed "the Redneck Way" by author Howell Raines, has had on America in the last twenty-five years of the twentieth century? Country music went mainstream and line dancing drove out disco. Denim replaced crushed velvet, while chewing tobacco took hold on college campuses. NASCAR racing began drawing bigger audiences than NFL football, and bass fishing swept through the nation's waters like a tidal wave.

In fact, over the past three decades, bass fishing has arguably become the largest, fastest-growing participatory sport in the United States, fueled by the popularity of a professional bass tour developed in the late sixties. In the first year of the new millennium, more than thirty million anglers spent approximately $60 billion in pursuit of the wily bass. That's more money than was spent during the same period in the United States on golf and tennis, combined!

This burgeoning industry has spawned many successful businesses and entrepreneurs, but none have been as colorful and visible as Bill Dance, an avid fisherman who rode the wave of bass fishing to fame and fortune. A charter member of the first professional tour, Bill Dance has since become an Outdoor Life Network regular with his own national television show, along with his own magazine and newsletter. His numerous videos and seven books tell his followers where the big ones live and how to catch them. His popularity is confirmed by his endorsements of more than twenty-five products. Bill Dance has literally become an industry himself and yet through it all, he has retained the humility and trademark self-deprecating humor that have made him an American icon.

I first had the pleasure of fishing with him on Lake Erie in a bass/walleye tournament that we set up to raise money to find a cure for cystic fibrosis. Not only was he great fun to spend time with, but I watched him charm everyone in the tournament, whether they were avid professionals or rank rookies. Throughout the event he remained as engaged and excited as if it were his first fishing trip, instead of just another fishing event in his remarkable thirty-seven-year professional fishing career.

In 1954, a Frenchman named Jacques Barzun wrote, "Whoever wants to know the heart and mind of America had better learn baseball." Today I think that expression should be modified to the following: "To understand the heartland of America, you must first understand bass fishing." One of the fastest ways to do this is to try to understand Bill Dance, but only after first understanding bass themselves.

My own database on these critters increased exponentially in 1996 during an afternoon visit to a Bass Pro Shop when I met an angler/author by the name of Homer Circle who was there signing his new book, *Circle on Bass*. Quoting from his book he told me, "Don't think of bass as being smart because you can't catch them when you know they're there. Think of them as wary creatures that have learned to survive in a dangerous world where not detecting a predator means death."

The bass was a natural to become the most popular American freshwater gamefish. They are native to every state in the union except Alaska, and are found in Mexico and southern Canada as well. Voracious feeders that will literally strike any bait out of hunger or territorial protectionism, they are hearty, aggressive, and, I believe, bad tempered—three traits that make them great fighters.

Largemouth bass, *Micropterus salmoides*, are around three and a half pounds on average, but have been known to range up to twenty pounds or more. In fact, the world record was a twenty-two-pound, four-ounce monster caught on Montgomery Lake, Georgia, in 1932 by a nineteen-year-old named George Perry. That record eclipsed the previous world record by less than a pound and still stands today.

The largemouth's cold-water smallmouth cousins, *Micropterus dolomien*, tend to be much smaller. From my experiences fishing in the Great Lakes, a three-and-a-half-pound smallmouth bass is a dynamite catch to brag about. The world-record smallmouth weighed eleven pounds, fifteen ounces and was caught in Dale Hollow Lake in Tennessee by D. L. Hays in the mid-1950s.

Both largemouth and smallmouth bass feed at all levels in the water and tend to seek the cover of overhanging rock ledges, fallen tree branches, roots, and other debris. They seem unable to resist plugs, jigs, and other lures bounced deep by their hiding places. They are also known to crash surface plugs, lures, and flies, giving the angler an acrobatic display of their incredible talent for multiple jumps.

These hearty battlers are found in all kinds of freshwater, from huge lakes like the Great Lakes to rivers and canals, to small lily ponds on golf courses in water ranging from thirty to ninety degrees. While they have been known to feed day or night, in clear water during the heat of the day, they tend to seek refuge from predators in their safe hiding places.

Equipped with incredible sensory equipment, bass will strike lures in even the murkiest water, once again assuring their reputation as the consummate freshwater competitor.

Like bass fishing itself, Bill Dance was born in the South. His mom and his dad, a doctor, lived in Memphis, and split up when he was nine years old. Although he lived with his mother, he spent "a tremendous amount of time" with his dad's folks in nearby Lynchburg, Tennessee.

"How big was Lynchburg?" I asked him one day as we searched for bass in Lake Erie.

"Well, Moon," he said, using his nickname for me, "the sign comin' into town says 'Welcome to Lynchburg, population three hundred ninety-nine.' My granddaddy was a doctor over there, so I knew everybody. I spent every possible minute I could there, and it was probably the greatest time of my life.

"My granddaddy was the greatest, sweetest, kindest, gentlest individual I've ever met in my entire life. I think about him all the time because he's the one who introduced me to fishin'."

"So he's been the greatest influence on your fishing life?" I asked.

"Well, my mother claims that she's kinda responsible for my fishin'. But my mother used to tell me, 'You're never going to amount to anything but a river rat if you don't get on those schoolbooks,' and I used to buy her rods and reels for Mother's Day and she didn't even fish. And I remember her line; she'd say, 'Well, I appreciate this wonderful gift but why don't you use them till I need them.'

"But my granddaddy, he was the biggest influence on me on fishin'. In Lynchburg, I fished every wakin' moment I could. I'd jump outta bed every mornin' and go fishin', but I always had to get back home for dinner at eleven-thirty A.M. That's what we southerners call lunch.

"Lynchburg was a glove manufacturing mill town and the home of Jack Daniel's Distillery. They blew a siren in the morning and I'd get up, and then they blew a dinner siren at eleven-thirty, and boy, I'd better be off the creek and at my grandfolks' home by then. After dinner I'd do my chores and then I'd be back on the water. But my biggest thrill was goin' fishin' with my granddad. He'd take off every Wednesday afternoon and every Sunday after church and we'd go out and he taught me the joy of fishin'—about walkin' up and down the bank, how sound was transmitted, what fish see, how to fish in clear water and muddy water, how fish react in the winter and the summer. He made a lot of sense, and I always think back to a lot of the things he taught me.

"He passed away when I was fourteen, and it was a terrible blow. It about killed me and it still hurts today even after all these years. I learned so much from him."

I asked Bill about the rest of his family.

"I had what they call a blended family," he said, "two full sisters and a half sister and two half brothers. Only my two whole sisters, Ann and Lisa, fished with me back when I was usin' live bait."

"Did your dad or granddad ever pressure you to follow them into medicine?" I asked.

"No," he said, "and actually, we had doctors in the family for five generations and I was fixin' to be a doctor too."

"What happened?" I asked.

"Well, it was just before entering premed. I was drivin' on a street in Memphis and there was a terrible motorcycle accident right in front of me. I slammed on my brakes, jumped out of my truck, and ran up, and when I saw what had happened it was one of the most horrible sights I've seen in my life. I looked at this guy and he was really, really messed up. There was blood everywhere. When I saw that, it did a one-eighty on me. I knew I could not do that. I *knew* I could not do that!

"Well, I always dreamed of working in the fishin' industry. That was before the nationally recognized tournaments came along, but I knew I wanted to get into the fishin' bait or tackle business in some way, shape, or form. I landed a job as a distributor salesman for a big distributor in Memphis that sold hardware and sporting goods. I went to some hardware stores that didn't even carry sporting goods and they'd take 'em on just to help me out. I had a real good friend in Memphis, Bill McEwen, who started Strike King Lure Company, and I'd even sell his spinner baits to lumber companies; I think they just bought 'em to be nice.

*Bill's wife Dianne caught this nice Kentucky bass fishing on a creek near their home.*

"Along about that time I got married to my wife Dianne, who has always been very supportive of my involvement in fishing. We've raised four great kids and now have six grandchildren."

## Ray Scott and The Bass Anglers Sportsman Society

In 1967, events took place that would help Bill Dance transform his image from that of a fine amateur fisherman to a nationally recognized professional bass champion, and, ultimately, a media personality and fishing legend. In June of that year, Ray Scott, a fast-talking, thirty-four-year-old insurance peddler from Montgomery, Alabama, hosted his first fishing tournament, expansively named the All-American Invitational, at Beaver Lake, Arkansas. Scott concurrently declared that bass fishing would soon become a major league sport.

Scott set up a temporary office in Springdale, Arkansas, and started calling around the nearby twelve or so states, looking for one hundred expert anglers who would be willing to put up $100 apiece as an entry fee. When he called the marinas in Memphis and asked them to recommend local anglers, the unanimous first selection was a young local fisherman named Bill Dance.

"Regardless of which marina I called, the first name they blurted out was Billy Dance," Scott said. 'This Billy Dance must be special,' I said. 'Why do you think he's good enough to come to the All-American Invitational Tournament?', I'd ask them.

"And the answer that I got was, 'Billy Dance is a young feller, only about twenty-four or twenty-five. But he's good. If there are fish that can be caught, he'll sure catch 'em."

Recalling that first tournament year, Bill said that he'd never met Ray Scott. "I'd had several write-ups in the local newspaper," Bill said, "and I knew the boat dock operators, and I'd been fishin' a lot. I was lucky at catchin' fish and stuff, and I got an invitation from Ray Scott to fish in that first tournament.

"Well, I wanted to go and my sales were up, fortunately, so my boss let me go to participate in that tournament at Beaver Lake."

It was only appropriate that Bill Dance would catch the first fish of the tournament within two minutes of "lines in the water." He then went on to lead the tournament for two days, ultimately finishing second. The winner of the event, Stan Sloan, collected the combined winner's check of $2,000 and a trip to Acapulco, which was a huge prize at the time. With this tournament, professional bass fishing was launched, as was Bill Dance's future direction. Scott put on two more tournaments that year and Bill again finished second in both of them. The stage was set for the young angler from middle Tennessee to dominate the professional tour for many years.

Ray Scott followed up his success in 1967 with the formation of the Bass Anglers Sportsman Society (BASS). The first chapter, the Chattanooga Bass Club, had fewer than one hundred members and a seemingly simple charge: to protect the future of bass fishing. Their membership got involved in a variety of programs including conservation, community involvement, tournaments, children's education, and lobbying (and perhaps a little beer drinking as well).

Under Ray Scott's leadership, that first club led to the federation of other clubs around the state and the eventual formation of nineteen state federations in five years. Today there are fifty-one federations around the United States, Canada, Japan, South Africa, and Zimbabwe, with more on the way. Its membership has grown to over 600,000 members, making them an extremely strong voice for what has become the bass fishing industry.

*Ray Scott admired this nice string of bass in a tournament at Lake EuFaula in the late '60s before catch and release.*

*Bill had a nice win at Sam Rayburn in Texas and was joined by Ray Scott and ten other finalists.*

In 1968, Ray Scott introduced *Bassmaster* magazine to promote his tournaments and clubs as well as the products of their growing list of sponsors, while Bill Dance won the first three tournaments of the year! As you might imagine, he was in great demand to endorse a wide variety of fishing-related products, including Bagley Bait, Creme Lure Company, and Heddon Fishing Lures. That same year, a guy named Cotton Cordell, owner of the nationally known manufacturer, Cordell Lure Company, offered Bill a job at twice what he was making as a sporting goods salesman. After six months working there, Cordell said to Bill, "We need a television show."

"I dove into the project headfirst," Bill said.

"Really, it was my wife Dianne who kept me goin'. She was one hundred percent supportive and she knew how much I wanted to get into this business. She always said, 'The mind is a powerful thing. If you believe strongly enough, you can do wonders. Don't give up.' Then one day she asked, 'What about ABC? Aren't they sports minded?' So I went

*Soon, Bill, flanked by Dianne and Ray Scott, was making winning a habit.*

to see our local ABC affiliate and got an appointment with the program director, Lance Russell. Well, he and I kinda hit it off. We had something in common—we both liked to fish—and he said they would give me a show, but they first needed a sponsor and a pilot.

"And I said, 'What do you mean, a pilot? I don't even have an airplane!' And he started laughin' and explained that a pilot was a sample show for a proposed new series.

"Then I decided to find me a sponsor, so I went over to the biggest place, called Fabulous Surplus City. They sold everything there. They had sporting goods, soap powder, garden rakes, clothin'. They had everything. I talked to the guy there and he said, 'I like the idea. Show me the pilot.' So I left and went to Toledo Bend and bought me a sixteen-millimeter camera. I went and shot a pilot and presented it to Surplus City, and they liked it. Lance said, 'All right, let's go for it,' so we went and filmed our first local show in Memphis."

Thus, *Bill Dance Outdoors* was born in 1968, first as a local show before going regional, and eventually national. Today *Bill Dance Outdoors* airs four times weekly on the Outdoor Life Network (OLN).

"Man, I'll never forget that first shoot. I was so nervous you could have cracked a walnut between my kneecaps. I mean, man alive, me on TV is like pourin' perfume on a pig."

Actually, Bill Dance on TV is a natural. After introducing his first show, Bill started doing some other local shows for cities like Jackson, Mississippi, Baton Rouge, and Paducah, Kentucky. Bill was producing, shooting, and editing his own shows, lining up guests, doing promotional work, and "running around like a madman" with 208 outdoor shows a year while constantly fishing an increasing number of tournaments.

Then he was offered the opportunity to syndicate the shows, first into fifty network markets, and eventually to ninety. About that time cable was coming into its own, and Bill moved his shows to ESPN. He was there for three years before moving to TNN, which better hit his demographics, including NASCAR and country-and-western fans. Bill also picked up some great sponsors like Wal-Mart, and his shows were a tremendous success.

He stayed on TNN for sixteen years before they changed their format, and then moved to OLN where they debuted his new shows, four times a week on prime time, starting in January 2004.

Looking back on his career in television, Bill credits four early outdoor programming pioneers, all of whom he studied and got to know personally. First was Gadabout Gaddis and his show *The Flying Fisherman*; this was followed by Virgil Ward's *Championship Fishing*, Jerry McKinnis's *The Fishing Hole*, and finally, Lee Wulff's *American Sportsman*. "They are giants in the business," Bill said, "and all good friends who took the time to help me."

Fabulous ratings alone do not tell the story of the wild success of *Bill Dance Outdoors*. Their producers' target of one million viewing households a week seems modest compared to the millions of Americans who hunt and fish, all of whom know who Bill Dance is and love to watch his show. Dressed in his customary outfit of jeans and sneakers, a polo shirt, his trademark orange-and-white University of Tennessee baseball cap, and a pair of sunglasses, Bill Dance has become an American icon.

"Actually, I've never put a lot of faith in ratings," Bill told me, "but every once in awhile we'll do something to check out how many people are watchin'. Like one time we offered a free tackle box in a drawing, but you had to send in your name and address on a postcard to be eligible. We ran that announcement three times, only three times, and we got a stack of mailbags in the office that was so big a circus dog couldn't jump over it."

Television has seen many fishing shows come and go, and *Bill Dance Outdoors* has not only survived but prevailed, with more than 2,000 shows produced in thirty-five years. I asked Bill to describe the key to his success, and his answer was very interesting.

"Well," he said, "I've thought about that a lot, and thought a lot also about what people like to watch. If you can do three things on television it can help your success: relate, entertain, and educate.

"The bulk of viewers can't go to Honduras and fish for peacocks. They can't go to Alaska and fish for graylings or the exotic lodges for walleye, or Key West to fish for billfish. And I've done an occasional one of those exotic shows, but if you can do somethin' that the people can relate to, they say, 'Hey, I can do that,' or 'I recognize that kind of situation.' They can relate, just like seein' an old dirt road with a barefoot kid walkin' with an old cane pole and a can of worms. Then we put entertainment on top of that.

"But I believe the strength of *Bill Dance* has always been on our educational format, the graphics, the detail, why we're usin' a particular bait, why this bait works under certain situations, how to read water, what to look for in fish habitat, the anatomy of fish, how to balance tackle, how to fish bluffs, how to fish timber, how to night-fish, how to fish freezin' water, how to fish hot water. Subject after subject, it's going to hit someone's interests.

"I put a lot of stock in the advice of a friend named Peter Englehart, a senior vice president of programming and production for OLN, who used to work for Roone Arledge at ABC Sports. He's got a great eye for content, and he keeps tellin' me, 'Bill, keep on doin' what you're doin'.' "

*Bill Dance's viewers feel like they are 'fishin' with a pal.'*

I think it's an understatement to say that there are millions who are glad Bill Dance is following that advice. Humility is one of his most charming attributes. My theory is that Bill succeeds by being totally himself, by being passionate about his sport, and by treating everyone the same. In short, what you see with Bill Dance is what you get, and people like it and they like him. I especially enjoy his blooper shows. Unlike most celebrities with enormous egos, Bill is not afraid to show himself as a human being, banging his knee on a trailer hitch, breaking a fishing rod, or falling out of a boat.

As the success and popularity of *Bill Dance Outdoors* was growing, so too were the tournaments themselves, which were now drawing huge crowds. And believe me, they are something to see. From the competitors unloading their gaudy, fluorescent-orange outboards from their trailers to the hugely popular ceremonial weigh-ins, everything is larger than life, which works to refuel every bass fisherman's passion for the sport.

Carl Hiaasen, *New York Times* best-selling author, and a neighbor of mine in the Florida Keys, best describes the start of a tournament in *Double Whammy*, his wonderful novel on bass fishing:

> Bass anglers prepare for the blast off!" In unison the fishermen turned their ignitions . . . and the boats inched away from the crowded ramp and the procession came to stop at a lighted buoy.

*Bill continued to win. This time at the Ross Barnett Reservoir in Jackson, Mississippi. Flanked by John Powell, Ray Murski, Ray Scott, and EC Key, he was about to hear Scott's ideas on "catch and release."*

The starter raised a pistol and fired into the air . . . the race was on. The bass boats hiccupped and growled and then whined, pushing for more speed. With throttles hammered down, the sterns dug ferociously and the bows popped up . . . they planed off perfectly, forty boats rocketing at sixty miles per hour in darkness.

In 1972, the bass tournaments were flourishing, magazines were selling, TV bass shows were expanding, Bill Dance's legacy was spreading, and Ray Scott's bank account was growing. But the entrepreneur was far from finished. That year Scott would introduce an innovation that would forever impact the sport of bass fishing, if not all of angling. As so often happens, necessity was the mother of his invention.

As his Bass Master tournaments were staged in more and more venues around the country, the outcries grew from local fishermen over the amount of fish killed by the competitors. You see, in those days, fish were brought in, weighed, and discarded. Locals became angry. Ray Scott gave the dead fish to their charities "to feed the young, the old, the less fortunate, etc." The locals were not impressed, believing that the tournaments were stripping the fish from their fisheries. Ray Scott countered with "fun facts" designed to minimize the effect of the extraction of "a few fish" on the habitat. Once again, the locals were not appeased.

Realizing this issue could jeopardize his tournaments, Ray Scott searched for an answer, and found it from highly unlikely allies . . . fly fishermen.

Bass fishermen watch Monday Night Football, drive pickup trucks and prefer noisy women with big breasts. Trout fishermen watch MacNeil/Lehrer, drink white wine, drive foreign cars with passenger-side air bags and hardly think about women at all. The last characteristic may have something to do with the fact that trout fishermen spend most of their time immersed up to the waist in cold water.

—Anonymous

One could write many books on the difference between bass fishermen and trout fishermen, starting with plug rods and fly rods. From a literary perspective, many authors believe that there is an inverse corollary between fishing and reading, except of course when it comes to fly fishermen, who read too much.

That notwithstanding, Ray Scott found an answer to his fish kill problem when he was invited to be a guest at a fly fisherman event in Aspen, Colorado. There he saw fly fishermen carefully releasing their small caught trout so they could fight another day.

Shortly thereafter, Bill and Ray were flying down to Lake Amistad on the Texas-Mexico border to talk to the chamber of commerce about holding a tournament there. Bill remembers a thoughtful Ray Scott silently staring out the window and turning to him to say, "You know what, Bill—we kill a lot of stringers of fish in our tournaments, and I'm thinking of putting in a new rule that all fish must be brought in, weighed, and released, alive. What do you think?"

Bill told him he thought it was a great idea. "You see," Bill told me, "it's hard for me to kill something that's given me so much enjoyment."

Scott came home and demanded that all Bass Master tournament competitors install large, aerated live wells in their boats for transporting their catches to the weigh-ins. He then constructed a large portable tank for the bass after they were weighed, to be cared for before their release in local waters. Finally, he put out an edict that dead fish brought to the dock would cause a deduction in score. So began Ray Scott's "Don't Kill Your Catch" program, and the Florida National of Kissimmee Chain of Lakes Tournament became the first to practice catch and release.

The future of bass tournaments was secure, but more importantly, the attitude toward killing fish was changed forever. Now Saturday-morning television viewers were watching their heroes—like Bill Dance—releasing their catches live, and they began to emulate their actions. "At first, some of my viewers started calling in," Bill said. "They wanted to know what I was doin'. They thought I was crazier than a sprayed roach, but then they started releasin' fish too."

This certainly wasn't a new idea. Back in 1938, fly fishing's all-time guru, Lee Wulff, had said, "Gamefish are too valuable to be caught only once." But fly fishermen were and continue to be a small, rather elitist audience.

Howell Raines pointed out in his best-selling book, *Fly Fishing Through the Midlife Crisis*, that "it took a slip-sliding fast-talking apostle of the Redneck Way to put catch-and-release into the head of the masses." Raines went on to say, "Ray Scott is a major figure in American sportfishing . . . who has probably saved the lives of more fish than any other regulatory step since state governments first began putting legal limits on catches in the 1870s."

Ray Scott had certainly laid his claim on the title of father of tournament bass fishing. Then in 1986, he surprised many of his friends when he sold his ownership in BASS and retired to a big house overlooking a well-stocked lake. His many contributions to sportfishing were recognized when he was elected to membership in the prestigious National Freshwater Hall of Fame. He was soon joined there by his friend and first fishing superstar, Bill Dance.

Ray Scott has had his share of critics, but Bill Dance is not one of them. Bill enjoys talking about the special admiration and friendship he has for Ray, pointing out that a lot of the criticism stems from envy and sour grapes. Of Ray Scott, Bill Dance says, "Ray is a great salesman. My hat is off to him and I give him all the credit in the world because I know without him, Bill Dance, Roland Martin, and Hank Parker—all of us—wouldn't be doin' what we're doin' today. I'd probably still be sellin' hardware or somethin'. He's a straight shooter and an honest, honest, honest individual. He plays straight by the book."

To make his point, Bill tells a story about the last day of a tournament in which Bill and a few others were trying to cross Rayburn Lake to get to the weigh-in. The wind had built the waves up to a point where they couldn't get back. So they went to a small marina and called Ray Scott, told him what was happening, and asked for a little more time. "Ray said, 'Bill, please don't ask me that, please. I've got to go by my rules. If you're not here on time, your catch is disqualified. It kills me to do that, but I've got to go by my rules,'" Bill told me. "And I respected him for that," Bill went on. Scott sent a big boat for his tardy anglers, who arrived twenty-five minutes late and had their catches disqualified. "Of course I felt badly," Bill said, " 'cause it dropped me from first to seventh. It was tough for me, but I know it was tougher for Ray, and I respect him for his decision.

"We've had a lot of fun together at all those tournaments. Ray is a great talker and a great salesman and a wonderful friend. You don't become so successful by trying to con everyone. He's never told me one thing he's going to do over the thirty years I've known him and then done something else. The best thing about Ray is that he does what he says he will. If he tells you a flea can pull a plow, you better hitch 'em up."

It's often said that luck plays a role in a fisherman's success. Other events started unfolding in the seventies that would also prove fortuitous for Bill Dance.

## Johnny Morris—An American Success Story

One of Bill's good friends from the professional bass tour, Johnny Morris, from Springfield, Missouri, was receiving a little pressure from his dad as to when he was going to give up the tour and "get a real job."

"Of course, I first met Johnny through the tournaments, and I got a call from him one day askin' how'd I like to stay at the Floridian Sports Club. John's daddy owned a bunch of these liquor stores in Springfield called Brown Derby's, and sold a lot of Schenley's whiskey, so he had access to the Floridian, a beautiful lodge Schenley owned on the St. John's River in northern Florida. John used to invite four or five of us to come over there and spend a few days, and we had a great old time," Bill recalls.

"Boy, we were livin' in a castle. The food was great and that's the home of the drink Johnny invented, called the Basseroo."

"The what?" I asked.

"The Basseroo. It was a famous drink, some concoction of, like, thirty-nine different liquors, and twenty-eight kinds of whiskey, and probably fifteen kinds of gin. You'd drink it and howl at the moon for three-quarters of the night. Buddy, you drink one of those and the cares of the world are forgotten. It was like one-hundred-and-fifty octane. It woulda made a freight train take a dirt road.

"I remember we'd sit around at night talkin' about fishin' and what we wanted to do in our lives, and Johnny told me how he wanted to get in the sporting goods business."

Frustrated by his inability to find regional favorite lures around the country, in 1971 John L., as he is known to his family and friends, took a career idea to his father. He told his father, John A., that he wanted to buy popular regional fishing lures and resell them nationally. His dad asked him where, and Johnny said, "Why, in your liquor store, of course." His father said okay, and asked his son what he would use for working capital. John L. thought for a minute, and then asked John A. for a $10,000 loan to get started. His father said yes, and the young angler/entrepreneur was in business; Bass Pro Shops were born.

"Shortly after that, I'm at home and Johnny called me and said, 'I'm opening my first store, and I want you to do some promotions there for me.'

"So, I said okay, and flew up to Springfield. Johnny drove me over to his store and I'm lookin', and it said Brown Derby Liquor. I asked, 'Is that the store?' And he says, 'Yup. It belongs to my daddy, and half of it is full of liquor and the other half is fishin' goods.'

"So we pull into the parkin' lot and I look up at the marquee and it says, 'Welcome Bill Dance, Seagram's VO quarts six ninety-five, Jack Daniel's nine ninety-five.' There I was on the marquee with Seagram's and Jack Daniel's—I guess those were pretty good names to be with. Johnny asked me what I thought and I said, 'Buddy, that's stronger than a hundred acres of fresh cut garlic—that's big time.' "

Three years later, in 1974, Johnny published his first Bass Pro Shop fishing catalog, which featured many products endorsed by his good pal, Bill Dance.

In 1977, Johnny Morris made his first acquisition with the boat manufacturer, Tracker. He would later expand his boat-building holdings to include the makers of Nitro, SeaCraft, and Mako.

*In spite of his growing workload, Johnny Morris can still find the big ones.* PHOTO CREDIT: BASS PRO SHOPS.

Then in 1984, he broke ground in his hometown of Springfield for what would become the world's largest outdoor store and single largest destination attraction in Missouri: Outdoor World.

If you haven't seen a Bass Pro Shop, you should go. In a style that would become signature Johnny Morris, the first store included many features that made it a memorable outing for outdoor fans of all ages. A breathtaking three-story waterfall replenishes several freshwater aquariums that are home to many species of fish, including Ethel, a seventeen-pound largemouth bass that grew to over twenty pounds before her demise of natural causes at the age of twenty.

Interactive attractions like archery ranges appeal to anyone who loves the outdoors. There are also plenty of restaurants and live fishing demonstrations by pros like Bill Dance, Roland Martin, Stu Apte, and others.

Using Springfield as a model, Johnny began building new stores around North America. His is a true Horatio Alger story of a man who has parlayed his passion for the outdoors into one of the world's largest distributors of fish tackle.

I'll always remember a story that Johnny told me sitting by a campfire on the Tree River in the Northwest Territories of Canada—a story of how he almost lost his life before Bass Pro Shops got started.

"I was fishing the Arkansas Invitational at Beaver Lake," Johnny said. "My partner that day was Bob Craddock from Kentucky. We were having a pretty good day, but it was cold and the wind started to blow up the lake pretty good.

"Eventually we headed back for the weigh-in. About halfway across the lake my bilge pump failed, and soon my battery shorted out because we'd taken so much water, and then a couple of big waves hit us and we capsized.

"Buddy, that water was cold! Must have been in the forties. I saw an empty gas tank floating and managed to swim out and get it, and Bob and I held onto it for dear life. Thank goodness we were wearing the life jackets that Ray Scott had ordered as part of his tournament rules, but it was so cold I thought we were going to die. I reached in my pocket and got a coin out and tried to scratch a message in that gas can to my parents. I wanted to write, 'Mom and Dad, I love you,' but the paint finish on that Mercury tank was too good and my hands were going numb.

"We were in pretty rough shape. I think I was starting to pass out when this big hand reached down and grabbed me and threw me in his boat. It was another angler named Billy Westmorland, who just happened to be fishing in this remote area, saw the floating gas tank, and came over to investigate."

Billy Westmorland clearly saved both Johnny and Bob Craddock's lives. Back on the dock they were treated for hypothermia, thawed out, and recovered completely with a story to tell that neither man would ever forget.

"Johnny and I have kept up our close friendship over the years," Bill Dance said. "The thing that has impressed me more than his incredible success is that he has never changed. He could sit in the White House and have dinner with the president, or go to London and have dinner with the Queen of England, or sit on a boat dock and eat a can of pork and beans, and he is the same Johnny as he was. He's a very shy person, the sweetest man with a heart as big as a bread basket. He's a prince of a guy, a class act with a 'Capital K.' Do you know, he even ended up buying the Floridian Sports Club where we used to drink those Basseroos!"

Johnny Morris credits Bill Dance with help in sales through his product endorsements. But as always with these two longtime fishin' buddies, it's not all about business. It's about friendship, and business just seems to come along for the ride. Of Bill, Johnny says simply, "He's a heck of a guy, and no fisherman ever drew a crowd like he does. He's got a huge, well-deserved following, and is a great ambassador for our sport, and I'm proud to say that he is a friend of mine." Eventually, Johnny Morris's Bass Pro Shops would become the largest sponsor of *Bill Dance Outdoors*. Like Bill, Johnny to this day continues to treat everyone he meets the same way.

*Bill Dance (left) with his good fishin' buddy, Johnny Morris.*

A few years ago some northern pals of mine and I were starting a celebrity charity fishing tournament in western New York. I invited John L. to fish it as my guest, knowing full well he'd cancel if the bluefin tuna were running in the Bahamas. This retired bass tournament guy has developed a passion for pulling on 1,000-pound tuna when they're around.

Sure enough, Johnny got the call from the Bahamas and I got the call to cancel. Now, for all his success, Johnny is still the thoughtful, kind of shy person he was before he sold his first lure, and as I often do, I decided to have some fun with him. So I feigned sadness, if not outright abysmal sorrow, at his rejection.

"Oh, Bubba," he said over the phone, "you can find someone else."

"No way," I shot back, "it's way too late, and I was really counting on you."

Johnny said, "I'll get you someone good. I promise."

"Like who?" I sniveled.

Johnny thought for a minute and rattled off five or six bass professionals; I rejected one after the other. I could sense some exasperation in his voice. Then he said, "Okay then, Buddy, who do you want?"

"Bill Dance," I said emphatically.

"I'll see what I can do," he said.

Less than half an hour later, my phone rang and a voice on the other end said, "Hey, this is Bill Dance. What time does the kick-off party start for the tournament?"

I couldn't believe it. I knew he and Johnny were good pals, but here he was, ready to pick up and fly to Buffalo, New York, for a "Ham-Am Tournament" in June, which had to be in the heart of his busiest season. When word got out that Bill Dance was fishing our inaugural tournament, our success was insured. The tournament filled up fast and our kick-off dinner sold out.

The day of the event arrived, and there he was, the world's most highly recognized fisherman, complete with his signature white University of Tennessee baseball cap with orange bill and block "T" signing autographs and swapping stories with a room full of strangers, just like they were old fishin' buddies, which in fact many of them were. These were hard-core *Bill Dance Outdoors* fans that had gone on dozens of fishing trips with Bill through the wonders of cable TV. In the winter in Buffalo when every body of water freezes more solid than the HSBC Arena's NHL ice rink, frustrated anglers either take to the ice with a drill or to the couch for some vicarious bass fishing. That comprises a pretty good TV audience when you consider that more hunting and fishing licenses are sold in this county than in any other county in the country.

The weather was beautiful that day as we climbed into Captain Jim Hanley's boat. Jim is a Buffalo guy who used to fish the bass tournament circuit twelve years ago. One of his proudest moments during that time was meeting Bill Dance. Imagine Jim's delight when Bill recognized him after all those years. Why wasn't I surprised? Bill Dance seems to have developed an encyclopedic memory of sportsmen he has met.

The conditions were perfect for fishing. There was not a ripple in an often turbulent Lake Erie, nor a cloud in the sky, with temperatures in the mid-seventies. Seagulls flew overhead as new friends smiled and caught—and released—some beautiful bass. By the end of the day we had caught three walleye and about twenty-five good-sized smallmouth bass. While a few other boats caught more fish, I don't think anyone had more fun. Conversation came easy. We took turns talking about fishing and our lives and laughing at each other's stories. At the end of the day I felt like I'd spent the day with an old friend—that I'd just appeared on an eight-hour version of *Bill Dance Outdoors*.

*We have larger walleye than this on Lake Erie but none have gotten kissed by as popular a fishing celebrity.*

While we were driving to the airport I asked Bill about his positive attitude. "Bill, you're so up all the time. Don't you have any sad stories?"

"Well, yes," he said. "I do have one. It was at Clark Hill in the Bass Master Classic which I'd never won. I can't remember the year, but I was leading on the last day and Lee Wulff of *American Sportsman* was shooting it. In the afternoon I hung a nice fish that would weigh a solid five, five and a half pounds, and the film crew pulled up and started filmin'. I got the fish up to the boat and was fixin' to reach for it—and could have gotten it—and the camera crew said, 'Bill, let him swim out one more time so we can get a tighter shot of it.' This fish had basically given up, but I gave him a little push out with my hand and he swam out five or six feet, jumped, and threw the hook and I lost him.

"Well, I went ahead and weighed in and I was still in first place until the final angler, Rayo Breckenridge, weighed in, and I lost the Classic by three and half pounds. Now that's a sad story."

On that note we arrived at the airport. I thanked Bill for helping kick off our charity tournament. He said he'd had a great time and we promised to stay in touch, which we have.

Since then we've had some great chats during which Bill has shared with me some of what he considers to be the highlights of his fishing career. While he lost that Classic because of the camera crew, he has won twenty-three National Bass Titles, qualified for the Classic eight out of nine years, and was BASS Angler of the Year three times, in 1969, 1974, and 1977.

He also enjoyed being honored in 1978 with the Congressional National Water Safety Award, which was previously given to such famous recipients as Lloyd Bridges and Jacques Cousteau. "That was great," he told me, "but my biggest thrill in fishin' was being present when all of my children caught their first fish. In fact, my three-year-old granddaughter Grace Ann came over the other day and I got to watch her catch her first two fish, and that was a thrill."

There came a time when Bill decided to retire from tournament fishing. "Why did you do that?" I asked him.

"Anxiety," he replied without a pause. "Ray Scott and my wife Dianne said the exact same thing to me at different times without knowin' it. Both of them said one day tournaments are not going to be my number-one priority. They're goin' to drop to number two, number three, and maybe to number four, and that's exactly what happened.

"I used to eat, breathe, and sleep those tournaments, but with all my shows and promotions and travel, I was literally passin' myself on the road. I knew everyone in every airport and was goin' three and four months at a time, only bein' home four or five days.

"I was just too busy. The pressure was huge and the anxiety continued to build up as my performance declined. So I went to my sponsors and they said, 'Hey, the time to quit is when you are on top,' and so I did. And they all stayed with me and you know, the only thing I miss now about the tournaments are the people."

Since leaving the tournament circuit, Bill is staying busier than ever with shows, promotions, and appearances, and he has found time to write several more magazine articles and seven books on bass fishing. Most importantly he has found more time to spend with his growing family, including his son Bill Jr., who has joined him in the business.

Today, the popularity of bass fishing continues to grow with no end in sight. Wal-Mart, a longtime tournament supporter, has now created its own series called the Wal-Mart Fishing League, allowing the anglers to compete for "big money."

I asked a question of Bill, like someone might ask of a baseball great like Ted Williams, Joe DiMaggio, or Mickey Mantle, about the modest earnings in those early days versus today's megamillion-dollar bass tournament prizes.

"I'm livin' the life I want to live right now, and I couldn't be happier than I am," he said. "Those tournaments opened the door for me and offered a steppin'-stone to bigger and better things in life. They afforded me the chance to make a good livin', raise my family, educate my children, and give them many things that I never had as a child.

"If the young anglers today can make a million dollars catchin' a fish, more power to them, but my first thousand-dollar prize money meant at least that much to me. I think it's good for the sport, but I don't miss it. I'm lovin' my life and have no regrets."

Bill and I were in a kind of melancholy mood one day while talking on the phone, and I asked him if he could tell me what it's all about—what drew him to fishing time and time again.

He took a deep breath and thought for a moment and said, "It's that jitterbug on top of the water. That really turned me on. The key word is challenge. I know you're like me on this, you're a competitor, and as such you know how we all compete. In fact, I believe that we as humans compete no matter whether we sell insurance, or sell automobiles, play football, play golf, tennis, or Ping-Pong—I'm tryin' to beat you, you're tryin' to beat me. We're tryin' to hit the million-dollar club; we're tryin' to be the number-one salesman sellin' cars. When we're drivin' our car or truck from home to work, we make six lights and say, Now let's see if we can make eight. Let's see if we can make them all.

"From the time we wake up, we're playin' these little mental games. We're sittin' on a couch watchin' the Buffalo Bills play against the Tennessee Titans. And you say, 'Hey, Bill, I bet they score on this drive, or I'll bet I make this putt. That's just the way we are, and we're the same way when it comes to fishin'. We're competin' against another living creature, tryin' to match wits with him. We're tryin' to lure him out of his world into ours. I think the key word is challenge."

"Okay, Bill," I asked him, "what about success? How have you prevailed and succeeded over so many years?"

"Well, Bob," he replied, "the one thing I've learned is that you can't buy, borrow, charge, or steal fishin' success. I love Vince Lombardi, and I'll never forget the words he engrained into the minds of the Green Bay Packers when he said, 'Winnin' is achieved through determination.'

"I've always believed so strongly in that, because motivation plays such a huge role when you're competing with Mother Nature—motivation, along with positive attitude and desire to win. Add to that a good dose of knowledge and experience. Good anglers can work and study hard to be consistent, but even then you're never going to be one hundred percent successful when you compete like we do with Mother Nature and her creatures. But that's where the word challenge comes in, because you're always challenging that.

"So why do we fish? The bottom line is that we're competitive and we love the challenge. It's just a wonderful, wonderful sport that gives us the chance to experience those two things over and over again," Bill concluded.

Watch *Bill Dance Outdoors* and you'll feel like you've made a new friend, a fishin' buddy who you want to spend more and more time with. Through his homespun humor comes a wisdom that transcends regionality. While his self-proclaimed passion and irrefutable skills revolve around the hunt for fish, I believe his life's larger success comes from his ability to relate, entertain, and educate—because of his humble nature and genuine interest and caring for people.

*Good company and good discourse are the very sinews of virtue.*

—Izaak Walton

Without exception, they are tenacious, persevering, and keenly in touch with their native instincts. To them, fishing is a reflective act, a state of mind, and a metaphor for life in how each one views herself in alignment with the universe.

—Lyla Foggia, *Reel Women* (1995)

4

# JANE COOKE: URBAN ANGLER

*One day I was out fishing the Connetquot River on Long Island with my friends from the Women Flyfishers Club. It's a hatchery in a state park and there are fish all over the place, but some are harder to catch than others. You fish on predetermined beats like on the rivers in England, and I was teamed up with my dear friend Barbara Mallory, whom I met fishing in Russia and fish with a lot. She's about six feet tall and is a wonderfully talented angler. So she makes this beautiful long cast and puts her fly right under an overhanging willow branch on the bank, and you just know there is a helluva fish in there, and sure enough, as the fly glides past a submerged log, there is this huge strike and she has her lunker. This fish runs upstream, jumps, runs downstream, and jumps again. We see him and he is huge—a sea run brown trout.*

*So Barbara and I followed the fish and we're both struggling. It's getting late and cold and dark and we have to get back to our group, and it's my job to net the fish. It was a simple matter of my just having to reach down and scoop up the fish, and for some reason I had my hand up, and I don't even remember touching the leader, but I must have—and the leader broke, just like that. That was all the extra tension that it needed—it was so taut and the fish was so big.*

*I don't remember to this day what Barbara said to me, but it was something like, "I don't ever want to fish with you again. You better leave now. You better go home."*

*We've had wonderful times fishing together but I've never seen a closer friend, someone I care about so much, so mad at me. It was awful. We laugh about it now, but I'll never forget the chill on the river that day.*

—Jane Cooke

In 1653, THE VENERABLE IZAAK WALTON established the male-dominated order of angling in his work, *The Compleat Angler*, amicably portraying a Brotherhood of the Angle scouring the local streams and rivers for fish while women cavorted as milkmaids in the meadows, a la John Donne. While baggy tweeds gave way for the most part to more modern garb, and the anglers' equipment changed substantially, the image of fishing as a men's sport—a guy thing—remained substantially intact for three centuries, well into the 1950s.

Today the old order has changed dramatically. In streams, rivers, ponds, lakes, and oceans across the country and around the world, women are emerging in great numbers, not only discovering the sport, but modifying it to suit their own needs and tastes. Barriers to entry still exist, from men's fishing clubs in the Northeast to men-only bass tournaments in the heartlands, but more and more, women are establishing their own clubs, tournaments, heroes, and mentoring programs, and their numbers are growing at an unprecedented rate.

There is, however, an historical and geographical precedent for the involvement of women in fishing. I'm sure few Brothers of the Angle know, and fewer care, that the first book ever written on fishing was written by a woman and predated Walton's work by 157 years. Dame Juliana Berners, the abbess of the Sopwell Priory, wrote the "The Treatyse of Fysshynge with an Angle" in her *Booke of St. Albans* in 1496.

Her work contained a wealth of practical angling advice, as well as information on equipment. Also in many cultures, inshore commercial fishing has been the sole domain of women. The economies of India, Africa, Asia, Laos, and the Philippines have been enhanced by women in aquaculture.

In the United States, a quiet, self-effacing woman named Joan Wulff, widow of the legendary Lee Wulff, has literally become the patron saint of women anglers, and many men as well. After winning a variety of tournaments since 1937 and a national distance fly-casting championship in 1951 against an all-male field, Joan Wulff appeared in many films, and has written several books and co-founded the Wulff School of Fly Fishing. Most important, she has served as a quiet but authoritative spokesperson for fly fishing as an art and conservation as an imperative.

Wulff has been a teacher and a mentor and role model to many younger women who have taken up fly fishing and brought their own personalities to the sport in unique and interesting ways. One of those

*Nobody's face lights up when they catch a fish like Jane Cooke, here with a small striped bass with a taste for flies.*

women is Jane Simoni Cooke. In her mid-forties and married with a young son, Jane may be the consummate New Yorker. Witty and urbane, multidimensional and independent, Jane appears to be the master of her world, juggling parenting, a home life, a social schedule, passion for the arts, awareness of the less fortunate, and a love of the outdoors. She's one of those people who seems to be constantly on the move, searching for answers, with a good heart and an insatiable appetite for information—one of those people you meet and say, "Wow, how does she do all that?"

Jane is a passionate angler whose husband has no interest in fishing. She is currently teaching her five-year-old son how to fly-fish. She has demonstrated her strength and self-reliance in learning the intricacies of fly fishing and breaking down its barriers of entry that have intimidated other women. While there is no doubt that Jane is a strong person, she is also very vulnerable. She has led an interesting life with plenty of change and relocation, but fishing for her has been a constant, a safe place, a refuge from turmoil—all of which she defines with great eloquence.

*Jane won the women's division of the first annual Montauk Redbone Tournament and posed here with tournament director Captain Scott Holder and her guide Bob Sullivan.*

Every year Jane celebrates opening day of trout season in Roscoe, New York. She will meet friends, including Joan Wulff and Judy Van Put, on the banks of the Beaverkill at six A.M. with a glass of champagne. Fishing legend Paul Dixon says that "she is the most unabashedly enthusiastic woman I know in fly fishing. She's the future of the sport."

Another of her fishing pals, prolific author Nick Lyons, says of Jane, "I just adore her. She's a beautiful woman and a perfect enthusiast, so ebullient and fun to be with. She brings a sense of humor and curiosity to everything she does. I once sat on a hillside and watched her try to catch a trout for an hour. Another time I saw her put her rod down to watch two otters playing. She has such a great love of the natural."

While her fishing career started in freshwater streams, she has become intrigued with pursuing the bigger fish found in salt water, and has tried her hand in a few saltwater tournaments. It was at one of these events in Montauk, Long Island, where we first met. She won the women's division, catching several bluefish and striped bass on fly. Her score placed her very high in the overall standings and I remember her accepting her award with understated grace.

In her own quiet way she has become an articulate spokesperson for fly fishing, which is clearly more to her than just a sport. At Montauk we began our talks about fishing and her life on streams, salt water, and, of course, in New York City. I'll never forget those conversations.

One of Jane's grandfathers and her father were engineers who worked on major projects in New York City, including the Pan Am Building and Kennedy Airport. This may explain why she feels so rooted in the Big Apple. In addition to engineering, her dad was intermittently both a banker and a businessman, explaining in part why her own professional path had many detours. She also vividly remembers long conversations she had as a child with her uncle, who was also her godfather and an avid fly fisherman.

"I was always interested in the natural world," she told me, "fascinated with bugs, plants, and trees. I remember memorizing insects' names early on and talking with my uncle about how they related to fishing."

She also remembers going on her first fishing trip when she was in second grade with her grandfather, who owned a vacation home in Harbour Island in the Bahamas.

Jane was born in 1957 and adopted, as were her brother and sister. She speculates that her own adoption might be linked to her love of fishing. She only recently made this connection which she explained to me one snowy day in New York when I was finishing up my story of her interesting life.

Thinking back on her years at Smith College, Jane's memories are ironically the most vivid when she recalls some of her summertime jobs, like working two years on a ranch in Cody, Wyoming, and another at the Mashomack Fish and Game Preserve on Shelter Island off Long Island. "I knew then," she said, "that I wanted to spend a lot of my time out of doors. I was a history major, a so-so student, but I loved the Connecticut River Valley and being outdoors."

"So you spent some time out West; but to me, you seem to be the consummate Northeasterner," I said one day at that fishing tournament in Montauk.

"I have a confidence here," she told me. "Confidence in the schools, the suburbs, the theaters, the museums, the restaurants, and the trout streams as well, and I truly love it here, just like my mom did. That wasn't true of my dad; even though he worked here on major projects, he always wanted to get out, to get away."

Jane's graduation from college left her more confused than focused. "A lot of my friends headed for training programs on Wall Street. I headed for San Francisco with two college friends," she told me, "with some vague idea of working in food service. I got a job running a restaurant called Quinn's Lighthouse in Oakland. One night we got robbed at gunpoint and I got locked in a freezer. That ended my food-service career."

After a few other jobs on the West Coast, Jane decided she wanted to be back in New York, where she took one of those Wall Street training jobs that she had earlier rejected. Success followed in the form of promotions—along with loneliness. "I was working too hard with no time for myself, and never even seeing natural light," she told me.

Frustrated, she took a battery of profiling tests. While the results offered various career options, they did indicate she should avoid anything too three-dimensional or structured, like architecture.

"So what did you do?" I asked her.

"I signed up for architecture school at the University of Virginia," she said with a smile. "I guess I've always been a bit of a rebel. That's one of the things that drew me to fishing, by the way—that I could be excelling at something not many women did."

Jane graduated from Virginia in 1988 with a degree in landscape architecture, moving her closer to her goal of spending more time outdoors.

She married a writer who she'd known for several years and defined as "a liberal's liberal." Jane's work in landscaping design was going well, but she felt like she was being smothered in a restrictive marriage.

"I wanted to take up fly fishing," she told me, "but my husband forbade me, saying it was too elitist."

Later that year, her dad died, and she was devastated.

"My marriage wasn't strong enough to sustain itself in a tragedy," she said, "and we divorced."

The New York girl headed for Salisbury, Connecticut, where she started her own landscaping company.

"I felt like I needed a fresh start in the country," she said. "My business was struggling, so I decided to start teaching in the local high school."

Throughout her metamorphosis, Jane and her mom stayed very close. One day her mom called and said, "Janie, now you need a sport," and Jane told her that she wanted to go to the Orvis Fly Fishing School in Manchester, Vermont. Her Mom treated her to the tuition.

"I called Orvis," Jane told me, "and I said, 'Look, I want to learn to fly-fish, but I don't want it to be a dating thing,' and they said, 'Why don't you come up for one of our family weekends around Easter. No one will bother you and you'll love it,' and I did. It was snowing and we were casting through snowflakes and it was great walking through the fields along the Battenkill. I just loved the whole thing—being outdoors, the equipment, casting, technique, the flies, the store, the people, studying bugs. I found it was virtually meeting all my needs."

Six months later, Jane's mom said she wanted to get Jane something for Christmas for her new sport, and Jane said that waders were essential. Her Mom got her an Orvis gift certificate, so she headed into town to the Orvis Shop on Vanderbilt at 44th, not realizing that fate was at her side.

She asked for help from one of the people working there. Her salesman turned out to be Paul Dixon, who has become a legend in saltwater fly fishing. Paul is an ex-California surfer who made his way east, went to work for Orvis, opened his own fly shop on Long Island, and became one of the first people to catch striped bass off the shores of Montauk using an eight-weight fly rod. As Peter Kaminsky would say about Paul in his great book about Montauk, *The Moon Pulled Up an Acre of Bass*, "It was the striped bass that put Dixon on the angling map." Now nearing fifty and having spent most of the last decade on the East End, he is a fair-skinned, curly-haired, Southern Californian with a quick laugh, a suave gentleman sportsman's manner, and an encyclopedic knowledge of every aspect of fly fishing, gathered, as he often says, "from time on the water."

*Paul Dixon catches big fish in both fresh and salt water.*

Eventually Paul would end up splitting the year guiding out of Montauk in the summer and fall and Key Largo during the winter and spring—but I'm getting ahead of myself. On this day Paul, the salesman, was in the store for Jane Simoni Cooke.

"I remember the first time I met Janie," Paul told me. "I was working for Orvis and in walks this girl and says, 'My mom owes me a Christmas present and I want to buy a pair of waders so I can fly-fish.' You could tell she was passionate about the sport. She started coming in all the time to buy flies and equipment, and we'd have long, long talks about fly fishing. She was really into it like no other woman I'd ever met."

Jane had no idea then who Paul was, but remembers him as being very nice and very attractive. "He helped get me the right size waders and while I was trying them on, I heard him talking on the phone to the basement, saying, 'Nancy, you better get up here, we've got a live one.'"

Nancy, it would turn out, was Nancy Zakon, who after starting at Orvis, was promoted to designing women's clothes for the catalog. She became a great spokesperson for women in fly fishing, started Juliana's Anglers in New York, the Bonefish Bonnies in Key Largo, and eventually would become president of the International Women Fly Fishers (IWFF).

Little did Jane know when she walked in looking for those waders that she would become a member of the "Orvis family" that day. She and Nancy became great friends, and Jane soon joined Juliana's Anglers, where she learned the art of fly fishing through outings, demonstrations, and lectures, which she would eventually go on to present herself. She found the mentoring that the organization offered to be very helpful.

She soon became a member of the board and helped others learn the sport. "It was all about teaching women not to be intimidated by their instructors and to build up their confidence. For me it wasn't about confidence, but it was a huge barrier for others. Many felt it was a man's sport, and it was, but I think we helped change that."

She and Paul Dixon also became great friends and she sees him in the role of her mentor as well. "I had my first little personal fly-fishing tragedy that day at Orvis," Jane said, laughing. "The waders fit fine and Nancy was ringing them up, and I was talking to Paul, who I thought was so attractive, and he said, 'I'm going to Long Island this weekend to get married.' My heart just broke. You see, in ten minutes I'd already developed a crush, fallen in love, and imagined myself married to this wonderful guy behind the counter, Paul Dixon. I figured, there goes another dashed hope for salvation—but we did become friends."

Jane continued her teaching, dating, and "floundering around" in Connecticut, buoyed by her growing interest and search for knowledge in fly fishing. One day Paul called her and invited her to come down to New York. He said, "We're having a book signing and there's someone I want you to meet." The someone was Howell Raines, the author of *Fly Fishing Through the Midlife Crisis*, who was at the time the editorial page editor of *The New York Times*. Paul remembers the signing like it was yesterday. "I introduced them (Jane and Howell), and there was immediate chemistry, like love at first sight."

Jane got her book signed, and Howell told her that he wanted to go fishing with her. They both had a good time talking, and then exchanged phone numbers. She took the book home, read it, loved it, and got some insights into Howell Raines as a fisherman and a man who had been married, had a family, and gone through a painful separation.

Howell began calling Jane to go out but she resisted, not wanting to get involved. Eventually he prevailed, and as Jane says, it turned into "a wonderful romance." Still teaching, she had plenty of time for travel, and they started dating and fishing all around the country. Of Howell Jane said, "He was a great guy, a great teacher of life as well as fishing, very organized and a gifted writer. I remember watching him write a piece on Robert McNamara—that was nominated for a Pulitzer—in about forty-five minutes. Having summers off was great. We fished for trout in Montana, redfish in Louisiana, and bonefish in Florida and the Bahamas." But ultimately, the relationship didn't work out and the couple soon separated.

It was a very tough breakup for Jane, who found a new apartment in New York. She remembers writing Christmas cards to fly-fishing friends she had made who were members of the "extended *New York Times* family," like Tom and Lori McGuane, Meredith and Tom Brokaw, Barbara and Arthur Gelb, and young Arthur Sulzburger. "I felt like I was no longer part of that family and felt devastatingly lonely. I spent Christmas with my sister who was seven years younger than I and had had her first child, and visited with my mom who had earlier been diagnosed with Alzheimer's. I felt all alone at thirty-something, wondering what the heck was going to happen to me."

These were difficult times for Jane, who was realizing how much she wanted to start a family of her own. As the winter receded, Jane did as she had done before in time of crisis: she turned to fishing. More aptly this time, fishing came to her. A friend of hers named Jane Timkin, knowing she was blue, invited her to go salmon fishing in Russia; her pal Nancy Zakon invited her on an Atlantic salmon trip to the storied Miramichi in Canada; and, of course, Paul Dixon was there, inviting her to fish the local streams and raising her spirits. "Paul was a steadfast friend through all this," she told me. "Everyone knows he's a great fisherman, guide, and teacher, but he's also fun to fish with, and he loves to tell stories and gossip. I love to fish with him. I was getting better and feeling stronger. I even started flirting with guys again."

*Jane caught her all-time favorite fish, this large male Atlantic Salmon, in the Upper Umba River in Russia in August 1977.*

The Russia trip was great for Jane. She found the Panoi River to be beautiful and the salmon plentiful and tough. While she doesn't count fish herself, the manager there told her she had caught the most fish on the trip and was therefore "high rod." Her confidence was returning. Also on that trip she killed her first fish to feed the camp. "I'd never killed a fish before, but when they cooked it for everyone, I felt like I was Diana the Huntress. It was great to feel like a provider." A feeling probably heightened, I thought, by several months of feeling inadequate after a high-profile romance gone awry.

Fall came, and Jane got a call from a friend she had dated for awhile after her divorce, Patrick Cooke, the editor of *Forbes FYI*. She said that the timing hadn't been right before, but they shared a romantic dinner in the city and soon they were dating again.

In the meantime, Jane's mother's health was failing and she was in assisted care in Baltimore. Jane started thinking about a move to be closer to her. She interviewed and was accepted for a job at the World Wildlife Federation and the National Trust for Historic Preservation in Washington. She was to report for work after an August fishing trip she had planned to Crystal Creek in Alaska to look for silver salmon.

"Alaska was great, the weather was sunny and clear, the fish were biting, and Patrick, my new boyfriend, called every day on the satellite phone," she said with the biggest smile I'd seen from her since we met.

"What'd he say?" I asked her. " 'I love you, over'?

"No, it wasn't 'I love you' yet. He said he was just checking in to see how the fishing was," Jane said.

"When I left Alaska, I knew I'd be back, but I also knew what I wanted," she told me, "and when we landed, I called Dick Moe at the National Trust and told him I can't take this job. I'm thirty-nine years old and in a relationship and I think I'm in love, and I've got to go for it."

Jane and Patrick eloped to Harbour Island where she had fished with her grandfather as a child. They were married at a pretty little Anglican Church on the top of a hill.

Two days after Jane and Patrick were married, she went fishing there with an old family friend, the legendary Bonefish Joe, who said to Jane when she got in his boat, "You're pregnant, I can tell," and she said, "No, Bonefish, that's impossible." Nine months later, to the day, their son Ronan was born, adding a new dimension to Bonefish Joe's enormous skills.

Jane told me that they stayed at Pink Sands in an oceanside cottage called Cabbage Key, so from then on, they've called Ronan their "Cabbage Key Kid."

I shared my own story about Bonefish Joe that made Jane laugh. Two years ago I was fishing with him and said, "Now, Joe, I'm a

*Harbour Island's famous first son, Bonefish Joe.*

conservationist into catch-and-release, and I don't want to kill any of these bonefish; I want to get this straight with you and be sure that you're in agreement before we leave the dock."

"Oh, yes, Boss," Joe responded. "Catch-and-release. Me too. That's what I'm into. No problems."

We sped out of the harbor to a little cove and immediately spotted a big Bahama bonefish tailing in the shallows. I threw a crab pattern fly and he slurped it up in a flash. I landed him in about ten minutes. Bonefish Joe reached gently into the water, hoisted him into the boat, and still holding what looked to be about a six-pounder, said, "Boss, you know I'm going to keep this fish," and I said, "Yeah, I figured you were," and nothing more was said.

Now I'm a major advocate of catch-and-release, but I also understand that many underdeveloped islands have been dining on certain fish for centuries, and change comes slowly. Anyway, Jane and I got a chuckle out of my story.

Knowing Jane's love of angling, I thought it strange that Patrick didn't fish. Patrick told me that he was happy for his wife—that this was her thing. He'd never have to worry about her having a sport she could pursue if anything ever happened to him. As you might imagine, Jane had a different take on the subject. "I'm delighted that Patrick doesn't fish. It makes fishing even more precious and personal for me. He loves to know how I did, which is nice, but it's not what our relationship is all about. To coin a phrase, there's nothing fishy about it," she said with a smile.

"I'm very happy now with my routine," she told me, "but every once in awhile I've got to get away, like last winter when I took Ronan

*Paul Dixon and Ronan at Ocean Reef.*

*Jane showing off "the world's smallest bonefish."*

with me to fish with Paul Dixon at Ocean Reef, and we caught the world's smallest bonefish one day, along with four permit."

One afternoon I got together with Jane in New York and asked her some very pointed questions about women in fishing in general, and her interest in angling in particular.

"What's this Women Fly-fishers Club," I asked her, "some kind of secret society?"

"No," she laughed, "it's not secret, but it is private. It was started in 1932 by a woman named Julia Fairchild whose husband was a member of the all-male Anglers Club who have a beautiful facility in the Fraunces Tavern on Wall Street. Today our club has about one hundred members. My name was proposed by my friend Barbara Mallory, obviously before I broke off that big fish of hers on the Connetquot. We have fishing outings and two meetings a year. This year I'm on the board and serve as entertainment chairman. It's fun. I love a good *girl twirl*."

"A what?" I asked, almost afraid to know.

"A girl twirl," she said, "is a good giggle with a bunch of gals. I love my time spent with women as well as my time spent with men. Each is special, but our women get-togethers are more relaxed and easy-going. There isn't the pressure, and we can laugh about things that we think are funny, just like men have things they think are funny."

"What do you have to do to get in?" I asked.

"Well, there's no initiation or secret handshake, but we do have a test," she said. "You have to be able to demonstrate that you can fish—not just cast, but actually fish by yourself, which means making leaders, choosing flies, tying knots, and all of the other things that go along with catching and releasing a fish. We're looking for women who can fish by themselves and not be dependent on others out there.

"Last year we started a new youth mentorship program that I'm very excited about. We seek out and identify young women interested in learning about fly fishing, help them get started, and break down the barriers to help them enjoy the sport."

"How about feminism in fishing?" I asked.

"I'm not a fan of feminism," Jane said. "Growing up, our generation of women was very much into it, but I believe that the feminists shortchanged me with all their talk of equality and the push to get into the battle for the boardroom. They overlooked the importance of having family and how difficult it is to bear children at an older age.

"Now I believe there is neither a place nor a need for it in fishing. We've come a long way, and smart manufacturers are realizing the market need for lighter rods and smaller, more fitted waders. People like Nancy Zakon, along with others like Christy Ball and Lori-Ann Murphy, are helping to remove equipment barriers, but as far as the sport of fishing itself, I think it should be totally gender neutral."

"And who are your heroes?" I asked.

"Well, Joan Wulff is right up there," she said. "She epitomizes women in fly fishing. She's what it's all about. We talk a few times a year and I look forward to our opening-day ceremonial champagne. Maybe some day many years from now Nancy Zakon will succeed her in what she has done to help women enjoy the sport, but for now Joan is without equal. She developed her own style, her own technique, and she persevered even after her husband's death. She competed at the very highest level of fly fishing, always with the grace and elegance of a ballet dancer, which she was. I just think the world of her and at the end of the day, I think it's the tastefulness of Joan and Nancy that attract me to them because there still is, or should be, a gentlemanly or gentlewomanly quality to fly fishing. Fly fishing is still a place for good manners and people behaving well, and you don't find many places like that anymore today."

I asked Jane if she thought women could keep up with men in fishing, both physically and emotionally.

"Physically, no; I don't think we have the strength or the stamina," she said. "Emotionally perhaps. Paul Dixon always speaks of women being better listeners who don't wear their egos on their sleeves and aren't about to take instruction from other men." She went on to say that women are more apt to stay within the limits of their capabilities and be more precise, and that helps them with the sport. "But then every once in awhile a woman comes along like Joan Wulff, and she breaks out from the norm," Jane said. "As a former dancer, she knows how to use every muscle in her cast, and she throws a fly line one hundred and sixty-one feet!"

I asked Jane what message she would pass along to young women considering taking up fishing. She told me, "I can only go by my own experience. It is like anything else, not necessarily a woman's sport— neither good nor bad for women. It's more about your personality, and mine happens to work. I don't need a mother or father or someone else to fish with me now, or in the past, and I think that there are a lot of women out there like that.

"You need to have a sense of independence because you're going to some places that are pretty out there. You have to love that isolation, a long walk in the woods along a stream, and ultimately, you're catching fish on your own. In essence, it's a loner sport. You may go with people, but that cast, that tug on your line—it's your own personal thing. It's a great challenge, and I love a challenge."

*Boy*, I thought to myself, *this woman has thought about this sport a lot, and lived fishing more than anyone I've ever talked to.* Just ask the right question or maybe even the wrong question, and Jane has wonderful, thoughtful answers.

"So, Jane," I continued, "what does it all come down to? What is the major thing that draws you to fishing?"

She looked me in the eye as if she had been waiting for me to catch up with her and to ask her this question. She took a deep breath and said, "It's about the fish—the fish in its underwater lair beneath a submerged log, protected by overhanging brush in a New England stream. It's about floating a little Adams to him, watching him feed, and feeling the little tug, the pull on the rod, and every time it happens, whether it's a sunfish on my son's line or a trout or a salmon, my heart flutters.

"So it's about the challenge, the connection, and the catch. For a second the fish becomes a pet. Maybe it comes from being adopted, and what I've actually done is adopt this little spirit myself. I'm working on a personal theory about adopted children and animals, and I think fishing may be a part of that."

"So what's the big deal about opening day, Jane?"

"It's ceremonial," she said after a pause. "I've started taking my son Ronan with me now because it's a celebration of faith, love, rebirth, and renewal, the return of spring and new fish. And faith in the new year and love of the sport. It's so appropriate that it comes at that time of year along with spring and Easter, and everything is new and fresh and clean after a winter's rest.

"Every trip can be like that. I feel close to my dad in the cathedral of that stream. I'll always say a prayer for him, and that's vital to my being there, and what I want my son to understand about me and about himself as well."

Our talk in New York ended, and Jane rushed to get back to her house in Pelham before Ronan got home from school. I wrapped a scarf around my neck, put on a coat, and took a walk in Central Park. As I watched the horse-drawn carriages carrying their passengers through the lightly falling snow, I thought about Jane Cooke and how wonderfully unique she is. Her background and perspective are quite different from those of Bill Dance and Don Tyson, two country boys at heart, although she definitely shares a love of fishing with them. And like them, she said that the challenge of fishing was one of the things that draws her to the sport. Maybe challenge is the common driver that I was looking for.

Still, there didn't seem to be an immediate link to any common draw to the pastime. Jane's fishing psyche definitely seemed to be in sync with John Bailey's. Separated by the Atlantic, they were both avid outdoors people caught up in the thrill of fooling trout with a fly rod.

Throughout her life, good fishing water has provided her with a stage when she's happy and a refuge when she is sad. Fishing has been a constant medium in which Jane can exercise her independence.

And while rooted in New York, Jane now has many domestic and international causes she champions, like an organization she told me about called Trickle Up, which helps the lowest-income people break out of poverty with capital and business training. Her enthusiasm for their work was infectious.

Now, watching ice skaters twist and twirl on one of the park's frozen ponds, I thought about our conversation and how much she'd taught me that day about fishing, and much more.

*Nothing is so strong as gentleness and nothing is so gentle as real strength.*

—RALPH W. SORKMAN

# 5

# ANDY MILL: WILDE HUND

---◆◆◆---

*I was fishing my second Gold Cup in Islamorada, Florida, the most prestigious fly-fishing tarpon tournament in the world.*

*We had a 125-pound tarpon totally subdued. It was lying on its side by the boat when my guide and pal, Captain Tim Hoover, reached over and lip-gaffed it so that we could pull it into the boat for a measurement. Halfway into the boat the fish shook its head as only a tarpon can. It threw the fly and ripped the lip gaff out of Tim's grip—then swam away with it, adding insult to injury!*

*My shock from that moment of madness turned to utter heartbreak when we ended up losing the five-day tournament by a mere eight ounces!*

*Just prior to the awards banquet, I was feeling so emotionally drained, I called my wife to share my disappointment—and hear some words of encouragement.*

*What I got, instead, was a long pause and silence on the other end of the line before Chrissie said, "Andy, get over it! Martina beat me in the finals of Wimbledon six times! Now get your butt home and help me with these kids!"*

—Andy Mill

OF ALL THE DANGEROUS SPORTS IN THE WORLD, I've always been intrigued by downhill racing and the athletes for whom it becomes a passion. "Downhill racer" is a title that seems to put someone in a special place of respect, admiration—and questionable sanity. To fly down the world's highest, steepest, and most dangerous mountains at speeds approaching 100 mph dressed only in Lycra long johns, helmet, and goggles, competing against a field of the world's best and fastest is a sensation we mere mortals can barely imagine.

I've always wanted to ask one of these racers some pointed questions that would reveal their innermost selves. How'd you get started? What's it feel like? Aren't you afraid? How do you deal with injuries? Are you crazy?

I figured I'd probably need to speak German, as world-class downhill racing always seemed to be the domain of a small handful of young athletes who grew up in or near the Alps in central Europe. The Austrian, Swiss, and Germans seem to take turns dominating their sport, punctuated by an occasional incursion from northern Italy or France. Over the past thirty years only a handful of Americans like Billy Kidd and Phil Mahre have won championships and established their skiing reputations. But none were ever as charming and colorful, as disarming and joyous, as gleeful and quixotic as Andy Mill, a sure gold medal winner in any competition to identify a real-life Peter Pan.

I got my chance to ask Andy the above, and many more questions, on an around-the-world fishing trip we took together with stops in Christmas Island, the Australian Outback and the Seychelle Islands. A trip to not only catch some interesting species of fish, but also to raise some money to help find a cure for cystic fibrosis—a deadly condition that shortens the lives of young people. A trip that we would film for three segments of Andy's award-winning TV fishing show, *Sportsman's Journal*, on the Outdoor Life Network.

Champion ski racer Andy Mill has reinvented himself as a world champion sportfisherman after a fascinating life which has taken as many jumps and turns—none of them boring—as a world-class downhill course.

*Andy has developed great technique for beating large tarpon fast, like this 150 pounder.*

An accomplished and passionate angler and a scratch golfer, Andy is married to Hall of Fame tennis star Chris Evert, the father of three irrepressible boys, and best friends with a beagle hound named Lucky, who cheated death by electrocution when he bit through the wire on a set of Christmas tree lights. "When I get home," Andy told me, "I love to drop down on the floor and bite his ears. It drives him crazy."

At fifty-one years old, going on sixteen, Andy's race through life has been even more exciting than the mountains he skied, and certainly more diversified. Andy is Hollywood handsome, standing six feet tall with an athlete's wiry physique. His dark hair is long and wavy, his green eyes sparkle, and his toothpaste-commercial perfect smile is warm and inviting. He is perpetual motion and never seems to stop, let alone sit still. If Andy had a motto, I'm sure it would be "Growing old is mandatory; growing up is optional." In fact, I am sure that when J.M. Barrie wrote his epic story *Peter Pan* in 1911, he had a premonition about Andy Mill when he said "all children, except one, grows up."

Andy (not Andrew) Ray Mill was born in Fort Collins, Colorado, in 1953, the second of four children. Andy Ray's siblings were named Kandy Kay, Cindy Fay, and Randy Jay. When asked about the motivation in name selection by his folks, he emits an expletive, tosses his head back, and laughs a laugh that draws everyone in earshot into the story.

His parents were "working people," and followed the job market to Laramie, Wyoming, when he was two, and then to Aspen, Colorado, years later when his dad got a job managing a lumber company. The

Aspen of Andy's youth was a small ex-mining town of 1,200 year-round residents tucked in the Rockies—a far cry from the glitzy playground of millionaires and movie stars that it has become today.

Ironically, Andy's first skiing experience came on a weekend visit with his family to Medicine Bow where his dad bought him his first set of skis at the age of eight. But his fishing memories began even earlier: "I remember being five or six years old and hiking up to the high country with my dad to fish a beautiful lake above Laramie," recalls Andy. "When I got tired, he'd give me a piggyback ride. My dad was a fly fisherman, but I think I caught my first fish, a trout, while trolling.

*Andy Mill, age 5, on his first fishing trip with his dad.*

"I have vivid memories of cleaning a fish. He showed me how to cut upward through their bellies to their throats to be able to take the guts out. It seems I could never get the hang of it and kept pulling their heads off. I hated that part of our trips. Maybe that's what influenced me early on to catch and release."

*Andy learning how to clean fish (and not enjoying it).*

"I got my first fly-fishing lesson when I was ten from Ernie Schweibert, who was quite renowned. He taught at Princeton and has written several popular books on fly fishing," Andy recalls. "Another famous angler, Chuck Fothergill, gave me fly-tying lessons when I was twelve, and I ended up tying for the Country Store in Aspen that was owned by Phil and Joan Wright. I learned with their three sons and we would often ride our bikes to the river and fish till well after dark."

While Andy played about every sport growing up in Aspen, he excelled at skiing. Instead of going to college, he made the United States ski team and skied competitively for ten years, participating in two world championships and two Olympic Games, in one of which he finished sixth in the downhill.

Andy was called Millstone by his teammates but that wasn't his only nickname. A few years ago, we went barramundi fishing together in the Northern Territory of Australia. When we arrived at the Bullo River Station, a ranch that we were staying at, the manager, originally from Austria, said to Andy, "Wilde Hund, it's really you—great to meet you!"

"Andy, what'd he call you?" I asked.

"Wilde Hund," Andy said with a chuckle. "That was what the Austrians called me on the circuit. It means wild dog, and that's what they say I looked and skied like. At the time I had long dark hair and a full beard and used to live life on the edge, on and off the slopes."

*Andy Mill during his downhill ski racing days, known in Aspen as "Downhill Jesus" and in Europe as "Wilde Hund," the Wild Dog.*

One night over an Australian campfire I asked Andy about the risks and rewards of downhill skiing, knowing that in his career he had had nine knee surgeries, two broken legs, and two broken arms, as well as a broken back and a broken neck.

Andy said that from his point of view, "You're not capable of living without experiencing all of the extremes. You won't know the highs and lows if you don't take the risks, and I think that's true in life, love, and business as well. I know that some people say that all downhill racers are nuts, but that all comes from those who've never had that ultimate level of passion to take risks," he said.

Andy says the exhilarating thrill of skiing a fine line at a high rate of speed—which usually determines the difference between winning or losing—is all but unexplainable. "When you are in the upper echelon of anything, you are driven to be the best and finish first," he says. "After I started getting hurt I lost my feel for winning. Through fishing I rediscovered that feeling. When I asked my wife, Chrissie, why she was so good, for so long, she replied, 'I think I hated losing more than I like winning.' I now know, through fishing, exactly how she felt.

"I wish I'd been able to experience the level of skiing success I've had as a fisherman," he added. "I very much needed a mentor. My folks were always supportive and I had some good coaches, but I've always wished that I had someone, to help me emotionally and spiritually as well."

Andy had hoped to have some of that from his first wife, a former Miss California. They were married for eight years, the first three of which he remembers as happy, and the last five—challenging.

The end of his skiing career was coming soon, along with the end of his marriage. In 1981, Andy went to Switzerland for a race at the famous Lauberhorn. In his first run, he caught an edge, careened off the course, and crashed into a retaining barrier, breaking his neck and back and tearing the ligaments in his right knee.

No doubt suffering from shock, he somehow managed to walk to the emergency helicopter.

"Right then," he said, "I knew that I was walking away from competitive skiing. That accident was really tough on me, as I had always defined myself as an athlete.

"Later, lying in the hospital, I thought, Here I am, twenty-eight years old, injured, in a bad marriage, with no career, no education, no money, and no job. I knew I had to pick myself up and start again. That accident was the death of an athlete and the birth of a man."

Andy came home and began looking for a job. Realizing there was nothing available on teaching skiing technique on television, he put together a program for TV syndication called *Ski with Andy Mill*, and his media career began. In 1986, five years after his accident, Andy turned another page in his career when his divorce became final.

Andy went on to work for the networks covering World Cup skiing—including the 1992 and 1994 Olympics for CBS. He was also a segment host for *Good Morning America* and hosted some specials for the Outdoor Life Network before signing an exclusive contract to host and produce his own fishing show, *Sportsman's Journal*, in 1996. Before the program would be born, however, Andy had some work to do on his social life. While he had successfully launched a second career, he knew something was missing. Then he met Chris Evert at a New Year's Eve party in Aspen. They fell in love and were married in 1988. In life as in sports, they are somewhat opposites.

"I've always been about speed and risk," Andy told me, "and Chrissie is conservative. Look at her tennis game—controlled hitting and patience from the baseline. But we balance each other. I think that our differences are what make us whole as a couple."

"Does Chris like to fish?" I asked Andy.

"I cannot say she's wild about it," Andy said smiling, "but we've talked about it and she realizes what it means to me."

The more time Andy put in on the water, the more passionate and professional he became as a fisherman. In fact, almost without recognizing it at first, Andy had started a process of transferring his love for skiing into fishing. "The sport has become very important to me," he says. "In fishing as in skiing or golf, I love the chance to see just how good I can be. There are a lot of anglers who can catch fish and a lot who can catch big fish, but who can catch those fish when it matters? This is what separates the good from the great anglers!"

The numbers speak volumes about Andy's success as an angler. He has finished first or second in thirteen of fifteen major tarpon tournaments he's entered. He's been first and second in the Florida Keys Fall Fly Bonefish tournament, and he's come in second three times in the Spring Fly Tournament.

> *"What is your name?" Wendy asked.*
> *"Peter Pan."*
> *Then she asked where he lived.*
> *"Second to the right," said Peter. "And then straight on till morning."*
>
> —J. M. BARRIE, *PETER PAN*

Andy and Chris keep busy raising three young boys whose love of snowboarding and motocross are being tempered by their new interest in tennis and fishing.

"You should see Chrissie with those guys and with me," Andy says, "She's the conservative one that holds us all together. She's the greatest. I love her very much."

I made Andy laugh when I told him that for me, this somehow conjured up the image of Chris as Wendy with Peter Pan and the Lost Boys.

*Andy and Chris, with their three sons and pet beagle.*

Following his fishing dreams took time away from his family, and Chrissie—busy with her own schedule of running her tennis academy and appearing as a television analyst for major tournaments, not to mention raising their sons—began to push back. She shared her feelings and they talked. Andy told her, "If you allow me to be me without taking away from our family, I'll be able to give back more of myself to you and the children. Your reaction to what I do is very important to how the children will relate to me as well." They reached an agreement to remain sensitive to his time requirements and the needs of their family, and strengthened their bonds like never before.

With an important self-awareness and sensitivity toward the requirements of his young family, Andy embarked on a quest to learn and conquer the sport of saltwater fly fishing, with a special emphasis on arguably the greatest flats battler of all: *Megalops atlanticus*, or tarpon.

On his way to winning ten tarpon tournaments, including the prestigious Gold Cup five out of six years, beating the premier tarpon hunters in the world, Andy has absorbed fishing facts and information like a sponge. "I figured I've got a small window in the fishing world. I still have my eyes, my instincts, and my physical skills, and I guess I've got ten years to take advantage of them."

He chooses prestigious tournaments very carefully and his fellow competitors look forward to seeing his participation. "When you sign up for a tournament that Andy Mill is going to fish, you know that you are going to have to battle to win, and you know that the event is going to be a lot of fun," says fly-fishing guru, Sandy Moret, no stranger to the winner's stand himself.

*Catching big tarpon on fly is believed by many to be the ultimate light-tackle fishing experience. Here Andy prepares to release his catch.*

As he continued to gain fishing experience, Andy was approached by the Outdoor Life Network to produce and host a half-hour fishing show called *Sportsman's Journal.* "I never wanted to do a fishing show," he says. "I've done a lot of fishing in fresh and salt water, but I thought the idea of the show was very risky. Concentrating on fishing meant giving up the life I'd built from the broken-down skier I once was, and I was apprehensive of that.

"It had taken me twenty years to get where I was. Everything would have to go away— CBS, *Good Morning America*, and my ski show that I had in place. If I made this next step, there was no going back. What really sold me on *Sportsman's Journal* was the chance to tell a story from beginning to end. I guess without recognizing it, I had become a journalist. Besides, I was really sick of skiing coverage," he said. "Professionally, this fishing show is my third life. First I was a skier, then a voice and an apprentice of broadcasting, and now *Sportsman's Journal*—my final act, you could say!"

When I asked Andy what he considered to be the key ingredients for fishing show success, his animation grew. "If you can combine humor, fish, and information within a great storyline, you have the makings of a winner. The production side also plays a huge role with underwater cameras, cutaways, lighting, and weather.

"Overall, I don't think much of most of the fishing shows on television," he says. "I find them redundant without much creativity. I want *Sportsman's Journal* to take viewers on an interesting adventure in an artistic way," he said. Andy admits to being greatly motivated by the opinion of his peers.

"One of my proudest moments," Andy recalls, "was receiving a Teddy Award, recognizing *Sportsman's Journal* as the nation's most outstanding outdoor TV show. A year earlier, I was criticized as a host, as was my cameraman Kevin Tierney, for his work. I told Kevin that we should continue working from the heart and be inspired not by critics, but by our own aspirations and our peers, the real fishermen whom we represent. That following year, we won the award!"

I asked Andy if there were any of his shows that stood out more than the others.

"I'm proud of every one of the shows that has gone to air, but obviously they all can't be award winners. But I'd say the show we did with President Bush when I met up with you on the Tree River in the Arctic Circle was very powerful. The fishing was explosive, but to have our forty-first president talk about mortality and serving his country with honor—as he had—was a unique privilege for me.

"Another show which was eye-opening was catching two blue marlin over seven hundred pounds on day one, and backing that up on day two with two on a fly rod. That was a thriller. I supported this wall-to-wall fishing action with old film footage of Zane Grey and Michael Lerner from the 1920s, documenting man's quest of catching a 'grander'.

Our show is very diversified; even though we try to catch most fish on fly, the locations are as varied as the fish we catch."

I was intrigued to know what Andy thought was the one common thread among the many fishermen he's fished with.

"Well, I don't know if it's one-dimensional or the combination of many things to make the whole," he said. "Fishing for me is a sense of adventure where the elements of the unknown combine with hope. I'm also big on silence. A long time ago, high on the Continental Divide in the Rocky Mountains, I noticed how deafening silence can be, and how clear my thoughts became when surrounded by silence. I first heard my inner voice on a mountain, and then on a river.

"Over the years, since my early childhood, I spent many summers wading the rivers of Colorado, redefining and redirecting my life. And whether you're the President of the United States, or a street sweeper, everyone needs to be in tune with themselves, and I think fishing gives people the chance to not only find themselves, but to spend time with nature. It's been said before—fish have great homes!

"And for me, just like the mountains, water has become spiritual," Andy says. "I would still love to fish if it weren't for tournaments or my show, because I truly feel centered and alive when I'm on the water. It's amazing how electrifying it is when you get a big fish on the string."

*Wow*, I thought to myself, *pretty profound stuff for a guy who sometimes seems embarrassed by not having gone to college.* Why wasn't I surprised when Andy cited a sense of adventure as one of the biggest drivers in his love of fishing, as well as his love of life. I knew that I'd remember this conversation and wondered if any other anglers I spoke with would be as articulate about their attraction to fishing.

Back in the Australian outback, Andy and I stood together in a small sixteen-foot aluminum boat in a beautiful sun-drenched gorge in the Bullo River after catching two nice barramundi. "So, Andy," I said, "You had a great skiing career, you're comfortable with yourself; what would you change, if anything? Would you take a mulligan on life?"

"I've never been more content," Andy said firmly. "I've had highs, I've had lows, I've felt pain, and I've found love. I've triumphed, but I've lost some things along the way. I don't feel that I've changed, but I feel that I've grown apart from some old friends. Some people I've cared about for a long time now seem distant. And I don't really know why."

I think I do know. Outwardly, Andy's a devil-may-care kind of guy who seems to effortlessly glide down the slopes without ever bending his knees. He changes sports and professions with apparent ease and moves on to conquer new fields, constantly grabbing victory from the jaws of potential defeat—all the while living a glamorous life with the wind perpetually at his back, the sun in his face, and a smile on his lips.

I think that a lot of Andy's perceived problems with some of his

*Andy signals victory from the Outback.*

peers come from his stoic nature. In his inimitable style, he has not shared much of himself with many people. In modern-day parlance, "He sucks it up and deals," remaining a relatively private person in spite of his celebrity, always striving to be the best he can be.

For some in Andy's life the problem is one of jealousy— wrongly assuming, "This guy's so damn cool, he must be a jerk." I quoted a passage to Andy from *Peter Pan*, where Peter's archenemy, Captain Hook, reveals his true feelings about his young nemesis:

*The truth is that there was something about Peter which goaded the pirate captain to frenzy. It was not his courage, it was not his engaging appearance, it was not — . There is no beating about the bush, for we know quite well what it was, and have got to tell. It was Peter's cockiness.*

*Ignoring the crocodiles, Andy uses a cast net to catch baits on the Bullo River.*

As we enjoyed the afternoon sun in the outback, Andy contemplated my quote for a moment, then jumped out of our boat and into the knee-deep, nasty-looking, crocodile-infested water and said, "Watch my back for big crocs, Bubba, I'm going to run across that mudflat and try to net some bait."

*"No, no," he told Wendy decisively; perhaps she would say I was old, and I just want always to be a little boy and to have fun.*

—J. M. BARRIE, *PETER PAN*

Some years ago—never mind how long precisely—having little or no money in my purse, and nothing particular to interest me on shore, I thought I would sail about a little and see the watery part of the world . . . I quietly take to the ship. There is nothing surprising in this. If they but knew it, almost all men in their degree, some time or other, cherish very nearly the same feelings toward the ocean with me.

—Herman Melville, *Moby-Dick* (1851)

# 6

# KEN LONGAKER AND KARL BRATVOLD: THE NORSEMEN

*Ken: After freezing for three or four months at a time in Alaska and the Bering Sea, Karl and I love to get away for a week to someplace warm, like Mexico, where you can go sportfishing in just shorts and a T-shirt. We'd been doing those trips for about ten years and one day, Karl's wife Vicki was reading one of those sportfishing magazines that pile up around the house, and she said, "Hey, you guys love to fish; why don't you fish in one of those tournaments like the Western Outdoors Los Cabos Tuna Jackpot?"*

*Karl: Actually, she said, "If you're going out there anyway, why don't you win some money at it?" And Kenny and I said, "Okay, we'll win the dang thing."*

*Ken: So we went down there, and Vicki and my wife Sharon came with us and stayed on the beach while we went fishing. It was great; they had this shotgun start, and there were two hundred and fifty boats with me and Karl on one of them, fishing our very first tournament. We didn't know anything, but it was real exciting. I was, like, all goose bumps.*

*Karl: We had this captain who was real enthusiastic and worked hard, but the first day was kind of slow until around two-thirty P.M. We had seen some porpoises on the surface and figured there might be tuna under them. So we worked our way out to where they were and trolled some lures in and out of the schools. All of a sudden big tuna started busting the surface all around us, so we pulled in the lures and started pitching live bait at them. We weren't getting any bites, and Kenny started reeling in to go back to lures when I felt a tug. I locked up the reel to set the hook and then this fish started taking line. I mean, he was cookin'.*

*Ken: The grand prize was for the biggest tuna. You could tell this was a very big fish. I've got a stand-up fighting belt on, so Karl hands me the rod. It wasn't an IGFA [International Game Fish Association] tournament, so we could both fight the fish. So I fight him for forty-five minutes and then give the rod back to Karl, who now has a fighting belt on too.*

*Karl: I'd been haulin' on this fish for an hour when all of a sudden I hear this loud pop and I think, "Oh no, I broke him off!" I look up and this fish is still on, but I've broken the tip off the rod. Thank goodness it wasn't an IGFA tournament, when a broken rod would have disqualified our catch. So Kenny grabs another rod and starts peeling line off it so that we can tie our line on and fight him with another rod.*

*Ken: We tie a blood knot and I start fighting him again, and things are going well. Then after another hour we run out of room on the reel so we have to peel line off another reel and fight the fish on a third rod.*

*Karl: So I take the rod back and fight the fish for awhile, and then Kenny fights him for awhile, and after almost three hours we get the fish up to the boat. It is huge, and the mate takes out this rusty old gaff and gaffs the fish in the head, then Kenny and I gaff him a second time in the tail. We're trying to get the fish in when boom, the first gaff hook straightens out and hits the mate right in the mouth and he's bleeding all over the place. The fish is so big, the three of us can't get him in the boat. So we get him around to the stern and lash him down to the swim step.*

*Ken: By this time it's five-thirty P.M. and we're just wasted. We have to be back at the dock by six P.M. or the tournament scale is closed. Our captain looks at his GPS and says, "Oh no, it's a twenty-five-minute drive to the dock." So we take off and I called the committee boat and they said that they had a hundred-and-ninety-five-pound fish weighed earlier and asked if we still wanted to weigh our fish. Well, Karl and I look at each other, and we have no idea how much this fish weighs, but I said "Yeah, I think this fish will look pretty good on the scale."*

*Karl: So we're on our way in and the boat starts to overheat and the engine is smokin' bad, and I look at Kenny and he looks at me and we both look at the captain and he's really looking*

*nervous. But we finally reach Cabo, and the captain doesn't know where the scale is, but we see this crowd of two hundred and fifty or so people standing on the dock, so we head for the crowd.*

*Ken: And we look over and there are Vicki and Sharon standing in the crowd, and I thought, Wouldn't it be great if this fish was over one ninety-five with our wives watching? So we pull up to the dock at five minutes*

*Vicki and Karl Bratvold, Ken and Sharon Longaker at the Western Outdoors Los Cabos Tuna Jackpot weigh-in station with their winning 256-pound tuna.*

*to six and get the fish on the scale and it weighs* two hundred and fifty-six pounds, *and everybody goes crazy. We're so proud that our wives were there to see us win the tournament.*

*Karl: The first place prize was fifty-two thousand dollars, and that night we're talking with all these experienced tournament anglers and they're saying we have good karma, and they're inviting us to fish the next tournament. And we're looking at them and they're in their fifties with no wedding rings on and cute Mexican girls on each arm, and Vicki says, "Karl, you aren't going fishing with those guys. No way."*

—Ken Longaker and Karl Bratvold

WHAT ISN'T SURPRISING TO ME IS THAT two men, friends and fishing buddies since the third grade, would share the same favorite fishing story. What *is* surprising, however, is that two veteran commercial fishing captains, away from home for at least six months a year fishing the icy water around Alaska, would look forward to and plan their vacation sportfishing trips with so much enthusiasm. Talk about a busman's holiday! What's also surprising is that intelligent men like Ken Longaker and Karl Bratvold would commit themselves in the first place to such a dangerous and difficult life as commercial fishing in the Bering Sea. Surprising only until you get to know these guys and learn the truth about commercial fishing through their perspective. Their life stories are inextricably linked to the sea, like breaking waves and the smell of salt.

Ken Longaker and Karl Bratvold started at the bottom and worked their way up to become captains of two major 200-plus-foot fishing boats in the world's toughest fishery, the Bering Sea. Getting to know Ken and Karl meant getting acquainted with the past, present, and future of man's attempts to harvest fish from the ocean, and also, to better understand what motivates people to fish.

A United Nations report published in January 2001 labeled commercial fishing as the most dangerous profession in the world, with more than 25,000 fishermen dying every year—an average of more than seventy a day. The report says that the true figure might be higher if all countries kept reliable statistics. It points out that the risk increases as fishermen search farther and farther from home for depleted stocks of fish. The report concludes with an arguable case that "as vessels are made safer, operators take greater risks in their ever-increasing search for good catches."

Ironically, in spite of the danger to fishermen and the importance of commercial fishing to feeding nations and dealing with world hunger, no industry that I know of comes under harsher scrutiny. It seems like every "public interest" organization trips over each other to take shots at commercial fishing.

Of all of the bodies of water that men and women seek to harvest for its bounty, the Bering Sea is reputed to have no rival for abundance of fish—or danger. Spike Walker, himself a fisherman, talks about it in his book, *Working on the Edge*:

> Some 1,600 miles wide and 760 miles tall, the Bering Sea is almost 900,000 endless square miles of water. She is bordered by the Aleutian Islands to the south, the Alaska mainland to the north and east, and the Soviet Union to the west. Surrounded by primitive shores and crowned with a monotonous gray vault of sky, it is a cold wasteland of wind and sea.
>
> The Bering Sea is one of the planet's deadliest, with weather ranging from unendurable monotony to monstrous and incredible bursts of volatility. For days, the sea can lie calm and still as a graveyard, while the sky above her vast cold surface can remain cloudy for months. For weeks on end, however, violent sixty knot winds can blow unchecked through her arena. Gusts have been clocked in excess of 130 miles per hour.

"Beneath the Bering Sea's tumultuous surface," says Patrick Dillon, in his book *Lost at Sea*, "is the richest fishery left on earth. The very

*A view of the Bering Sea and ice on the bridge of the*
Starfish.

forces of competition between wind, temperature, currents, tides and variable density which cause havoc on the surface, cycle and recycle the water from top to bottom underneath. As a result no part of the sea is deprived of the oxygen, light and essential nutrients that attract and sustain the immense population of shrimp, crab, halibut, hake, herring, cod, pollock and salmon that keeps a billion-dollar local industry alive."

Every year all types of fishing vessels—crabbers, trawlers, long-liners, and bottom draggers—journey to the Bering Sea to ply their trade, and the small town of Dutch Harbor on Unalaska Island in the Alaska Peninsula becomes a hub, processing catches and providing fuel and supplies to the huge fleet of fishing vessels. Joel Gay points out in his work, *Commercial Fishing in Alaska*, that Dutch Harbor is consistently the nation's leading port in both value and amount of seafood landed, but that "more fishermen die after leaving Dutch Harbor than any other port in the country."

It was in the Bering Sea in the 1970s that crab boats earned the reputation as the deadliest workplaces in America, and it was an early stop in the career for two young fishermen, Ken and Karl, who journeyed fifteen hundred miles from Seattle to Dutch Harbor, twice a year, to make a living as crabbers. In order to understand the lure of fishing for them, one must go back for a look at their heritage and early years.

Norway elicits many different impressions depending on who you ask. Some say it is the home base of Vikings who sailed from its craggy shores to explore the world; or the capital of winter sports and host to the 1994 winter Olympics in Lillehammer; or an enormous northern country populated by attractive, blond-haired people, who are reserved but friendly.

Ken Longaker's parents were both born on the water on the southern tip of Norway, his dad on the island of Karmoy, and his mom in Kvinesdal, a town that was an hour and a half away by train. His mother's father was a carpenter, his father's dad a fisherman who fished for cod and also traveled to New Bedford for scallops.

In 1954, Ken's parents left Norway for the United States and settled in Brooklyn, New York, where Ken was born a few years later. "In the mid-fifties, there was a huge push to come to the USA, and my parents came for the American Dream," Ken said. "My dad worked as a carpenter, and my mom started working in Manhattan at a coffee factory and later at Chase Manhattan Bank."

Ken was born in 1958, and his brother Gary, who would later become the first mate on his boat, was born four years later in 1962. He has memories of summer trips back to Norway with his mom every year, where they would stay in the house that his grandfather built and go fishing in the rivers for trout with his grandfather and uncle. He also remembers trips out of Brooklyn with his dad to Sandy Hook, where they fished for striped bass.

"We spoke mostly Norwegian at home, especially in the early days," he told me.

"My uncle Noralf was a fishing boat captain in Norway who would fly to Seattle to pick up an American boat to run to Alaska for the crab season. He used to tell my father what a great city Seattle was, so in 1964, my dad took off with a buddy and drove cross-country to check it out. He was gone for four months, got a house, and got things settled. Then he sent a letter and said, 'C'mon out here.' I was ten when we left. I was really excited about the move. We lived right in Brooklyn, so having a dog or a bicycle was out of the question. For me it was like

*Karl's dad, Harold, on the docks in Westport, Washington.*

moving to the country. We moved to a small town in Washington called Ballard. It was like a Scandinavian center with a lot of Norwegians living there. Although I didn't know it then, fishing was a huge industry."

Little did Ken know then, but he was about to meet another ten-year-old with whom he would share an attraction to the sea.

Karl Bratvold is also of Norwegian descent, although he was born and grew up in Ballard. His mom and dad were also born and grew up in the United States. His father was of Norwegian descent and his mother was Swedish. She

*Karl, twelve years old, shows off a nice salmon to his sister Laura.*

grew up on a farm in the Midwest. His dad worked at Boeing and met his mother at the Young Peoples Organization at University Presbyterian Church in Ballard. Karl was born in 1958, and his sister Laura was born two years later.

Karl's first memory of fishing was with his father on the opening day of trout season on Lake Meridian in Kent, Washington. "I was six. It was pouring down rain; it was miserable, and we didn't catch a fish," Karl told me, laughing. "Also, I remember my dad's friend, Spence Wivag, who he'd kind of grown up with. We used to go salmon fishing out of Westport, and my dad used to get seasick every time; the first time I went, I got deathly sick. I was ten years old."

"So," I asked him, "is that the first year you met Ken Longaker?"

"Yeah," Karl said. "I went over to a friend's house, and Kenny and his mother were there. I remember she was a beautiful blond woman and they spoke a different language, but I understood it because my grandmother is Norwegian. Then Kenny and I started third grade together at Loyal Heights. We became pals. I guess the Norwegian [heritage] was part of it, but there were a gang of us, and we really bonded.

"We were also in Boy Scouts and would hang out at one of our other pals' houses, Craig, whose dad was a fisherman," Karl said. "It was there that we first tried smoking cigarettes. We'd all ride bicycles together and then we went through our trials and tribulations of junior high together. We were a tight bunch right into high school."

"We all went to Ballard High," Ken told me, "and we screwed around a lot."

"Yeah," Karl added, "we drank a lot of beer and chased a lot of girls."

"There were about seven of us," Ken remembers, "and we were really tight and fished a lot together as well. I think in the back of our minds, we knew we wanted to be fishermen, and it makes me smile when I think that five of us are actually captaining big commercial boats today."

But there was one person who didn't buy into the professional fishing idea: Karl's dad. "He was an engineer at Boeing, and wanted me to be an electrical engineer," Karl says. "Every summer I would mow lawns in the neighborhood and one of my customers, Per Eide, owned a seventy-foot salmon trawler called the *Antoinette L*. He invited me to spend the summer fishing with him offshore. I said, 'Oh yeah, man, I'm goin'.' I figured my dad would never let me go. It was one thing for the two of us to go out in Puget Sound in a rented boat from Ray's Boat House, but it was something else to go out for a few weeks at a time to fish commercially. But he surprised me and said okay. I guess he figured I'd get seasick and that would be the end of it."

"So, what happened?" I asked.

"Well, I went and got deathly seasick for the first week," Karl said. "I was sick as a dog. I never wanted my mom so much."

"And what did Per say?"

"Things like, 'Get back to work, you little ——!' He had no sympathy for me at all," he said. "He'd just cuss me up and down. It's not like today. We can't talk to our crews like that. Hell, now we even have to take sensitivity training."

"So, what's a good cure for seasickness, Karl?" I asked him.

"Hard work and a paycheck," he answered, laughing. "You've got to get your mind off it. Lying around in your berth is the worst thing you can do."

"What were your duties on the boat?"

"There were only two of us on board," he said, "so I did quite a bit of everything, including cooking breakfast."

"And what about your dad's plan to see you give up on the life of a fisherman?"

"Obviously it didn't work," he said smiling, "but he didn't give up. One day after my sophomore year, my dad took one look at my report card, saw all my absences, and decided to send me to a private school. I still hung out with the old gang, but I just didn't go to school with them.

"After graduation, I tried college—Seattle Pacific University. More drinkin' beer and chasin' girls. I lasted one year. I think my dad got the idea that electrical engineering wasn't in my future."

Ken's memories of high school were similar to Karl's, except that his mom and dad went through a painful divorce in 1974.

"It was tough for all of us," he recalls. "Things got a little tight. My brother Gary and I continued to live with my mom. I remember doing a lot of king salmon fishing on the Puget Sound with my dad, in his boat that he kept at Ray's. The fishing was awesome."

Ironically, in 1976, the same year the boys were graduating from high school, the government was drafting legislation which would greatly change the face of American commercial fishing. That year Congress passed the Magnuson Act, which established that only U.S. vessels could fish within two hundred miles of American shores. This meant that hundreds of crabbers, long-liners, and trawlers from seafaring countries like Japan, Norway, and Russia could no longer fish in what now became "our waters." The act also established eight regions, each with the authority to establish annual quotas for that region's fisheries. These two actions created huge opportunities for American fishermen.

The Starfish, *a crabber owned by Ken's uncle Noralf who gave him his first job fishing in Alaska.*

"After graduation I took off several months to figure out what I wanted to do with my life, although in the back of my mind, I already knew," Ken told me. "My uncle Noralf was running a crab boat called the *Starfish*, and he invited me to join him in 1977 to fish the Bering Sea. I'd always admired him and looked up to him. He gave me my first crabbing job and I was really excited. It was something I'd always wanted to do."

I asked him to tell me about his first trip to Alaska.

"Well, we left Seattle and it was flat calm," Ken said. "Then we went through the Strait of Juan de Fuca before busting out right into the Pacific Ocean. It's about a twelve-hour run till you're outside Cape Flattery, and from there, it's seven days of the Gulf of Alaska till you reach the Aleutians. We hit that open water and I was as seasick as I could be," Ken recalled. "I was embarrassed because my uncle was the captain, and I wanted to do my best. The *Starfish* was a hundred-and-eight-foot Marco boat with a crew of five. There were four older Norwegians and me, so Norwegian was spoken on the boat. It was tough work, and it seemed to be blowing all the time, but I'd thought about it so much and there I was doing it. I just loved it.

"Most of the crew had been through Brooklyn in the old days, and they all knew my folks through a club called the Sons of Norway. I worked real hard like they did and they were good to me; I felt that I fit in well," Ken said.

"Worked real hard" is an understatement. In Ballard, they would load 125 seven-by-seven-foot metal crab traps called *pots* on their boat, which they would later bait and then drop in the Bering Sea, with lines attached to marker buoys. Then they would run to Dutch Harbor, pick up another 125 pots, run to the fishing grounds, drop the pots, and repeat the procedure. By this time the season would open, and they would go around the sea, retrieving their 375 pots—or, as they call them, "seven bys"—by hydraulic winches. Then, they would deposit the crabs in their saltwater storage tanks and reset the pots before taking their catch back to Dutch Harbor. Ken described to me how they would often

*Ken and Karl smiling before unloading a "7 by" on the* Starfish *with their crewmates.*

work side by side on the deck for twenty hours straight in freezing conditions, without even a quick break for a hot meal.

"Weather?" Ken told me. "It was always cold, and it seemed to blow all the time. But there was work to do and we just did it."

Karl joined the full-time commercial fishing ranks later in 1977, working for his old neighbor, Per Eide, who had bought an eighty-foot bottom dragger from the estate of Karl's friend's dad who had passed away. The boat, called the *New Washington*, had a crew of five, including Karl, who was hired as a cook.

"Weren't you intimidated cooking for five guys?" I asked him.

"Not really," he said. "I'd learned to cook from my grandmother, and I got help from this old halibut fisherman on board named Albert. We'd go into town and buy groceries, and I introduced Per to a dish he'd never tried before—pizza—frozen pizza that I'd stock in the freezer before we left port. He loved it."

Then the next year, 1978, Karl too made his first trip to Alaska as a crab fisherman on the *Mar-Gun*, owned by his friend Gunnar Ildhuso ("Mar" is for Gunnar's wife Mariam, and "Gun" for Gunnar).

"I loved it," he told me. "I absolutely loved it. I knew this was what I was meant to do in life."

One day, fishing for striped marlin together off the shores of Mexico, I had the opportunity to ask Ken and Karl about their motivation "to weather the storms" and take on the challenge of such back-breaking work as fishing for crabs in the Bering Sea.

"Fishing in Alaska," Ken told me, "was like the last frontier—a chance to literally go somewhere and do something that many Americans had never done before. King crab was plentiful, and we were young. Sure, there was some danger, but none of us really thought much about it."

"It was a giant adventure," Karl added, "like a second gold rush. Guys were going up there and making over a hundred grand a season and buying new Corvettes. There was some risk, but when you're young, that's less of a consideration. Let the wind blow. We were living the life we'd always dreamed of."

In 1979, Ken married his junior high sweetheart, Sharon Lundli, who knew what she was committing to since her father had been an Alaska fisherman as well. They put off their honeymoon for three months while Kenny fished the fall crab season in Alaska.

Karl would get married fourteen years later at the Seattle Yacht Club, to a woman he'd dated earlier for about a year, Vicki Edderkin.

I asked him why he hadn't married her earlier.

"Well, I would have, but she told me she missed me while I was away fishing and gave me the ultimatum and . . . I went fishing."

"What changed?" I asked him.

"Well, we were young," he said, "and I guess we both grew up."

Karl's comments about the lure of commercial fishing made me think of Philip Wylie's great passage on making a living on the ocean in his wonderful book *Crunch and Des*—one of my all time favorites:

> That was the sea. Fierce and indecent and unjust. He knew he shouldn't try to associate justice and luck. It was permissible, when you have a bad day, to say you weren't living right "or you ought to go to church." But the man who began to believe that

the deserving should get the sea's bounty, and the mean and the stupid its infinite misfortunes; the man who tried to act as if he and not the ocean, were arbiter of such things, was riding for trouble. You had to take it, like it or not. And if a day came that you couldn't take it—well, it was time to think about quitting the fishing business.

By the late seventies, the king crab which had provided such a lucrative "gold rush" for American anglers had become far less plentiful. But the fishing fleet adapted and started catching tanner crab, which had always been in great abundance but literally rejected by the fleet. Then in early 1981, tanner crab seemed to follow the king crab.

"The year before," Ken told me, "we were pulling up pots full of crab, and then all of a sudden, the pots were almost empty. It was as if someone had turned off a light switch. Then, 1982 was a really bad year."

"Overfishing?" I asked him, stating what I thought was the obvious.

"Absolutely not," Ken said. His answer surprised me. "We do not overfish the Bering Sea," Ken continued. "In truth, the amount of crabbing may have even decreased since the Magnuson Act limited crabbing to American vessels. It also established conservative quotas which we honor religiously. In fact, those quotas had been declining for years. In my almost thirty years of fishing, I've found the Bering Sea to be one of the best-regulated fisheries left in the world—a real model for others."

"So what happened to the crab?" I asked him.

"Well, marine biologists were all over it," he said. "There are hundreds of theories: perhaps a problem with the females and their eggs, or maybe overpopulation of pollock eating all the crab larvae. No one really knows for sure, but one thing I do know is that fishing is cyclical. While stocks of some species diminish, stocks of other species grow. The biomass of pollock, for example, is greater than ever."

"So what did you do?" I asked them.

"We became pollock fishermen," Karl said.

"Yeah," Ken added. "Many of the premier owners of crabbers converted their boats to pollock trawlers by adding a gantry, net rails, and winches."

"Did your uncle Noralf convert his boat?" I asked.

"No," Ken said, "he was pretty set in his ways; but Karl and I both saw the handwriting on the wall and went to work for the same company on two different boats. We're very fortunate that our partners were fishermen and understand our business."

Other sweeping changes came to Alaska fishing as well. Many of the foreign fishing companies which had been precluded from fishing the Bering Sea began entering into joint-venture contracts with the American trawlers or catchers, to provide the fish that they would process at sea.

Like all industries, Alaska fishing went through its own consolidation as well. In the 1970s, the quota system was known as the "Olympic style." This meant that one quota was established for everyone, and it was a race to catch as much as you could. All boats kept records, and when the fleet hit that number, fishing for the season was over. This gave way to provisions of the American Fisheries Act of 1998 that installed Individual Transfer Quotas (ITQs) for each of the licensed fishing boats.

"We know now at the beginning of the season what our quota is," Karl told me. "One of the net effects of this was fewer, larger, more efficient boats that caught and processed as well, like the boat I captain now, *Starbound*. It was previously known as a factory trawler. Now it's called a catcher processor. It's two hundred and forty feet long and forty-eight feet wide, built in Anacortes, Washington, in 1988. We have a crew of one hundred and fifteen, and can catch, process, freeze, and hold eleven hundred tons of frozen fish, in any combination of filets, minced, or surimi style which is later marketed as a seafood salad similar to a crab salad. Our average trip away from Dutch Harbor, which we just call Dutch, is two weeks.

"Kenny's boat *Defender* is a two-hundred-foot catcher, with capacity for holding seven hundred tons of round or unprocessed fish," Karl said.

*Karl's boat,* Starbound, *a 240-foot catcher processor.*

*Ken's boat,* Defender, *a 200-foot catcher.*

"Freshness has always been very important in our business," Ken told me. "With our joint ventures, we used to go out for three days and supply our fish directly to processor ships. They became our lifeline and supplied us with fuel and all the supplies we needed so that we could spend over one hundred days at sea. Now we go out for three days and return to Dutch for offloading at one of our onshore processing facilities."

"Can you explain to me how trawlers work?" I asked them, feeling somewhat ashamed of my ignorance.

"First," Ken told me, "our boats are equipped with incredible electronics for finding schools of fish, including down-looking sonar and forward-looking sonar. Pollock swim in huge schools, and as professionals, we know exactly what we're looking for on our sonar. Once we spot the fish, we set out our mid-water net behind the boat. This is called a *tow*. The net also has sonar attached for finding the fish. At the end of the net is a detachable *cod end* which looks like a wind sock. The fish come into the net and end up in the cod end. Mine holds two hundred metric tons, and I have catch sensors to let me know when it's full. Then we go through the haul-back, pulling the cod end on the deck; once it's over the hold, we open what's like a big zipper and the fish go down a conveyor belt and are dispersed into refrigerated seawater tanks.

"Now, as a two-hundred-footer," Ken added, "we have a National Fisheries Observer on board at all times when we're fishing. Most of them are just out of school where they studied marine biology, and they seem to have this preconditioned bias that we're bringing in all kinds of other species. The first time out, they are amazed at how 'clean' our catch is."

"What does that mean?" I asked.

"It means that our catches are literally pure pollock. You see, everyone lumps all commercial fishing into one category, and it's just not fair. We get misbranded as pillagers and plunderers. Our ocean is regulated, and we target species and have very little if any bi-catch, but the negative image persists and it's frustrating."

*A tow of "almost pure pollock" on the* Defender.

"Tell me how you guys learned to operate the boats?" I asked.

"Well, it's like being an apprentice," Karl said. "The boats work around the clock and the captains have to sleep sometimes. So their mates get to oversee what we call *night tows* while they sleep."

"It's really something," Ken added. "Karl and I got to be first mates on our boats at the same time, and we used to be on our bridges talking all the time to each other and three other high school pals who were in similar situations."

Someone else must have been talking as well, because at the end of a season in 1985, Ken and Karl's captains retired and turned over command to their first mates on the very same day. Talk about careers in parallel.

"Is pollock fishing a lot safer than crabbing?" I asked them.

"Yeah," Kenny said, "especially crabbing in the seventies. There was a huge amount of deck work on those crabbers. Handling those crab pots under difficult conditions, that's when a lot of bad things happened."

"Loading the pots on deck and getting the proper balance could also cause problems," Karl added.

His comments reminded me of the two sister ships, *Americus* and *Altair*, two state-of-the-art crabbers that sunk mysteriously the first day out of Dutch Harbor in 1983, their decks stacked with crab pots headed to the grounds. While the evidence may never have been totally conclusive, balance was clearly an issue. Patrick Dillon masterfully explored the tragedies that took fourteen lives in his 1998 book, *Lost at Sea*.

"Safety in the Bering Sea has improved one hundred percent since we started fishing, and the Coast Guard has played a major role in the process," Ken told me. "In 1989 new military technology led to EPIRBs [Emergency Position-Indicating Radio Beacons] which could be attached to life rafts. Then in 1991, primary safety equipment regulations mandated that immersion suits and life rafts be carried on every boat. Prior to that, many boats were going out with PFDs [Personal Flotation Devices] only. Today our boats even have satellite tracking. The captains that Karl and I worked for were always way ahead of the game on safety equipment. That's the way we learned to captain our boats as well," Ken said.

"The Coast Guard has also done a great job on dockside inspections," Karl added, "and in 1999, they started inspecting each boat's stability books as well. In 2000, they added firefighting equipment inspections."

"The relationship between fishermen and the Coast Guard is excellent," Ken said. "They're like doctors. If you're in trouble out there, you're really glad to see them just like a doctor if you are sick. Now they're helping us keep from getting sick in the first place."

"They also do a great job on investigating accidents," Karl told me, "so that all of us can learn from bad things that happen—more preventive medicine."

"I'm also very proud of how our own industry has addressed its problems," Ken said. "The owners got together and formed the North Pacific Fishing Vessel Owners' Association in Seattle in 1986. We have a terrific ongoing training program, teaching all kinds of subjects like onboard safety, ship safety, first aid, and fire training."

The River Test, where the author fished with John Bailey, is a beautiful ribbon of blue that winds its way through southwest England and provides a great home for rainbow and brown trout, grayling, and royal swans.

IGFA's beautiful headquarters in Dania, Florida, by night, built in large part thanks to the dedication and largesse of Don Tyson. (PHOTO CREDIT: INTERNATIONAL GAME FISHING ASSOCIATION).

Jack Emmitt (left) and country western legend Porter Wagoner (right) flank their friends Johnny Morris and Bill Dance.

Bill Dance, the world's first bass fishing legend, with a supersize largemouth and his trademark University of Tennessee hat.

Jane Cooke fished Balsam Lake and the upper Beaverkill with former Federal Reserve chairman, Paul Voelcker, and her friend and mentor, author Nick Lyons (to her left).

Here's Andy Mill (right) and me (center) helicoptering to big fish on the Bullo River in Australia—a river that gets absolutely no pressure from anglers.

A proud President George Herbert Walker Bush with his young grandson Jeb (to his left) and their Inuit guide showing off one of the arctic char that they caught on the Tree River in the Northwest Territories in Canada.

Ken Longaker (left), Karl Bratvold (center), two marlin, and a shark they caught a few years ago fishing in the Pacific.

Three fishin' pals, (from left) Dennis, Mr. Haefner, and Mr. Bradley, at their favorite fishing spot on the Niagara River at the foot of Ferry Street in Buffalo, New York.

At this printing, Sandy Moret has caught 106 permit on fly including this guy in Belize in 1999 who fell for one of Sandy's crab patterns.

Sue Lowry, soon to be Moret, has always had an angler's instincts, as she demonstrated when she caught this nice bonefish at Deep Water Cay in the Bahamas in 1995.

Scott Keller (right) guiding longtime friend, Yvon Chouinard, founder and owner of Patagonia, Inc., on the Rio Grande River in Tierra del Fuego.

Captain Lee Baker (center) shows off a nice Ted Williams's caught permit before the Hall of Famer moved out of the Florida Keys.

Toby and Anita Cosgrove (right and center), with fishing mate Rusty Albury off the Atlantic coast of Marathon, Florida.

Bob Rich proudly shows off an Australian barramundi from the Northwest Territory, perhaps the first ever caught on fly on Australia's Bullo River.

"Yeah, Kenny, and don't forget sensitivity training," Karl chimed in, smiling.

"Right; and we do safety drills on the boats all the time," Kenny said, "so that, God forbid anything should go wrong, we'll be ready. I think as a fishery we're a lot safer and the numbers will show it."

Ken is absolutely right. I called Sue Jorgensen, Fishing Vessel Safety Coordinator of the Alaska Coast Guard, and got the facts. Fishermen deaths in the Bering Sea have gone down dramatically in the past thirty years, highlighted by 2004 when there was only *one* death—a huge turnaround since "the boys" started in 1977 and 1978.

"Still," Ken said, "the sea is still the sea, and when you're on her, you always have to keep your guard up."

Many writers have tried to describe the perils of the ocean. In his chilling book, *Lost at Sea*, Patrick Dillon quotes the words of an early oceanographer, R. M. Snyder, that I'll never forget: "There are things about the sea which man can never know and can never change. Those who describe the sea as 'angry' or 'gentle' or 'ferocious' do not know the sea. The sea just doesn't know you're there—you take it as you find it, or it takes you."

"You've each had harrowing experiences, then?" I asked the naïve question, knowing the answer.

"Sure," Ken replied. "Like one night in December of 1986. I was captaining a boat called *Starlite*. We were doing an extended joint venture with the Japanese for yellowfin and sole. We were attempting a routine nighttime transfer of our cod end to the factory ship in the yellowfin grounds, thirty or forty miles northeast of the remote Pribilofs in the Bering Sea, when our two-inch steel transfer cables got stuck in growing seas. So instead of hauling in just our cod end, they were hauling in our boat as well. We had to torch the cable and dump the fish. After that, we laid into the wind to ride out the storm, and I went to my cabin for some rest.

"There seems to be an unwritten rule in the Bering Sea that if something goes wrong, it will happen between two and five A.M., and that's just what happened," Ken said. "All of a sudden, we got hit by a huge wave. It felt like we'd run into a brick wall. I got up from my berth and found an inch and a half of water on the floor. I went to the bridge, and as I suspected, the wave had taken out all our windows and fried our electronics, even our radio. I did keep a single sideband radio in my cabin, and luckily, we were able to raise our partner ship, *Westward I*, which happened to be nearby. We were able to board up the windows, and the other boat came over and led us on a two-hundred-and-fifty-mile trip to Dutch Harbor.

"As we limped in, I thought a lot about how powerful the ocean is and how it can overcome the most thorough plan," said Ken. "The winds in that storm reached seventy-five miles an hour, blowing the tops off thirty-five-foot waves. I was just glad we got back to Dutch safe and sound with nobody hurt. Others weren't as lucky. When we got back toward port, the Coast Guard was out in force. Two boats didn't make it back."

*This eerie picture of Karl's boat iced up in Shelikof Strait sits behind his desk. A boat nearby iced up, rolled over and sunk. All hands were lost.*

"The night I remember most," Karl said, "was spent riding out a storm in the Shelikof Strait between Kodiak Island and the mainland in 1984. It was rough conditions and the boats were icing up real bad. One of them rolled over and sunk. All hands were lost."

"What do you guys think about the most when you're at sea?" I asked them.

"Safety first," Ken replied. "Making sure our crews are safe, and of course, catching fish. But I'm always thinking of my family as well, especially in the quiet times. Sharon and I have three great children, Kirsten, Siri, and Torin. I'm very proud of all of them. My daughter Kirsten just finished her last semester at the University of Washington with a perfect 4.0, and she's on her way to law school at Seattle University. My wife Sharon has done a great job with our kids, and I love her very much."

"When I'm fishing in Alaska," Karl said, "I have the same priorities as Ken, although he had a fourteen-year start on me with family. Vicki and I have two great sons, Kristoffer, my fishin' buddy, and Tristan, my ballplayer."

"Is it tough to be away from them so much?" I asked.

"Of course," Ken said, "and I love getting back to be with them and taking our sons to Mariners' games. But after awhile some things 'down there' get to me, like traffic and television and politics, and when the fishing season starts I'm ready to go back."

"How long will you guys do this?" I asked them.

"I haven't thought much about it," Ken said. "I guess as long as I feel like doing it."

"Not me," Karl said. "I'd like to be out of it in ten years. Buy a little sportfishing boat and find someplace warm. I love the heat. Vicki says I'm like a lizard. All I need to do is find a gray rock to lie on in the sun."

"So," I asked them, "when it comes to fishing, what drives you? Besides the financial return, are the motivators the same in commercial and sportfishing?"

Ken thought for a moment and then seemed to answer for both of them.

*Karl puts the wood to a Cabo striped marlin.*

"Yes, I think so," he said. "It's the thrill of the adventure. The excitement of a great catch, whether it's a pot full of crab, a two-hundred-and-fifty-six-pound yellowfin tuna, or a cod end full of pollock. Those are moments that you never forget," Ken said.

"I agree," Karl added. "It's definitely the 'thrill of the hunt.' I also love the ocean and being on the water. And the planning is fun too, getting ready for your next tow or going through a catalog and pricing a new spinning rod. There's a lot of regulation in our industry now. The 'cowboy' days are over. It's big business. But in spite of it all, there are still some days when it's just great fun. We'll cruise around and find a huge school of pollock and fill our net after a ten-minute tow of these beautiful fish. It's just great, great fun."

And it has been fun for me getting to know Ken and Karl. Their industry, I feel, has often been unfairly maligned, and yet they answered my questions with patience and honesty. It's hard to believe that two young men could be so well educated by the ocean, their university. It was interesting to discover that like Andy Mill, a tournament-tested fly fisherman, Kenny and Karl, two seasoned commercial fishermen from the Bering Sea, both spoke of the thrill of adventure as what had lured them to fishing. Maybe I was closing in on the elusive common quality shared by all anglers.

I also cannot think of any two friends who I would rather go fishing with, storms or no storms.

> *They that go down to the sea in ships, that do business in great waters; These see the works of the LORD, and his wonders in the deep. For he commandeth, and raiseth the stormy wind, which lifteth up the waves thereof.*
>
> —PSALMS, 107: 23–25, THE BIBLE, KING JAMES VERSION

# 7

# GEORGE HERBERT WALKER BUSH: ANGLER AND CHIEF

*Last summer, I took my grandson Jeb on a trip to the Tree River in the Northwest Territories of Canada in search of arctic char. We were fly-fishing together from the riverbank in a place they named the Presidential Pool in my honor. Jeb, who was fourteen, hooked up a monster. You should have seen it—a big male, bright red, underslung jaw in the height of the spawn. The fish sprinted out of the pool and headed downstream. He was really flying through those big rapids. Jeb didn't miss a beat, and followed that fish right down the bank, keeping the pressure on the fish while jumping from rock to rock.* Gee, I thought, I'd love to be able to do that.

*In sixteen or seventeen minutes Jeb had won the fight, subdued the fish, and brought him to the net. It was the biggest fish of the trip. You should have seen the look on my grandson's face. I'll never forget it!*

—President George H. W. Bush

*President George Bush fishing the surf in Kennebunkport, Maine in 1989.*
PHOTO CREDIT: GEORGE BUSH
PRESIDENTIAL LIBRARY AND MUSEUM.

FAMILY AND FISHING ARE TWO SUBJECTS that the 41st President of the United States understands very well, so I wasn't surprised when George Bush combined them into his favorite fishing story. I was, however, surprised that he spoke enviously of his grandson's agility. Notwithstanding the hip replacement he went through recently, President Bush, who commemorated his eightieth birthday in 2004 by once again parachuting from a plane, is one of the most energetic and agile people I know. His jump was just another symbol of courage and fitness from a man who, considering his age, has kept up perhaps the most grueling schedule in history, since departing from the White House in January of 1993.

A highlight of my fishing career has been the opportunity to fish around the world. Two or three times a year I manage to fish with President Bush in places as cold as the Arctic Circle, as warm as the Florida Keys, and many places in between—from South Carolina to Great Britain. He possesses all the qualities you'd look for in a "best fishin' buddy." He combines optimism and patience with an almost childlike enthusiasm for the pursuit of fish. He's a great tactician and loves the preplanning that goes into an outing as much as the actual trip itself. On the water or at the camp, he is warm and congenial, always pitching in to help and solicitous of everyone's success and enjoyment. He has boundless energy and is usually the first on the water and the last to leave it. "Around the campfire," he is engaged and engaging, and mixes wonderful stories of the fishing day—or fishing days gone by—with tales of events from his life, punctuated once in awhile with some of the world's oldest, corniest jokes.

"How did you do today, Mr. President?" always draws some interesting responses, ranging from "We got our uniforms dirty today" to "Those fish out here had lockjaw today." Usually, he does get his uniform dirty. He's been a passionate angler for a long time. A lefty, he's become proficient with a variety of tackle including fly, spin, plug, and conventional bait casters, and he's caught fish with family and friends throughout the United States and around the world.

Born in 1924 in Milton, Massachusetts, George Herbert Walker Bush was named after his mother's father. "My mother couldn't make up her mind which of her father's names (George Herbert Walker) she wanted me to have. When christening time came, she decided not to decide."

The future president first developed a love for fishing and boating at his family's vacation home in Kennebunkport, Maine. His first memory of the sport was in 1930 when he was six years old, fishing for cod or pollock off the rocks in front of his house with long poles and snails. (Maybe that's one of the reasons why seeing his grandson hopping along the rocks fighting a big fish in the Arctic Circle elicits such fond memories for him.)

By the time he was ten, he was often invited to fish with his own grandfather on a converted Maine lobster boat call the *Tomboy*. Their target species was mackerel, which they caught trolling jigs on twine with small pieces of torn rags as bait tied to their hooks.

Soon, he was allowed to drive the boat himself, elevating his love for boating to the same level as his passion for fishing. He still runs a boat off the shores of Maine in the summer. Now he prefers fast outboards so he can get to where the fish are quickly in the limited time he has available to fish on any given day. Stories abound, in fact, of him outdistancing press boats full of photographers, and, occasionally, his own security boats, full of exasperated secret service agents assigned to protect him. When I asked him about one of those episodes recently, he replied laconically, "You have to get to the fish," while one of his ever-present agents rolled his eyes and then smiled.

Sports were always important to George, who captained the Yale baseball team. One of his fondest baseball memories was meeting Babe Ruth, the same year the slugger died, before a Yale–Princeton game in 1948, where Ruth presented Bush with an autographed copy of his new autobiography that he was donating to Yale's library.

*Baseball Captain George Bush accepting an autographed copy of "The Babe Ruth Story" from the Babe himself in 1948 on behalf of Yale University.*
PHOTO CREDIT: GEORGE BUSH PRESIDENTIAL LIBRARY AND MUSEUM.

Long before President Bush became a ballplayer at Yale, he nearly lost his life in Japan's Bonin Islands. During his senior year in high school, the Japanese attacked Pearl Harbor. After graduation and on his eighteenth birthday, he enlisted in the Navy as a seaman second class. He took flight training and became a torpedo bomber pilot and, still at the age of eighteen, the Navy's youngest pilot. He went on to fly fifty-eight missions over the next two years before his nightmare began. Flying over one of the Bonin Islands, Chichi Jima, his plane was shot down by Japanese anti-aircraft fire. His two crewmen were killed and he parachuted into the sea and spent several hours drifting in a rubber raft before he was rescued by a U.S. submarine. I asked him how he could love ocean fishing so much after that, and didn't he ever have nightmares about it. He said that he didn't, and that his trip back there a few years ago "brought closure to the whole thing."

*Congressman Bush and his family in Washington in 1967.* PHOTO CREDIT: GEORGE BUSH PRESIDENTIAL LIBRARY AND MUSEUM.

*George Bush campaigns for the U.S. Senate in 1964.* PHOTO CREDIT: GEORGE BUSH PRESIDENTIAL LIBRARY AND MUSEUM.

While still in the Navy, before the war ended, George Bush married Barbara and enrolled at Yale where he got the nickname Poppy. They went on to have six children, one of whom died in infancy in 1953. His account of her loss in a touching letter to his mother appears in one of his books, *All the Best, George Bush,* and reveals him to be a strong, articulate man, not ashamed to show his emotions.

After graduation, George Bush moved his wife and son, George W., to Texas to work in the field of oil exploration. He lost his first run for the Senate in 1964, but was elected as a congressman in 1966, and reelected in 1968 before losing a second senate bid in 1970.

President Nixon appointed him U.S. Permanent Representative to the United Nations in 1971. How ironic it is that he was the one chosen to ask Nixon to resign while he was head of the Republican National Committee in 1974.

That same year, President Ford asked George Bush to fill the top diplomatic post in China, as chief of the U.S. Liaison office. He moved to China and lived there until late in 1975 when Ford brought him back to the States to become director of the Central Intelligence Agency—a post he served until newly elected President Carter began his administration in January of 1977.

In 1980 Bush ran for the Republican nomination for president against Ronald Reagan. Although Bush lost, California governor Reagan asked him to serve as his vice president. They were elected in 1980 and then reelected in 1984.

*President Ronald Reagan and Vice President George Bush on June 11, 1982.*
PHOTO CREDIT: GEORGE BUSH PRESIDENTIAL LIBRARY AND MUSEUM.

George Bush was elected president in 1988, and his presidency will most be remembered for several actions on the domestic front:

- The Americans with Disabilities Act.
- The bailout of the savings and loan industry.
- The Clean Air Act Amendments.
- The president's agreeing to a budget reduction package to try and deal with the huge deficit inherited from Reagan. (This

violated his famous "Read my lips—there will be no new taxes" promise, and negatively impacted his popularity with the conservative wing of the Republican party.)

- The nomination and bitter confirmation hearing of Clarence Thomas to the Supreme Court.
- The civil rights bill of 1991.

President Bush will no doubt be best remembered for many of his bold initiatives abroad. For example, he dispatched U.S. troops to Panama to oust their corrupt, drug-dealing dictator, Manuel Noriega, who was later tried, convicted, and jailed in the U.S. on charges of trafficking. In the process democracy was restored in Panama. He signed the North American Free Trade Agreement with Canada and Mexico, and he stood up to Saddam Hussein and drove the Iraqis out of Kuwait in 1990. The entire military action known as "Desert Storm" took thirty-one days and resulted in minimal coalition casualties.

But President Bush's days in the White House were numbered. He lost the 1992 election to Bill Clinton and returned home to Texas.

*President Bush eating with the troops in Saudi Arabia on November 22, 1990.*

*George H.W. Bush, the 41ˢᵗ president of the United States, on January 9, 1991.* PHOTO CREDIT: GEORGE BUSH PRESIDEN-TIAL LIBRARY AND MUSEUM.

Always a gentleman, he congratulated the new president elect and refused to "go negative." His feelings for one-time supporter turned third-party spoiler candidate, Ross Perot, were not as generous.

I first met President Bush when he was director of the CIA and a parishioner at St. Columbas, my minister brother's Episcopal church in Bethesda, Maryland, but it's through fishing that I've gotten to know him best. Unlike tennis and even golf, the tempo on the water is usually perfect for one-on-one talks, and I know he's

*President Bush receives a salute from General Norman Schwarzkopf during the Desert Storm Homecoming Parade, Washington, DC, on June 8, 1991.* PHOTO CREDIT: GEORGE BUSH PRESIDENTIAL LIBRARY AND MUSEUM.

*President and Mrs. Bush arrive in Houston, Texas after the inauguration of Bill Clinton, January 20, 1993.* PHOTO CREDIT: GEORGE BUSH PRESIDENTIAL LIBRARY AND MUSEUM.

shared several of these times with many leaders of the free world, occasionally in some comical situations.

For instance, the year before Andy Mill interviewed him for his TV show, Canada's then prime minister, Brian Mulroney, was along on the aforementioned trip to the Arctic Circle (when Jeb caught the biggest fish). This account left out the part about a very large and aggressive black bear that was menacing the fishing camp. Bush and Mulroney were both accompanied by a contingent of security folks, secret service for the president and Mounties for the prime minister. With the bear coming ever closer, a few satellite phone calls were made. It was decided that it would not look good if the former president and/or the prime minister were eaten by a Canadian black bear, so the threat should be eliminated. Then another round of calls was made while the former president and prime minister were out fishing, to determine which security force should kill the bear. In spite of their well-honed sense of

Canadian hospitality, it was decided that the Mounties as hosts should do the honors, as this was their domain (and probably to minimize the risk of any international episode that could arise from foreigners coming in and "whacking" their livestock). This cast a bit of a pall over the security contingents who had been carrying on some interesting dinner debates about the efficiency of their weaponry.

At any rate, one of the Mounties pulled the trigger and dispatched the unwelcome intruder to black bear heaven. While the safety of the anglers was restored, it was reported that the relationship between the secret service guys and the Mounties was a tad strained—every one of them had wanted to test his weapon on a real target.

After Desert Storm and before Operation Freedom, my wife and I shared an interesting trip to the coast of North Carolina with President Bush for some false albacore fishing. Also known as little tunny, these fish are a member of the tuna family and provide a great offshore sight-casting target for fly fishers. They hunt for small baitfish in large schools and when they find them, they drive the baitfish to the surface and attack them simultaneously. This bait-eating technique creates what's known as a *bait shower*, allowing keen-eyed anglers in fast boats to approach within casting range. When hooked, these fish, ranging from twelve to fifteen pounds, fight frantically in and out of the water. The battles often last between fifteen and twenty minutes, and the fish, which aren't especially palatable anyway, are released to fight another day.

The flurry of the fish is matched only by the flurry of the anglers and the boat captains to speed to the showers. It's a miracle there aren't more collisions, but there is a lot of good-natured yelling accompanied by the snapping of graphite fly rods. I'm sure a freshwater fly fisher used to the serenity of his or her stream would be appalled, but we love it, and so does President Bush.

After a late arrival by private plane at Cherry Point Marine Base and a good night's sleep at a friend's house, we all got up and enjoyed a homemade southern breakfast. President Bush disappeared into the kitchen and my wife whispered to me, "Can you believe it? The former president of the United States just cleared my plate and is in the kitchen doing the dishes!" That's just the way he is.

After a great day of fishing, still in old fishing clothes, we returned to our plane at Cherry Point to find what looked like the entire force standing at parade rest by the runway. As our SUV approached, the marines snapped to attention and President Bush got out to talk to the base commander, who was saluting the former commander in chief along with his executive officers. President Bush came back to the car and asked if we minded if he took a few minutes to review the troops. He said, "I'm sorry for the delay. I didn't think they knew I was going to be here."

We said not to worry, drove to the plane, loaded our fishing equipment, and stood by watching from a distance as this tall man in camouflage pants, sneakers, an old golf shirt, and a Bass Pro Shop baseball cap walked up and down the rows of America's finest, stopping to shake hands and chat with everyone.

An hour later a pale, sad-eyed President Bush climbed aboard the plane and sank down in one of the seats, a tear rolling down his cheek.

"Mr. President, you don't look so good. Are you all right? Do you want a drink?" I asked him.

President Bush, who limits his alcohol to an occasional cocktail, surprised me and said he'd like a beer. When I sat down with him he said, "I'm sorry. I'm okay. This is the base where we launched Desert Storm. I haven't been here since the day in 1991 when I came to see the troops off that were headed toward Iraq. It was unbelievably emotional. We didn't know then what the outcome would be or how many of them would be coming home. And now nine years later here they are, safe and sound. Their CO is a great guy and he's retiring soon, but he and his men wanted to tell me how proud they were to have served . . ."

President Bush's voice trailed off. I got him another cold beer and buried my nose in a newspaper so as to not further interrupt his private thoughts.

I've hopped around the wet, slippery rocks with Jeb Jr. at President Bush's house in Kennebunkport, on the peninsula known as Walker's

Point, but I much prefer fishing with the president at the George Bush/Cheeca Lodge Bonefish Tournament that he hosts every fall in Islamorada in the Florida Keys. The proceeds from this and other tourneys he fishes go to some of the good causes that he champions. He's an avid participant and while he's never won it, he's on a roll, and for two years in a row, has caught bonefish weighing in at over thirteen pounds.

*President Bush heading out for a day of fishing with his friends, veteran Florida Keys guide George Hummel and the dean of sportscasters, Curt Gowdy.*

The tournament in 1998 provided a most memorable moment for those in attendance, as well as the press corps covering the event. General Norman Schwarzkopf, one of the heroes of Desert Storm and himself an accomplished fisherman, accepted an invitation to fish. Some avid watchers of the political scene noted that Schwarzkopf and Bush had literally not been seen together since the war ended in 1991. Some speculated that there might even be some ill feelings between the two which, of course, was totally untrue. After the relentless bombing of Baghdad, Iraq appeared to have lost its will to resist. Cloaked in patriotism and the growing popularity of this one-sided war, many around the country argued that we should continue on to Baghdad and finish the job once and for all by ousting their dictator.

Flush with understandable pride for the efficacy of their battle plan and the resulting victories, the U.S. generals were reported to be chomping at the bit to continue their course. It was then that President Bush, knowing that our mission was completed and aware of the geopolitical consideration of our involvement, ended the war. Rumors swirled that the coalition commander, General Norman Schwarzkopf, was particularly miffed by this decision, although as the consummate professional soldier, he obeyed the chain of command absolutely and said nothing to indicate that he felt anything short of full agreement with his commander in chief. In fact, the president talked personally with General Schwarzkopf the day the war ended and was assured that General Schwarzkopf and the other commanders all said, "Mission Accomplished."

As the tournament entrants finished their entrees at the kick-off dinner, master of ceremonies Curt Gowdy, the legendary host of ABC's *American Sportsman*, got up to welcome everyone, say a few remarks, and introduce some of the assembled celebrities. The first person he introduced was General Schwarzkopf, and then without notice he asked the general if he wished to make a few remarks.

General Schwarzkopf made his way to the podium to a warm welcome from the crowd, and then put everyone at ease with a fishing joke. He said that he felt it would be tough for him and the president to catch these bonefish and win the tournament. "You see," he said, "these bonefish are like Saddam. Every time the president and I come around, they shut their mouths."

After a round of laughter and applause, General Schwarzkopf gave an impromptu five-minute speech that began a dialogue with his commander in chief that would turn out to be the highlight of the tournament. The general honored his former boss with words of highest praise. He said that if it hadn't been for Bush's willpower and prompt action, this war may never have been fought and won. He also credited Bush with giving the generals the support they needed to not only win

*General Norman Schwarzkopf pays tribute to his "Commander in Chief"*
*President George Bush.*

the war, but also to minimize the loss of lives. Then he complimented
the former president for staying the course and having the courage to
end the war once the mission had been accomplished, even in the face
of growing public sentiment to oust Saddam. Finally, he ended his remarks by saying publicly to President Bush, "Sir, I'm proud to have
served you," and walked over and shook his hand. General Schwarzkopf
returned to his seat with a standing ovation.

Sitting across the table from the president, I could see that he was
greatly touched by the general's remarks. When it was his turn at the
microphone, he was no less open and articulate in his praise of General
Schwarzkopf, calling him "a great American and great leader," and saying how happy he was to be able to spend some time together in the
next few days. My wife, who was seated next to the president, later confirmed President Bush's sharing with her that this was in fact the first
time since the war in Iraq ended that he and General Schwarzkopf had
had the chance to sit down together and "get caught up."

*President Bush compliments his friend General Schwarzkopf "on a job well done."*

*George Hummel (right) explains the attraction of fishing bonefish with live crabs to President Bush and an amused General Schwarzkopf.*

As the dinner ended and we started to think about bonefish, there was no doubt for any of us in attendance that any rift between these two men had either been put to rest there in the dining room of the Cheeca Lodge, or indeed, had never existed (and President Bush has assured me that the latter is true).

Many of us felt that we'd just shared a moment in history as well as having been afforded the opportunity to collectively honor and thank two true American patriots.

After last fall's tournament we flew out of Marathon together, and the president's people cleared it with a county policewoman for me to drive to the airport with the motorcade. I was feeling pretty proud of myself, driving along in my ten-year-old blue Buick Roadmaster with a police escort. (Two weeks later, that same lady cop gave me a ticket for speeding on that same route, thereby bursting my bubble. I guess she must have been a Democrat—but that's another story.)

On the plane out of Marathon, President Bush and I talked a lot about fishing. While he's fished all around the world, his favorite place to fish is still his family home in Kennebunkport, where he operates a thirty-one-foot Fountain outboard powered by two 225-horsepower Mercury Opti Max engines. He tells a story of getting skunked there for two and a half weeks on a vice presidential working vacation, joking that it was the fault of all the press and security boats surrounding him. Then, when he finally caught a bluefish, "You should have heard the horns, bells, and whistles from that flotilla," he jokes.

"I've played a lot of sports in my life and I've always loved to fish," he said. "Now, fishing is number one with me—probably because I've gotten so bad at golf. I've fished with everyone in my family," the president says. "All of my kids and all of my grandchildren. Even Barbara joins me once in awhile. She's the only person I know who can read a book and fish at the same time. Once when we were fishing together on a lake in Alabama, she out-fished everybody and caught a six-pound largemouth bass.

"The president," as he now refers to his son George W., "is a good bass fisherman. We fish together on a new bass pond he built at his ranch in Crawford, Texas. All the kids love to fish. One of my favorite fishing trips was to Venezuela with my daughter Doro [Dorothy]. She did great both for bonefish at Los Roques and Peacock Bass at Camp Manaka.

"And the grandchildren are into it also. You should see Jeb Jr. with a fly rod. He can throw it a mile!"

Both President and Mrs. Bush realize the value of fishing for a family. "Bar says that it builds bonds between men and women too," he said. "The tranquility and fellowship experienced while fishing tran-scends generations," he said. "There is nothing like a grandfather expe-riencing the wonders of nature through the eyes of a youngster. I guess you could say that more than ever, fishing has become a passion for me."

*Mrs. Bush joins her son Marvin, Brent Scowcroft, and her husband on his boat,* Fidelity, *off the coast of Kennebunkport on September 3, 1990.* PHOTO CREDIT: GEORGE BUSH PRESIDENTIAL LIBRARY AND MUSEUM.

A few years later, the president and I went on a fishing trip I'll never forget. My wife and I had a chance to introduce the president to one of our all-time favorite venues: the Test River in England. Our pals Johnny and Jeanie Morris, Bill Wrigley, and Allie Nimmer from

Chicago joined us. It was mayfly season, and the trout were feeding on dry flies like mad dogs. Everyone in the party was catching them, but it appeared that the president was especially lucky. Every time I looked down the river at him, his rod seemed to be bent. We were catching rainbows and brown trout of three to four pounds on every other cast!

On our third and final day, as the sun was setting in a beautiful, cloudless sky, I contented myself to sit on a bench streamside and reflect on the good friends I'd made fishing, the beautiful places I'd seen, and the wonderful fish I'd fought. But reveries don't last long when big trout are slurping everything in sight. I picked up a three-weight fly rod and threw a spent mayfly pattern to what seemed like a huge bust in the middle of the stream.

There was no drama in the wait. A monster-sized brown trout inhaled my fly and took off swimming and jumping for parts unknown (maybe Liverpool). After a twenty-minute fight, where she went into the backing three times, got tail wrapped, freed herself, and went to the backing again, I hauled in a thirteen-pound brown trout that the guides and the riverkeeper excitedly agreed had to be a Test River record on three-pound tippet. And the most excited angler of all that night was President Bush, a veteran angler, who has caught a lot of big ones, will catch many more, and was as excited for his friend's good luck as if he had caught the big fish himself.

We posed while our guide pal, Stan Conway, took the customary "hero" picture. I later sent that photo, which appears on the next page, to the president with a modified caption.

The president got a kick out of the caption but vowed, as I expected he would, to catch a bigger one on our next outing.

The trip was great fun, probably a far cry from some of the legendary extreme outings to Alaska, Newfoundland, Argentina, and Iceland, where the president has run circles around his fishing partners, some of them half his age.

During some beautiful streamside luncheons and casually elegant dinners at the inn, the president shared stories about previous trips to England, enjoyable dialogue with Margaret Thatcher and other heads of

*"Unidentified ghillie" (a.k.a. Bob Rich) holds up a 13-pound brown trout caught by President George H. W. Bush while fishing the River Test with his good friends Bob and Mindy Rich, Johnny and Jeanie Morris, Bill Wrigley, Alyssa Nimmer, and Stan Conway.*

state, the treachery of Saddam Hussein, the challenge of being chief of state, as well as accounts of other notable fishing excursions with family and friends. He also served up the invitation of a lifetime when he invited Stan Conway to come visit the Bushes in Kennebunkport for some striper fishing, which turned into a trip our English friend will never forget. One of the things I admire the most about "my fishin' buddy" President Bush is that for all he has done, he's never lost his humility. He remains a sensitive, caring man of the people.

We talked a lot about fishing on that trip, as you might imagine. Regarding types of fish, I remember the president saying, "The species isn't that important. Atlantic salmon, bluefish, stripers, bonefish, tarpon, bass, trout—they're all wonderful. There is a great thrill in catching fish. For me the real thrill, though, is time spent with family and friends. It's about great fellowship and camaraderie. I also love the solitude of being alone in nature. I can cast for hours and never catch a fish—that's okay. I love the opportunity to commune with nature and now, more than anything, it's about experiencing the joy of a grandchild."

*President and Mrs. Bush with their family in 2000.* PHOTO CREDIT: GEORGE BUSH PRESIDENTIAL LIBRARY AND MUSEUM.

So being outdoors with family and friends is now a key driver for President Bush, as opposed to challenge and adventure. Perhaps, I thought, as we get a little older, the motivation changes and we become a little more reflective about our feelings on the subject of fishing. The next friend I plan to talk with is a retiree, and I hope that he can shed some light on this subject as well.

*Fishing is more than fish; it is the vitalizing lure to outdoor life.*

—HERBERT HOOVER

The art of bottom fishing is that of letting the fish come to the fisherman, instead of vice versa . . . Bottom fishing, in short, is the Thinking Man's fishing.

—Louis D. Rubin, *The Even-Tempered Angler* (1983)

# 8

# WILLIAM BRADLEY: GENTLEMAN FROM THE SOUTH

---

*Well, sir, I been fishin' in this same spot on the shore of the Niagara River where the ferryboat used to land to take folks back and forth from Buffalo to Canada.*

*One day last year I get this huge tug on the end of my line, and it's heavy, but it don't jump, so I know it's not a bass. And my pole is all bent over and everybody's runnin' over to see what I got. And I bring 'im up near the surface and we see it's a wall-eye—a giant walleye, mind you. It musta been thirty-five or forty inches long—musta weighed eighteen pounds, maybe more.*

*When everybody saw that fish they started runnin' around lookin' for a net to help me, and do you know, nobody had a net that day. Can you believe it? And it's about ten feet down to the water from this pier.*

*Well, I decide to pull him up and I lift and I lift and I get that fish out of the water right up to the fence, and guess what? That walleye looked me right in the eye and winked at me and jumped off the hook. Jumped right back into the water and swam away.*

*Hey, I'm tellin' ya the truth; he looked me right in the eye and winked at me and jumped right off the hook. It's true, ask any of these guys. Hey, if I'm lyin', I'm flyin'.*

—William Bradley

*The aging Peace Bridge connects the U.S. to Canada from Buffalo, New York to Fort Erie, Ontario.* PHOTO CREDIT: JIM MCCOY

MARINE BIOLOGISTS TELL US THAT FISH don't have eyelids, but if Mr. Bradley says that his walleye winked—I believe him. The current in the Niagara River still runs thirteen knots per hour under the half-mile-long Peace Bridge, which more than fifty years ago replaced the ferry-boat that used to carry cars and passengers from Buffalo, New York,

USA, to Fort Erie, Ontario, Canada. Now the debate rages on about adding a utilitarian twin span to the bridge or replacing it with a spectacular signature bridge—a new international landmark for all to behold, which its proponents say would miraculously erase Buffalo's image as a decaying rust belt city. At some point a decision will inevitably be made, leaving half of the arguers happy and the other half disappointed. As the controversy continues, the only constant is the beautiful, raging river itself, which connects the shallow, treacherous Lake Erie to the deeper, more picturesque Lake Ontario thirty miles away, after a spectacular eighty-four-foot drop over Niagara Falls.

Along the way groups of avid anglers come together almost every day for about eight months a year at special fishing spots on the shore, unfazed and disinterested in the politics of bridge design, focusing instead on camaraderie and catching the favorite fish of the river, whether it's black bass, walleye, perch, or pike.

No one is more of a regular, more revered or more constant, than Mr. William Bradley. Nearly every day, weather permitting, Mr. Bradley takes his place sitting on the cold concrete slab next to the big cleat that was used to tie down the stern line of the 120-foot ferryboat, which has now become no more than a very distant memory to the local senior citizens known as Buffalonians. Without a word spoken, his place is always saved, although a group of regulars jockey to be in close proximity to this seventy-year-old sage, a fun-loving philosopher who exudes warmth and friendship with ever-ready humor for the unsuspecting.

*William Bradley sets up on the pier for a day of fishing.*

Originally from South Carolina, William Bradley moved to Buffalo in 1951 and has been fishing in this same spot for forty-one years. He's now got more fishing time on his hands after retiring from local Bethlehem Steel Company following a forty-two-year career.

He has a sturdy build from years of hard work in the now closed steel mill, but today sports a little paunch around his midriff—no doubt a by-product of his hard-earned retirement. When you say hello, he introduces himself almost sheepishly by his last name only, as is the custom with many older working men. His handshake is warm but tentative—not like those developed over many years by practiced hand shakers who seem to feel an imperative to let you know everything good, trustworthy, and admirable about themselves with the first grip of their hand. He also saves his big broad smile for awhile until, I guess, he feels a comfort level with a newcomer to his personal fishing domain. When the smile arrives, it comes effortlessly and lights up his face, putting you at ease.

He's seen a lot of things in his lifetime and shares his experiences openly, concentrating on the positive and the good and quickly passing over the ugly and the sad. He's happy enjoying the sunshine and looking forward to the next fish as opposed to dwelling on subjects like the death of the steel mill or a loved one, or his early life in a segregated rural southern community.

When he speaks of his youth, he smiles as he recalls his earliest memories of fishing. "I was one of two children," he says. "I had a younger sister who passed. We came from a broken home. I was raised by my grandfather who took me fishing all the time on a small river near our house. He used to wake me up at like four-thirty in the morning, before the sun came up, to go fishin'."

"Why'd you get up so early, Mr. Bradley?" I asked him one morning. "Is that when the fish bite best?"

"Oh, no man," he said. "We'd slip off to avoid working in the fields. Fishin' was a lot more fun than pickin' cotton, tobacco, or corn. We'd fish all day for sunnies. I guess you call them brim. We'd leave early and come home late. My grandfather took me in when I was eight. We were close. He lived to eighty, and then when he passed, I took it hard. I felt more like I'd lost a brother than a grandfather."

"Do you know why they say grandparents and grandchildren get along so well?" I asked him. "It's because they both have a common enemy." He smiled, then looked wistfully across the Niagara for a minute—just long enough for me to wonder if I should feel badly about asking him questions regarding his youth.

Then he sighed and said, "Well, that's just the way it is. I learned a lot from that man while fishin' together. Two things he taught me: 'Your life is only as good as what you put into it,' and 'Do unto others'— the golden rule. That's what I live by."

"How about school, Mr. Bradley?" I asked. "With all that fishing, did you get a chance to go to school?"

"Oh, yeah," he replied. "I finished ninth or tenth grade, I can't remember which, at Blakely Grade School in Kingstree.

"Then when I was eighteen years old, my uncle from Buffalo came to visit, and he brought me back to live with him and his family. That was in 1951, and I've been here ever since. That was a great move.

"I got my first real full-time job here. I went to Bethlehem Steel in Lackawanna and they hired me to do what they called 'yard work.'

That means I walked around the property all day pickin' up papers in their yard, but it was okay. I did that for about five years, and then they taught me to operate cranes and bulldozers. I had a good career. I was makin' top dollar."

I remember those years at Bethlehem Steel, from my own youth. The company, south of the city on the shores of Lake Erie, were the largest employers in the area with over 20,000 people working there in shift work around the clock. But time caught up with them. They were paying

*Steel milling was a huge industry in Buffalo, N.Y. in the early 1900's.*
PHOTO CREDIT: JIM MCCOY.

huge wages for the times, $30-plus per hour in the sixties with a strong union, and under siege from foreign imports.

Rumors started to fly that they were going to close the plant, a fact that their owners and management vigorously denied, even though they cut their capital expenditures to the bone and retooled other least-cost facilities, allowing the Lackawanna plant to become obsolete.

"I saw it with my own eyes," Mr. Bradley said. "My last eight years, I spent goin' from building to building, tearin' out motors and sendin' them to their plant in Johnstown, Pennsylvania. I'm helpin' to tear the place down and they're tellin' everybody they're not closin'. It just didn't add up.

"But I'm not complainin'. I had a great career and I met my wife Paula here. I've been blessed," said Mr. Bradley. "She was younger, a friend of my cousin's. I first saw her ridin' the Ferry/Jefferson bus. I asked her out and we dated for awhile. Then one day she said, 'Hey, you goin' to marry me or not?' and I said 'sure.'

"So, we got married and it's been great. We argue some, but that's all right; I've learned my lesson."

"What lesson is that?" I asked.

"Well," Mr. Bradley said, "they can't argue with themselves. It takes two. From then on I just say, 'Oh, yes dear, you're right, you're absolutely right,' and we get along fine.

*Paula and William Bradley with their children.*

"Paula and I have had a wonderful life together," Mr. Bradley said. "She became a teacher at Bennett High School and taught there for sixteen years, and we have four wonderful children."

"Did you take your children fishing when they were young?" I asked.

"Sure I did," he said. "It gave me a great chance to stay in touch with them. You've got to talk to your kids—that's the most important thing that parents can do."

"Did Paula fish too?" I asked him.

"No, Paula shops; I fish," he said. "But she'd always come along and make lunches. We'd take family day trips to Canada all the time. We've always been close. And they still love to fish, even my son who lives in Florida. In fact, I think he fell in love with Disney World when we went down there in 1975. It was great except for those credit cards. I used them wherever I went, then I got home and the bills came in. I couldn't believe it! I promised the Lord—no more. We had a barbecue in the backyard with those cards right on the charcoal. That was it for credit cards!"

"So Paula doesn't fish at all?" I asked.

"No, man, but that woman can shop," he said. "She has an eye for bargains. I can't go with her, though, makes me crazy. And she got my daughter hooked. They love to go to garage sales. I've told her you won't be findin' any bargains in those white folks' yards. They smart, they know better."

"With the children grown up," I asked, "do you and Paula ever get away?"

"Oh, yes," he said. "We go to Las Vegas every year for a few days for some gambling."

"What's your game, Mr. Bradley?" I asked.

"Dice," he said. "I love to shoot craps."

"How'd you learn that game?" I asked.

He smiled. "Are you kiddin' me?" he replied. "Black men of my generation may not be able to spell their names but they can shoot those dice. It used to be a way of life. I learned early at the speakeasies on the east side of Buffalo, and I've done well in Las Vegas, even won money out there sometimes."

"Really?" I asked him, trying to look skeptical.

"Yes sir," he said, "at the Lady Luck Hotel." Touching his index finger to his lips and pointing to the sky in a familiar pose, he added, "If I'm lyin', I'm flyin'!"

When William Bradley starts to tell a story, everyone around draws a little closer and listens intently. I started to get the feeling that they've heard these tales before but it didn't really matter. It's the story-telling that gets you—the mirth, the timing, the suspense, the punch line, the laugh, and the ultimate oath of authenticity. The story itself just goes along for the ride, and the stories told by Mr. Bradley and his pals on the foot of Ferry Street may be one of the things that separate them from many other anglers I've known.

"Hey, Mr. Bradley," I said, "don't you ever move your fishing spot around a little or go out on a boat?"

"Why would I?" he replies. "I've got everything I need right here, and I might get seasick, and I don't even know anybody who owns a boat," he says, exaggerating a bit. You see, the charm fishing holds for William Bradley is not the lonely solitude of a mountain stream or a southern bonefish flat; it's the camaraderie of being surrounded by his friends, white, black, and Latino, men, women, and children, in a pleasant, familiar, and close location where everyone is treated as equals. Here there is no competition, only friends rushing for nets to help each other land fish.

"Of course I love to show off and catch a fish," he says, "but I'm just as happy to see my friends catch them, and I'll help them any way I can."

"So, what does fishing mean to you, Mr. Bradley?" I asked him one sunny morning as he and ten of his pals waited for a bite with a dozen hungry seagulls flying overhead "lookin' for a handout."

He thought for a moment and answered, "When I retired from the steel mill I needed something to do, just like my friends Mr. Haefner here and Dennis. I started a little vegetable garden at home—still grow my favorites like collard greens, black-eyed peas, and pinto beans, but you need more to do.

"People dream of retirement, but you can't just turn off work then. It'd be like turning off your medication. This is a place to go to keep you from goin' crazy when you have nothin' to do. And you know what, it ain't all about catchin' the fish—it's about the calmness of the water. It's a way to solve problems—although I ain't sayin' I got any," he says with a smile.

"And down here I've found true friends regardless of whether they're white or black. I lived through a lot of prejudice down South, and I never want to deal with it again. You meet good people fishin'. It transcends race. Like my friend Dennis here. We love to talk and fish and we don't care about the color of each other's skin."

"And what do you talk about?" I asked.

"Mostly fishin', but we talk about our families too."

"And what *don't* you talk about?" I asked.

"Religion and politics," Dennis chimed in, also smiling.

"Mr. Bradley," I asked, "what makes a good fisherman?"

"First, you've got to have inner peace in your heart; then you're ready to become a good fisherman," he answered.

"And what about luck?" I asked. "Are you lucky?"

"I'm lucky to be here," he said. "But I catch fish not because of luck, but because it's my time. It's just my time."

"And Bradley here's a good fisherman because he takes his time, and if he doesn't catch him today," Dennis adds, "he knows that he'll catch him tomorrow or tomorrow after that. There's no pressure."

"And how long do you fish every day?" I probed.

"Till the bait runs out," Mr. Bradley said, smiling.

"Actually, a lot of the guys like to use shiners, but I've always preferred worms myself. Goes back to the days of fishin' for sunnies with my grandfather. Also, I get to talkin' and lose my concentration and those fish suck that minnow right off the hook without my knowin' it. With my worms, they have to work a little harder the way I rig them."

"And what do you guys do when it rains?" I asked.

"We usually sit in one of our cars over there and talk about fishin'," Mr. Bradley said.

"And what about catch-and-release?" I asked.

*Mr. Bradley prefers worms to minnows because it's harder for the fish to take off the hook while he's talking to his friends.*

"We keep what we're going to eat and if someone catches a fish he doesn't want, he offers it up to everyone else before releasing it."

"Has fishing changed since you started coming here?" I asked.

"Everything changes, son," he said. "Now there's fewer of some species like pike, but more of others like smallmouth bass. That's just God's way."

"Are you a religious man, Mr. Bradley?" I asked him.

"Oh, I believe," he said. "A couple of weeks ago, my wife surprised me and said, 'William, I had a dream. I just don't think me and the kids are going to see you in heaven.'

" 'Just because I don't go to church with you every Sunday?' I asked her, and she said yes.

" 'Well, Paula,' I said, 'The apostle Peter was a fisherman, and he became a saint.'

" 'Yeah, but I never saw him fishin' at the foot of Ferry Street,' she said, just like that.

"Lord, that woman can argue," he said as Dennis and his other friends smiled.

"I thought you didn't talk about religion?" I asked.

"Only occasionally to prove a point," Mr. Bradley said, "but as long as people here treat each other right, they don't need to have a religion."

Mr. Bradley's well-thought-out philosophy and beliefs are disarmingly simple and straightforward. He and his friends have taken advantage of the warm summers on the Niagara River to forge deep friendships around the sport of fishing. They are close and caring and worry about each other if someone doesn't show up. They spend hours talking about fishing and teasing each other. If, for example, someone shows up with a new sports shirt like Mr. Haefner did one day. Mr. Bradley nicknames him "the model."

Dylan Thomas once said, "Somebody's boring me; I think it's me." I sometimes think of that quote and how occasionally when I'm fishing alone and it's really slow, I start to think that I'm getting bored with myself. I now know who I am going to seek out for fun company to recharge my batteries.

*Mr. Bradley reflects on the enjoyment he's found in life.*

Mr. Bradley and his friends also go out of their way to mentor the young anglers who seek their counsel with a little teasing thrown in for good measure. "Yeah," Dennis says, "this one young boy caught a big bass and Bradley told him if he caught another one like it, he could be on our fishing show on television. Can you imagine, me and Mr. Bradley with our own fishing show? Now the boy tries to catch another big one every day to be on our show. Then one day this Channel 7 TV news cruiser drives by as the kid is arriving, and Bradley tells him he missed his chance. The show had just ended.

"Another time he sends him up the block to Russ's Bait Shop to pick up some 'singing worms.' Russ is still laughing about that one," Dennis said with a chuckle.

"The kids are so important. You know what I'm really looking forward to?" Mr. Bradley asked me. "Fishing with my grandchildren and teachin' 'em just like my grandfather taught me. The oldest is already five. I'm sendin' my wife out to find a fishin' rod I can give him. She loves to shop for bargains, you know."

Calmness of the water, family and friends—my friend Mr. Bradley has this fishin' pretty well figured out. So much for challenge and adventure being the common thread. Like President Bush's fishing trips, Mr. Bradley is driven by more basic feelings which date back perhaps to his boyhood in South Carolina, fishing with his grandfather for sunnies.

*When you bait your hook with your heart, the fish always bite!*

—John Burroughs

*. . . not everything about fishing is noble, reasonable and sane . . . Fishing is not an escape from life but often a deeper immersion into it, all of it, the good and the awful, the joyous and the miserable, the comic, the embarrassing, the tragic and the sorrowful.*

—Henry Middleton, *Rivers of Memory* (1993)

# 9

# SANDY AND SUE MORET: FLORIDA KEYS OUTFITTERS

———◆◆◆———

*It was a real hot August day in South Florida. Flip Pallot and I had gotten up at 4:00 A.M. to go bonefishing in Flip's skiff to Elliott Key in Biscayne Bay. We caught a few each and by 9:30 A.M., it was so hot, the bonefishing was over as the fish went to deeper water.*

*We decided to stay out and look for some lobsters. Flip put on some goggles and I towed him behind the boat on a thirty-foot piece of anchor line. Flip waved for me to stop when he saw a big, empty oil drum that someone had sunk in about eight feet of water that was now full of lobsters. He adjusted his goggles, dove down, and got three nice ones.*

*Then we continued the drill and Flip started yelling again, 'There's another drum down there,' Flip yelled, 'with a twenty-pound jewfish in it.' Now this was before the ban on jewfish, and also before they started calling them "Goliath groupers" to be politically correct. But call them jewfish or Goliath grouper, these fish are great eating, and Flip and I decided that we were going to have him for dinner.*

*All we had in the boat were two eight-weight fly rods that were fine for bones but not for a fish this big. We scrounged around in our tackle bags and found a 5/0 tarpon fly and about fifty feet of hundred-pound test line that we had been using for tarpon shock leaders. So we tied the fly to the line, broke open one of the lobsters, and attached its tail to the tarpon fly. Then Flip swam down and literally hand-fed the tail to the unsuspecting jewfish, which slurped it in without even leaving the oil drum, while I held the other end of the line. Flip surfaced, gasping, "He ate it! He ate it!" I hauled that big fish into the boat in about a minute and a half—a great team effort, a great catch, and a great dinner, that I'll never forget.*

—Sandy Moret

*Flip Pallot (in the water) photographs Sandy Moret and their "tag teamed" jewfish.*

WHILE HAND-LINING A JEWFISH MAY BE quite different from the fishing techniques that Sandy Moret and his old friend Flip Pallot teach six times a year at Sandy's Florida Keys Fly Fishing School in Islamorada, it demonstrates the love of the outdoors and the thrill of the hunt that serves as the cornerstone for many passionate and talented anglers.

Sandy has become known as the "saltwater fly fishing guru" to thousands of wannabe anglers who have attended his school, shopped at his Florida Keys Outfitters store (also in Islamorada), or seen him on one of his many appearances on ESPN or the Outdoor Life Network. He's also substantiated his reputation by winning just about every backcountry fishing tournament in South Florida, and some of them in multiples.

If saltwater fly fishing were a corporation, Sandy Moret would certainly be its head of research and development. He has spent years defining and improving both tackle and technique with his friends and fishing buddies, who also serve as the faculty for his popular fly fishing school. Famous anglers like Flip Pallot, Steve Huff, Rick Ruoff, Stu Apte, Jose Wejebe, Chico Fernandez, and Steve Rajeff regularly take time away from the hunt to teach their skills at the Florida Keys Fly Fishing School, which Sandy started in 1989. The frequent return of the faculty speaks volumes about the anglers' love of the sport and their desire to pass along what they've learned, but also, their respect and admiration for Sandy, who is not only a master angler, but also the catalyst or "the dean" who pulled it all together.

While the art of "freshwater" fly fishing dates back more than five centuries and is documented in such early works as *The Booke of St. Albans* from 1496, saltwater fly fishing is far more contemporary, its roots dating back less than one hundred years. Proponents of fresh- and saltwater can each make a strong case for their respective sport. Freshwater fly fishermen can talk at length about mystical streams and storied waters, time-honored techniques, and the incomparable thrill of watching a trout rise to take a dry fly. Saltwater anglers, on the other hand, talk no less passionately about new flies, equipment, and techniques designed to subdue a large bonefish after a 150-yard run or beat a 190-pound tarpon on a sixteen-pound test line. At the end of the day, both sports are great. Saltwater fly fishing is just newer, and some of the best research and development comes from Sandy Moret and friends.

And some fly-fishing students, meeting Sanford Wiley Moret (his seldom-used full name) for the first time, might see his academic side. A self-described "marginal student at best," Sandy has always been a copious reader, not just of fishing books, but historical and contemporary literature as well, which he might discuss more openly were it not for his painfully shy nature. He stands about five feet nine inches in his Teva sandals and passed the half-century mark about five years ago. His brown eyes look out from above a scraggly salt-and-pepper beard. His hairline has been slowly receding for several years, but this hasn't prohibited him from wearing his hair in a ponytail, albeit a bit of a sparse one. He's still fit, but nowhere near as thin as he was when he finished second in the city high school hundred-yard dash championships in his native Atlanta. (Atlanta is a huge city and the birthplace of many Olympic athletes. It's hard to picture our hero Sandy lining up against some of those studs in the premier track event, the hundred-yard dash, and beating all but one of them. I asked one of my pals from Georgia about that and he said, "Don't forget—that was in old Atlanta before desegregation, and the field was, therefore, shrunk a little." Either way, I figure that Sandy must have been turning in some pretty good times on the track.)

Sandy almost always dresses, onshore or off-, in faded jeans or lightweight tan fishing pants and equally lightweight long-sleeved fishing shirts, often times imprinted with the Florida Keys Outfitters logo on the pocket and also on the visors he wears to shade his eyes. Many evenings, he discards the fishing shirts for colorful, flowered short-sleeved shirts. He completes his look with a gold bonefish earring in his left ear, proclaiming to all his favorite target species.

Sandy's baritone voice and unmistakable Georgia accent is ideally suited for telling fishing narratives or for singing the parts of Waylon Jennings songs that he remembers only after a few Jack Daniel's on the rocks—his beverage of choice.

One of the sidelights of being Sandy Moret's pal is receiving first notice of the many great trips that Sandy and his wife Sue set up to premier fishing locations around the world. The most recent trip took us to the island of Alphonse in the Seychelles off the coast of West Africa, where we went in pursuit of bonefish. Trips like this make you feel like a cross between a pioneer and an explorer, especially knowing that in many cases, armed with your fly rod, you are trying to do something that no one has ever tried before.

It's also great to fish with someone so talented who is not only willing, but anxious to share his expertise. He's also great fun to travel with and the stories come fast and furious, followed quickly by the late-night singing. All of Sandy's favorite songs remind me of that story about what happens when you play a country-and-western song backwards: your wife, your dog, and your pickup truck all come back to you.

One of our favorite Moret-led trips, which has now become an annual event, is a weekend visit for ten couples to Deep Water Cay, a small island off the northern coast of Grand Bahamas, which is teeming with bonefish, all of the small variety.

After dinner on our arrival day, it falls upon our fearless leader to give us our marching orders and housekeeping details. Disarmingly shy, Sandy hates this duty, but stands anyway to deliver his messages as quickly as possible. Having been a part of this trip for almost ten years now, I know his copy points as well as he does, and wait patiently for his comments on conservation.

Soon Sandy says, ". . . and don't let the guides kill any bonefish." That's my cue. I raise my hand, and in my most innocent voice, I ask, "But Saandee-Mon"—that's my Bahamian nickname for him—"how are we going to do that?" Sandy then rolls his eyes, smiles, and says to ask the guides, "Hey, if you were playing golf, you wouldn't eat your golf balls, would you?" By now his remark is legendary, and he delivers it almost in unison with the rest of the campers, who dissolve in laughter and repair to the bar. I haven't the heart to suggest to Sandy that his comment to the guides probably means nothing to them, as there are no golf courses on the island, and in any case, I'm sure none of them have ever played golf.

Happily, we have been thrilled to see how catch-and-release has been coming of age, not only in the U.S. but around the world. As more and more people travel in search of big fish and many locations start to benefit from this tourism, new attention to conservancy is spreading. One can only hope that for some fisheries, it is not too late.

Sandy Moret is proud to be a leader in protecting fish in their environment in South Florida. Besides belonging to several conservancy groups, he was one of the founders of an organization called "Bonefish and Tarpon Unlimited"—very loosely modeled after "Ducks Unlimited"—with a mission of protecting the species and insuring its long-range survival.

"The Keys," Sandy says, "are part of a very fragile ecosystem, and the fish will only do as well over time as their environment. There is a lot of room for knowledge, understanding, and education if we are going to pass this resource along to future generations, and that's very important to me.

"When I began earnestly fly fishing in salt water during the early seventies, there were two fly-rod tarpon tournaments," says Sandy. "The Gold Cup was started as an all-tackle tournament by the baseball/angling great, Ted Williams, in 1964. Anglers could use artificial plugs, jigs, or flies, but no live or dead bait. Ted won the tournament in '65 and '67. The Gold Cup went all-fly in 1972 and was in essence the world series of tarpon fly fishing. The Don Hawley Tarpon Tournament was begun in 1975 as an all-fly tournament.

"Angling luminaries like Carl Navarre, Billy Pate, Al Pflueger Jr., Stu Apte, Jimmy Lopez, Tom Evans, Flip Pallot, and Jimmy Bell competed for the gold. They fished with a who's who of skiff guides. Jimmie Albright, Eddie Wightman, Steve Huff, Jim Brewer, Clarence Lowe, Cecil Keith, Gary Register, Billy Knowles, and Hank Brown were among those on the pole and the gaff."

Sandy is the first to disclose that back in those days he was not always a poster boy for catch-and-release. Of that time, he says, "Both events were 'kill tournaments' where scoring was achieved by bringing a tarpon of over seventy pounds to the dock for weigh-in at the end of fishing each day. Over five grueling days an angler/guide team could enter five tarpon for weight. The tournament was limited to twenty-five boats setting the stage for a potential massacre of 125 dead tarpon. Fortunately, big tarpon are truly difficult to bring alongside a skiff with sixteen-pound tippet, stick with a straight eight-foot kill gaff, and then slide into the cockpit of a skiff while the fish is going berserk. About one out of four tarpon gaffed would snatch the guide overboard for an 'Islamorada Sleigh Ride' before being subdued. A dozen or fifteen tarpon were killed during the tournament week if the fishing was good.

"From '72 through '86 the average tarpon killed and weighed during the tournament weighed about eighty-five to ninety pounds," says Sandy. "There were two fish just over one hundred and fifty pounds caught in fourteen years. One of the three Gold Cup Tarpon Tournaments that Captain Steve Huff and I won together set a record score, with four weight fish and around a dozen releases.

"Our biggest fish that year was one hundred thirty-nine and a quarter pounds and snatched Steve right over the gunwale when he gaffed it fifteen minutes into the fight. Steve's gaff had a rope loop attached to his wrist so he wouldn't lose the fish. I cranked the engine, followed the bubbles, and reeled until they surfaced. Steve's arm was in the tarpon's jaws holding the fish when he handed me the end of the gaff. Unknowingly as I pulled on the gaff, a well-honed tip was sticking out the other side of the tarpon and went into Steve's forearm about an inch deep. We got the fish and won the tournament. In retrospect it was pretty barbaric, but kill tournament fishing was one of the biggest 'rushes' I've ever had, anywhere, anytime! At the end of the week there was no doubt about who caught what or how big they were because we laid their carcasses on the dock," Sandy recalls.

"I know all of this sounds pretty much like Hemingway/Roosevelt sportsmanship today. But you have to remember, these were the same anglers and guides who founded the Everglades Protection Association that effectively lobbied for banning commercial fishing in the Everglades National Park and pushed the Interior Department to restore some semblance of surface water flow through the 'Glades. EPA then later merged with the Coastal Conservation Agency to form the Florida Conservation Association.

"At the same time, along with the Florida Keys Guides Association, we were lobbying to require a fifty-dollar tag to be purchased in advance in order to kill a tarpon. Killing tarpon began as soon as anglers in the late 1800s realized they could be caught on rod and reel, or even harpoon. By 1980, an estimated five to eight thousand tarpon were killed in Florida each year. The fish were brought in and hung on the dock for a photograph at the end of a day or night charter. They remained on the dock until a tourist booked the next day's trip, and then they were discarded. What better advertisement could a captain have to insure a full charter for the next day?" says Sandy.

I have never had a conversation with Sandy and not learned something about fishing in general or bonefish in particular. I believe that he feels more and more that it is his mission to share information on his sport with people to protect the target species he has come to love and thus protect the sport itself. No one has a clearer historical view of catch and release fishing than Sandy as he demonstrates when he talks about the history of Keys tournaments.

"In 1986 the Don Hawley Tarpon Tournament anglers and guides voted to go to an all-release format, and The Gold Cup followed suit in 1987," he told me. "Around the state, anglers and guides rallied and pushed through the tarpon tag rule with the Department of Natural Resources, and today, the tarpon kill in Florida is under a dozen a year. Virtually all of the fish killed are submitted as potential IGFA world records.

"I haven't fished a tarpon tournament since the scoring format changed. Today the anglers and guides put a tie wrap around the fish, then turn the tie wrap in for measurement to determine the points. The size of the average fish went up about twenty percent with the new scoring format. And while I have no doubt about the intention or honesty of the anglers and guides using this method, I know that in the excitement and 'heat of the battle,' it's too easy to make an error. The scale had no emotions.

"I still buy a tarpon tag every year in case the big one comes along. I haven't used one yet, but I have no qualms about putting a record on the dock should the opportunity present itself. If and when I do, there will be no doubts as to what he weighed," says Sandy.

Here is where my pal Sandy and I disagree. I wouldn't even consider killing a tarpon, knowing that a hundred-and-fifty-pounder is probably fifty years old, and believing as I do that these wonderful prehistoric battlers could also become endangered. Like Sandy, however, I too have quit fishing any tarpon tournaments where the fish must be handled for the same fear of harming of the fish. I like the events that award anglers for most releases and allow you to let the fish go in the water, after taking a photo. As my friend Captain Gary Ellis (founder of the popular Redbone Fishing Tournaments) reminds us: "Release the fish and save the memory; it's bigger."

But what makes Sandy Moret such a superstar in his sport? I've asked that question of many of the best anglers in South Florida, like Rusty Albury, Craig Brewer, and Tim Klein, and their responses formed an interesting composite. "He has patience born of experience. He reads the fish and waits for the right opportunity. He has a compact stroke, places the right fly perfectly, and knows exactly how to move the fly to look like the meal that fish was looking for at that time. He makes his first cast count with the confidence of someone who knows there will always be a fish tomorrow, and tomorrow after that. He's the Cool Hand Luke of fly fishing, and he studies the sport constantly and never stops learning."

*I challenge anyone to come up with an earlier fishing picture of themselves than Sandy fishing the banks of the "Hooch," the Chattahoochee River, with a cane pole, at age one!*

Like others, Sandy wasn't born a great fisherman. In fact, he spent his youth in an area that isn't even known as a great fishery. As he tells it, Sandy grew up in a Jewish neighborhood in the Morningside area of Atlanta where he ran track, threw the javelin, avoided classes, and read all of the novels of Leon Uris and James Michener. He had two brothers and a sister and his first memory of fishing was long cane poles on the bank of the Chattahoochee River with his mom, trying to catch catfish and brim. He also remembers fishing for bass at a

*Sandy's mom was the first Moret to catch a billfish, in 1940.*

summer camp in Tennessee, and later on a johnboat in a lake in northern Georgia where his family had a retreat. Bass were also his target when he and his older brother Randy used to skip school—and later, work—every so often.

Less than a motivated student in high school, Sandy strategically selected the University of Georgia based on where his friends were going and who was reputed to have the best parties. A business school major in real estate accounting and finance, and a member of the Georgia Army National Guard (ROTC), Sandy married his high school sweetheart, Terri Orenstein, in 1967, before graduating in 1969 and going to work selling commercial real estate.

Sandy had contemplated going to work at his father's family business after school, but the family business "had an awful lot of family." Both of his brothers and lots of uncles and cousins worked at their very successful liquor, wine, and beer distributorship in Atlanta. After a few years, his brother and fishin' buddy Randy had become frustrated at that business and also wanted a change.

They heard about two failing beer distributorships in Miami handling Pabst and Miller, negotiated a purchase, and moved their families to Miami. At first things went well. They merged the franchises and grew the business from $4½ million in sales the first year to over $48 million. The more the business grew, the unhappier Sandy became.

"I think I was in a midlife crisis," Sandy says. "There was still too much family, I wasn't enjoying myself, my marriage wasn't working, and I wanted to go fishing, not shopping at the Dadeland Mall."

Feeling they had nothing in common except for the three children from their fifteen-year marriage, Sandy and Terri split up and Sandy sold his interest in the distributorship to his brother, gave his wife the house and an income, and moved into a one-bedroom apartment. He tried his hand at Miami business one more time when he opened a fast food restaurant called D'Lites. He opened a second and then a third on his way to franchising before the financial roof fell in and the business imploded.

"Miami had too much concrete," he says. "I wanted to fish. For me the city had become a traffic jam, and I didn't know how to disco. I picked up and moved myself to Islamorada in the Florida Keys." However, not before meeting some people who would become close friends and greatly influence the course of his life.

"I met Flip Pallot in 1972. My kids were taking swimming lessons from this lady who was the wife of the president of Burdines Department Stores. We were invited to their Fourth of July picnic and this guy named Flip shows up with a full beard. He seemed as locked

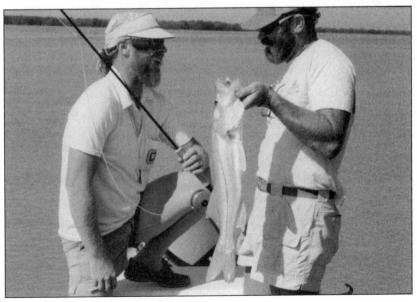

*Sandy (left) caught this snook on fly and was reminded by Flip Pallot that he was still Sandy's mentor.*

into an unhappy life as I was," Sandy shares. "He was a loan officer in his family banking business that would later sell out to Royal Trust Company of Canada, and all he wanted to do was talk about bone-fishing. I couldn't believe it; he fell asleep on their couch still talking about bonefish."

Flip good-naturedly tells a slightly different version of the story. "Sandy was pathetic," he says. "My wife was always after me to spend some time with him, so I finally said okay, and he became my project.

"He and his brother Randy were freshwater plug fishermen and clueless about fly fishing in salt water. I'd pole him around for hours and he couldn't catch a fish to save his life. Then he'd beg me to try my hand. We'd change places and *boom*, I'd catch a fish, and then back on the pole again for hours. Believe me, he was hopeless.

"But now look at him! He wanted it so badly and he worked hard. Now he's a great saltwater fly fisherman—maybe the best there is—and I'm proud that he's my friend. I love that guy!"

Using his ESPN show *Walker Cay Chronicles* as his vehicle, Flip has become a legend when it comes to turning phrases on fishing, and I couldn't let the opportunity pass by without asking him what has been his greatest draw to the sport. He smiled reflectively and said, "It's all about leaving the dock." I liked that a lot. It made me think about breaking away from our terrestrial world as we know it and starting an-other new adventure on the water.

Sandy and Flip became close friends and started fishing together three days a week, or they'd go duck hunting throughout South Florida, the Everglades, and Okeechobee. Many times their hunting trips would include others who have also become close pals of Sandy's, like John Donnell and Rob Fordyce, in addition to Sandy's brother Randy.

"So off I went for Islamorada," Sandy says. "I built a small house and started looking around for fish to catch and something to do, but a little harder for the former.

"I fished with a lot of interesting guys," he says, "including my first Gold Cup with 'Grouchy' Bob Reineman. Then I met one of the most interesting people I know who has become a close friend. Everyone in South Florida had heard of this guy, Captain Steve Huff, who was on his way to becoming a fishing legend in the Keys. They said that Steve thought like a fish and pioneered ways to catch the big ones that were way beyond their time. So I had a chance to meet him through Flip and

bought a day fishing with him at the Metropolitan South Florida Tournament (the MET) auction.

"I'll never forget that day, and neither will Steve," Sandy recalls. "We left the dock in Marathon and drove Steve's skiff to a tarpon spot called Loggerhead. By the time we got there, the wind was blowing fifty miles per hour. All of a sudden, the wind was gusting to ninety. We limped back to Tarpon Creek and hid out under a railroad trestle there, watching waterspouts and lightning and getting battered by three-foot waves as lawn chairs and coolers floated by. We finally weathered the storm and when I got home, I discovered that the two houses on either side of my house,

*Sandy and Steve Huff pioneered the sport, caught some big fish together including this one hundred pound plus tarpon and became close friends, even though on this day, Sandy stuck a gaff through Steve's arm.*

that were both under construction, had been leveled by the wind.

"I sent Steve a book called *How to Predict Weather*, and we've been close friends ever since. He's a great guy who many people call 'the Michael Jordan of fishing guides.'"

Sandy admits to a few blank spots during his early years in the Keys. "I bought some retail properties and fished a lot," he recounts, "and I remember a lot of late nights, Jack Daniel's—prime ingredients for Keys Madness."

Sandy was reported to have been a soft-spoken outdoorsman and lady's man in 1985 when he met Angie, the woman who would become his second wife. "She was an attractive outdoor person who was emotionally inconsistent. Our marriage lasted four years and there were no children," Sandy relates rather succinctly.

Then came a big break for Sandy. "I went to a place called Port of the Islands to attend a fly-fishing seminar that I'd heard about. Port of the Islands is a small place on the Fakaunion River, just north of Chokoloskee, an hour south of Naples, and the seminar featured Flip, Mark Sosin, and Lefty Kreh. It was held at a place called the Remuda Ranch. I loved it, and I thought, 'Why can't I do something like that in the Florida Keys?'

"I got home and called Flip, Chico, Steve, and Stu, and they said, 'Go ahead—set it up; we'll be there.' And the rest is history."

*Sandy opened his Florida Keys Fly Fishing School in 1989 with a world class faculty: seated (from left), Steve Huff, Flip Pallot, and Sandy; standing (from left), Chico Fernandez, Rick Ruoff, Stu Apte, and Steve Rajeff.*

Thus began Sandy Moret's Florida Keys Fly Fishing School in Islamorada. It opened in 1989 and was an immediate success, with students coming from all around the country to learn from Sandy and his pals. "Yup," he says shyly but with some uncharacteristic bravado, "I started the first organized saltwater fly fishing school on the planet!"

Like all subjects concerning fishing, Flip Pallot is very articulate about Sandy's school. "I love teaching at the school with Sandy and all those other great anglers," he says. "They're not only pioneers in the sport but giants in it as well. They're the Babe Ruths of fly fishing and all good friends. Getting to spend time with them is one of my biggest thrills in life."

*Coach Moret talks about leader length and strength.*

"It really went well," Sandy says, "but we had a problem. All our students arrived with small freshwater equipment, and I couldn't source any stuff to sell them. There were three shops in town that sold fly equipment, owned by Hal Chittum, Randy Towe, and George Hommell, and none of the equipment suppliers wanted to sell to me and upset the applecart.

"So I rented this little two-thousand-square-foot place next to Lorelei on the Florida Bay and started selling customized equipment," says Sandy. "The concept worked, and now we're doing classes at least six times a year and our shop is flourishing."

I think one measure of Sandy's success is the fact that the other three shops have now closed, and the big-name manufacturers of fly-fishing equipment have beaten a path to the door of his beautiful, expanded shop.

But enough about Sandy Moret, the recycled bachelor. John Donne penned an enormously famous poem, the words of which are infinitely better known to lovers than the poem's title. So I will use Donne's words from "The Bait" to introduce Sandy's love interest:

*Come live with me, and be my love*
*And we will some new pleasures prove*
*Of golden sands, and crystal brooks*
*With silken lines and silver hooks.*

In 1992, Sandy Moret, the soon-to-be twice-divorced/junior varsity scholar/ex-beer distributor/party specialist/fly-school dean/successful shop proprietor would meet a student who would complete his life and become his partner in and outside of his business.

Locked in a going-nowhere relationship with her offshore fishing boyfriend from Fort Lauderdale, Sue Walsh Lowry had gotten into backcountry fishing when her beau bought her a small flats skiff after renting a vacation home in nearby Venetian Shores. Despairing after a long series of failed relationships with men, Sue decided she needed a new hobby, and chose fly fishing. Little did she know that this decision would lead to her own version of "true love," a la *The Princess Bride*.

Sue, one of seven children, was born in a small town outside Philadelphia. She had a twin brother who drowned in a creek on their property when they were three. To this date, she doesn't remember that day—the day when she says her family started to unravel.

"I was happy to finally be off to college," Sue told me, "and I never went back—or looked back. After graduation from South Carolina, I married my high school sweetheart who had joined the Air Force, and I became a military wife. Our tour of duty included four moves. I hated it. During the fourth stop, we got divorced. Our two children stayed with me while I searched for a meaningful occupation.

"Eventually we moved to Fort Lauderdale where I found a job in food service and got my real estate license. My luck with men never seemed to improve. In retrospect I was always looking for projects and not partners. All of that changed when I met Sandy," Sue said.

"How did you meet him?" I asked her.

"It was really by coincidence. I decided I wanted to learn how to fly-fish and I enrolled in his school," Sue recalled.

While she thought Sandy "was very nice and cute," all did not go smoothly in their first meeting. In her first breakout session with one of the instructors, whom she refuses to name, everything went wrong. At the break she approached the woman who was handling the logistics and asked for a new instructor.

"Who do you want?" asked Angie, the woman who was handling the details.

"How about Sandy?" Sue said.

"Forget about it; he's my husband," Angie said.

"Hey, I don't want to marry him," Sue answered incredulously. "I just want to learn how to fly-fish."

Little did anyone know how prophetic this meeting would prove to be for the soon-to-be second ex-Mrs. Moret.

Sue could hardly be characterized as a home wrecker. Her incredible independence can be intimidating to some. She's about five feet six inches tall with light brown hair and a very caring nature. She loves the outdoors almost as much as she loves a good story, which she will tell with rapid-fire, staccato speed, followed by the question, "Can you believe it?" and her patented, captivatingly gleeful laugh that makes everyone around her laugh as well.

In any case, Sue says that she withdrew from the fishing class after just one day and spent the rest of her Islamorada weekend basking by the pool at the Cheeca Lodge where she was staying. She says that she didn't talk to Sandy again for about a year.

Always up for a new work challenge, Sue started a new line of ladies fishing clothing which she called Turtle Creek. She was the owner, designer, accountant, marketer, and sales force. Almost a year had passed since Sue's brief experience at Sandy's school, when she went to present the clothing line to Sandy, who was recently divorced. Sandy liked the clothing as well as the new company's owner, and the two became friends.

It was at a sportswear convention in Denver that their friendship blossomed into a full-blown love affair. Sue was at a booth selling her wares at this annual trade fair and Sandy was there buying products for his store. He invited her out for dinner (Mexican, Dutch treat) the first night, and every other night for four straight dinners (the last of which included champagne at the Russian Café, where Sandy paid the check). Somewhere along the way, as Sue tells it, there was some kissing in an elevator, and from then on, who knows. Sandy and Sue maintain strict radio silence on any more details.

Upon their return, the buxom brunette Sandy had been dating—who had been known to enjoy fishing topless—was nowhere to be seen. Soon, Sue went to work at the Florida Keys Outfitters where she took over merchandising and built up a terrific collection of men's and women's togs.

Sue and Sandy became roommates soon after, and as Sue recalls, they had very few spats. "I did run away once after an argument, got two blocks away, and realized this was my home and I had nowhere to go—nowhere that I'd rather be. I went home and we kissed and made up."

After three years or so, a shy Sandy got his courage up to pop the question. Sue recalls, "We had gone to Atlanta to visit his mom who was ill. We were on our way to the gate, and we stopped at the Hooligan's in the Atlanta airport. I was reading Sandy a very funny magazine article about second marriages, checking accounts, and credit cards. The next thing I know, he's dropped to one knee right beside the table in this restaurant full of people and he's proposing to me. I couldn't believe it! Of course I said yes, and we called his mom to share the news. 'It's about time!' his mother said."

Sandy adds, "Sue started laughing and told me to get up. I propose and she starts laughing!"

"Yeah," Sue chimes in, "can you believe it?"

Soon after, the two were married at a brief celebration on the porch of Sandy's home in Lower Matecumbe Key, overlooking a beautiful sunset on the Florida Bay. Their biker attorney, Joe Miklas, performed the ceremony in a clean Harley-Davidson T-shirt, and seventy-five invited guests enjoyed a sumptuous Keys feast of steak and lobster while the local band, Big Dick and the Extenders, supplied the sounds of the '70s—free of charge, of course, for their special friends, Sandy and Sue Moret.

After a quick honeymoon at Henry Kravitz's lodge in Meeker, Colorado, the two set up house in Islamorada with their families, Georgia the dog, and three cats.

"It's a great life," Sue says. "I've married a wonderful friend who I'm very much in love with. He's a pal and not a project—although I

*Sue and Sandy tied the knot and became saltwater fishing's premier couple.*

would like to help him quit smoking." Of the honeymoon, Sandy, the more laconic family member, says, "It was great; a beautiful place. We caught some trout . . . but I hate to fly."

So, one day a few years later, my wife Mindy and I were sitting by a pool with Sandy and Sue at the beautiful Alphonse Island Hotel in the Seychelles talking over an incredible day of catching bonefish on the flats of nearby St. François Island. Sandy took a long chug of a glass of Jack on the rocks and said, "Can you believe it? I haven't had a cigarette in over an hour!"

*Sue Moret, a lefty, has developed a great knack for catching big bonefish.*

Sue smiled and slugged him gently in the arm, saying, "And you better not, Bucko!" (This is her favorite pet name for him.)

"Sue," Mindy asked her, "what does fishing mean to you, and would you fish as much if you hadn't married Sandy?"

"Well," she said without hesitation, "I love being outdoors on the water and, like Sandy, I love seeing the fish and sight-casting to them. Without Sandy, I probably wouldn't fish as much, and I certainly wouldn't have learned half the things I know about the sport, or enjoy it as much. For me, fishing is total relaxation and a chance to get my mind off everything else."

"What about you, Sandy?" I asked. "Cut to the chase. Why do you like to fish?"

"Bubba, Ah loovve to watch water," Sandy drawled.

"C'mon pal, that's what you always tell me. Fishing obviously means a lot more to you than that."

Sandy leaned his head back, looked around, and spoke after a long pause. "Okay, for me it's all about the challenge. It's about competing against other anglers and nature—and, of course, the fish themselves.

"It's not about a body count. I lost interest long ago in fishing for numbers. The idea of trolling up a boatload of dolphin fish, for me, is totally meaningless. I want to set targets and then handicap myself with the very lightest equipment I can use. For me that defines excellence. I want to catch the biggest possible fish on the lightest tackle.

*Sandy demonstrated his skill with light tackle, as with this large Bahamian permit.*

"I want to travel too," said Sandy. "I want to master waters, to catch sea run browns in Tierra del Fuego and Atlantic salmon on the Ponoi River in the Kola Peninsula in Russia. But most of all I want to catch big bonefish at home in Islamorada. They're the most unique fish in the world and the biggest challenge, and there are only a few people on the planet who can fish them with any consistent success—and I'm proud to be one of them.

"But do you know what drives me the most about fishing for any species, Bubba? It's the 'bite'—the moment in time when you've done your thing and the fish has done his thing and you are connected.

"And always out there is that elusive 'biggest fish.' Even if you think you've caught him, there is another 'biggest fish' to find, and maybe as you search for him, you'll go somewhere that no one's ever gone, or do something that no one's ever done before. That's what fishing means to me."

There it is from Sandy "the Professor," another vote for challenge—the challenge of catching the "biggest" fish ever, although he tempered his response with his comments about the bite. This is the first time I'd heard one of my angling friends mention "the bite" since Jane Cooke had spoken so eloquently about "the little tug" that always makes her heart flutter.

I'd now spoken with eleven anglers and felt no closer to finding the one thing that drew them all to fishing than when I'd first started. In fact, I found myself feeling downright confused.

*The pleasant'st angling is to see a fish*
*Cut her golden oars the silver stream*
*And greedily devour the treacherous bait.*

—WILLIAM SHAKESPEARE, *MUCH ADO ABOUT NOTHING*

ghil·lie (gĭl′ ē) n. Also gil·ly pl. ies 1. Scottish. A professional guide and servant for sportsmen, especially in fishing and deer stalking. [Scottish Gaelic *gille*, boy, servant, akin to Irish *giolla*.]

—American Heritage Dictionary

# 10

# SCOTT KELLER: FISH HAWK

*My grandfather was a great teacher. I loved spending time with him. I learned so much—big things and little things, memories I'll never forget, like the smell of the great stuff he kept in a plastic tub to get your hands clean. I can still smell it in my mind.*

*I'll also never forget the first time he took me fishing. I was four or five years old and thrilled to be invited. We went to Kahn Lake which was created by the construction of a dam on the headwaters of the Napa River. We anchored up in the lake and then started rolling cheese balls in our hands. My granddad said that we were creating our own hatch.*

*When we had rolled more than a hundred cheese balls, we threw about half of them into the water and waited for what seemed to me like an hour. It was probably more like five minutes. Then we put cheese balls on our hooks and started fishing. We caught rainbow trout on every cast. The first fish I caught, my grandfather brought in and gutted—showing me that its stomach was full of cheese balls. He explained to me that we were basically "matching the hatch."*

*That simple lesson made everything clear and understandable, but it also changed my life. I remember deciding right there*

*and then how I wanted to spend my life—not only fishing, but
learning and teaching as well.*

—Scott Keller

WHAT WEEKEND ANGLER OR HUNTER has not looked enviously at
the life of a professional guide and dreamed of trading places, of giving
up the workaday rat race world of self-inflicted pressure and pain for a
life in the great outdoors? After enjoying time on the water or in the
fields, who among us hasn't questioned their own motivation and priorities and wondered what it would be like to shift gears and become a
full-time guide?

This is the career path that Scott Keller's grandfather started him
on so many years ago on their first fishing trip together. At the time, the
five-year-old boy had no idea that you could make a living guiding anglers, but the concept was already firmly in place.

Now at age forty-four, Scott Robert Keller has guided fly fishermen around the country from Michigan to Alaska, from Montana to
the Florida Keys, and around the world as well. He's also put his anglers

*Scott Keller and his ever present sunglasses at the lodge.*

onto monster fish in Russia and Mongolia and caught a world-record sea run brown trout in Tierra del Fuego off the tip of South America. He has lived every Walter Mitty's dream life as the consummate international fishing guide. He's a colorful character, and his adventures on and off the water have made for some interesting narrative. He gets my vote as the all-time most interesting campfire companion.

I first met Scott during a July fishing trip I took with three pals to Enchanted Lake Lodge, a beautifully remodeled cedar lodge located in the heart of Alaska's Katmai National Park. On the Alaska Peninsula, Katmai is made up of 4.2 million acres of breathtaking wilderness, making it the second-largest park in the United States.

*Darren Erickson oversees the loading of anglers on one of the camp's Beaver float planes for an unforgettable day of stream fishing.*

Enchanted Lake is run by Darren Erickson, an accomplished young fly fisherman and guide, and his wife, Tracy, a self-taught gourmet chef who manages the kitchen and the restaurant. The Lodge accommodates twelve anglers with six experienced guides and is beautifully located on the side of a hill overlooking Nonvianuk Lake in the shadows of the snowcapped Walatka Mountains, which are all part of the Alaska Range.

The Lodge's two DeHavilland Beaver floatplanes transport their guests to and from some of the best watersheds in the Bristol Bay regions. Glacial lakes seem to spring up in the barren tundra purely to serve as perfectly located floatplane airstrips, from which avid anglers can hike to nearby feeder streams and rivers. Short hikes put the anglers and guides on the shores of picturesque rivers like the Merrain, Little Ku, Battle, the American, and the Moses, which are known to fly fishermen from far and wide for the best rainbow trout fishing in the world. While other species like coho and sockeye salmon, char and grayling move in and out of these waters during the four-month season, it is the rainbow that keeps the lodge's rooms full.

The fishing is extraordinary, and wildlife viewing in the region is also without equal. During our trip, we got used to seeing bald eagles, moose, beaver, numerous species of sea- and shorebirds, as well as dozens of brown bear (which Alaskans seem to go out of their way not to call by their more common and menacing name of grizzly).

*A young, curious brown bear takes time out from gorging himself on sockeye salmon.* PHOTO CREDIT: JACK SHEWMAKER.

As our floatplane ferried us to the Lodge the first day on our final leg from the town of King Salmon (population 250), the staff lined up at the dock to greet us. It was a youngish group of clean-cut men and women who looked like they had just graduated from college. One of the guides stood out from the rest. A little older, Scott Keller packs 200-plus pounds on his six-foot frame and wears his wavy blond hair long in accompaniment to a full beard. He looks like a cross between Grizzly Adams, Jeremiah Johnson, and a California surfer/ski bum (which he actually was for many years). I'm sure that you would see an ever-present twinkle in his light blue eyes if they weren't covered night and day by his sunglasses. "I hate squinting," he would tell me later.

Even before I heard his stories I found him to be very knowledgeable about his trade. He not only shared what seemed to be a lifetime of information on Alaska fishing on our very first day together on the Little Ku River, but also directed me to books by some of his favorite authors so I could do some research when I got home. I especially liked the following excerpt from Tom Jay's *Initiation: The Storied Waters of the North Pacific.*

> Salmon are born in brooks, creeks, rills—the headwaters of greater streams. They run to the sea for a miraculous sojourn. Feasting, their flesh reddens in the richness of the sea. Mature, they awaken to the call of their natal waters, and follow clues subtle and disparate as magnetic fields and the bouquet of stones to the streams of their birth to spawn and die. Loving and dying in home ground is a primordial urge. Salmon embody this for us, our own loving deaths at home in the world. Salmon dwell in two places at once, in our hearts and in the waters, and they know the way home.

Arriving at the Little Ku River, about an hour's hike from where the floatplane dropped us off, we noted that the water was red with sockeye salmon who had come upstream to spawn. Ironically, their eggs provided food for the thousands of large and small rainbow trout, our target species, who followed them from the lakes below.

"There are five species of pacific salmon," Scott told me. Chinook or kings, sockeye known as reds, coho (silver), and chum that are called dogs, pinks, or humpies.

"When these sockeye are born, they are called *fry,* and they spend their first half year in the river. Then they wash out to the lakes below where they are called *smolt* and spend a year in the lakes. When they go to the ocean, they are known as *par*. They swim thousands of miles for three years before they return to the rivers to spawn and die. They are driven to return to the very same gravel beds where they were spawned. It's an especially incredible journey when you consider that only one in a thousand of the eggs that spawn actually return to the river as adult salmon to spawn," Scott said.

Scott's knowledge of fishing in Alaska and other great fisheries around the world is deep, and I wondered how he put it all together. The secret became evident as we pursued rainbows together and talked about life.

Scott's great-grandfather, a fly fisherman, had migrated from Scotland to Salt Lake City, Utah, where he was a rancher. There is a street there called Keller Lane where the family ranch was located. *A River Runs Through It?*

"Of course I loved it," Scott says. "It was the story of our family—without the religion, of course.

"My grandfather was born in Salt Lake City, the first of eight sons," he says. "His name was Reed Wilmott Keller. *Reed* means resolute of mind and spirit in Scottish. He and his brothers worked the ranch with their father and would travel the area by horse and wagon to fish all of the local water. His favorite river was the Madison."

Eventually his grandfather got married, became a plumber, and moved his family to Napa, California, where he bought a hardware store. He and his wife had two sons—Scott's dad, Robert, and brother Wally—and two daughters. The men in the family carried on the family fly-fishing tradition.

"My grandfather loved fishing for rainbow trout with dry flies," Scott recalls. "My dad loved to fly-fish as well," he says. "He worked his way through Napa Junior College, was drafted into the army, served overseas, and then returned to finish up his studies at Sacramento State. After graduation he became a sales rep for a company that made backpacking equipment.

"My mother was born in Idaho and met my father in Germany. Her father was in the army, a master sergeant who was also stationed in Germany. She has a heart of gold. While she was never into fishing, she played a huge role in our lives. She not only cleaned and cooked for our family, but fed half of the neighborhood kids as well. She always made sure that everybody around her had a good time.

"My parents moved to Elk Grove, California, and had twelve kids—ten girls and two boys. I was the second-oldest child, the oldest son. I had it good. I had my own room and was like king of the house, although I never spent a lot of time at home. I was always playing sports—baseball, basketball, and football."

Scott's dad went on to start a firm called Sports USA that represented all kinds of outdoor hiking, backpacking, skiing, and mountain-sports equipment from around the world. He built the company up and then sold it. "Made his million, retired, and started a nonstop fishing trip. He is one of the most talented fly fishermen I've ever known," says Scott.

"I went to Elk Grove High School," Scott says. "My marks were horrible. I was a complete knucklehead—there to play football. Elk Grove was a nice little town until the population boom in California took place and the developers took over. It went from a sleepy little cow town with one stoplight to urban sprawl—all tract housing and shopping malls. Now they call it Laguna Hills. What a joke; there aren't even any hills there."

Scott remembers a lot of fishing trips as a boy with his dad and his uncle Wally, himself a great teacher who had gone on to become a school principal in Carson City, Nevada. "We liked to fish Henry's Fork, the Madison, the Yellowstone, the Fire Hole, and our family favorite, the Red Rock in Montana. We used to buy two types of flies from an old guy near there named Pappy Wambacker. He tied Brown Bear Blacks and Brown Bear Browns. The brown trout and rainbows were huge, and they loved those two flies. Some of my first fishing memories were of sitting on my dad's shoulders on the Red Rock while he fished.

He would hook one up and hand me the rod so I could fight and land the fish.

"Then when I got older, my dad and uncle used to leave me on a gravel bed, fishing. I remember my waders used to fill up at least once a week, scaring the hell out of my uncle Wally and my dad. They would take turns fishing me out of the drink while I'd be doing my best frog kick back to the bank.

"Ted Turner bought Red Rock in the nineties and closed it down. We still poached it for awhile, but I don't think the fishing was ever as good again."

While Scott's grandfather passed away when he was nine, his great-grandfather was alive for several more years.

"Do you have any memories of him?" I asked.

"Well, I know that he was superintendent of schools in Utah and loved trout fishing, but by the time I knew him, he was too old to fish much," he said. "But he was a great fish eater—maybe the world's best."

"What do you mean?" I asked.

"Well," Scott said, "he absolutely loved to eat trout, so while we'd fish he'd start a small campfire, come and get our fish, clean 'em, cook 'em, and eat 'em himself. We'd have these huge fishing days, come back to camp, and he'd be napping and the fish would be gone. Man, did he love to eat fish, and we'd always fall for it."

Scott eventually graduated from Elk Grove and enrolled at Co-sumnes River Junior College in Sacramento, where he played football and did not distinguish himself academically. After his sophomore year, he'd had enough school and took a semester off to work in a ski shop. He soon became a ski bum in Kirkwood, California. "I never went back," he said.

He remembers a two-week camping trip to the Brooks River in Alaska with his dad and Uncle Wally that summer. "Wally was a lot younger than my dad," Scott recalls, "and I always thought of him as more of an older friend than an uncle. He had an incredible eye for game, like no one I'd met before. He could see fish in a river or mule deer on a mountain. It didn't matter which. I learned more about fishing from Uncle Wally than anyone else in my life. He was also great fun to fish with. Every time he'd get a hookup, he made the same little war whoop, real quietly—*Whoo hoo*, just like that.

"He had five daughters, and I think he really loved our getaway to Alaska as well. The Brooks River was beautiful. We shared time together cleaning fish and washing dishes. I saw Alaska that summer for the first time through his eyes, and fell in love with the place," Scott says.

"The next fall, instead of going back to Cosumnes, I went to Kirkwood and got a job repairing skis at a shop there," Scott says. "It was great. I was twenty years old and had a few girlfriends, and I skied every day. I hung out with a guy named John Klusing who was the head of the race department at Kirkwood. On our days off, we fished the Klamath and the Trinity together for steelhead.

"One winter John and I went to the San Mateo Sportsman Trade Show together and visited a booth run by one of the lodges in Alaska who were looking for guides. We both applied and were accepted. It was my first real guiding job. We skied every winter through the eighties and then guided in Alaska in the summer. We'd just take the people to the river, get them set up, and fish behind them all day. It was a lot of fun, but I still never thought you could make a living out of guiding.

"It was great. They paid us each four hundred dollars a month and room and board for four months. Even then I never really thought of myself as a professional guide until I met the head guide. His name was Ben John and he was half-Indian. He taught me things about guiding I'll never forget. Above all, he taught me that as the guide, I was in charge. It was my foremost responsibility to make sure that my anglers had a good time. He used to say, 'You're the captain of the ship and you make all the decisions, and you don't take any crap from anybody. Then, when someone gives you a tip, say thank you, put it in your pocket, and don't look at it till much later.' "

About that time, his dad was starting a company called Stream-line. "He had been retired when he met a guy name Jack Ellenberg, the owner of the company, at a sportsman's trade show. Ellenberg, a would-be surfer from Santa Cruz, made excellent waders, but the company was having financial problems and my dad invested a little money in the company. Then the company got in a little more trouble, and my dad invested a little more money, and on and on, till he finally took it over. My dad's retirement was over—not his first choice—and he started working again. He ended up moving the business to Bainbridge Island, Washington, where rod manufacturers Fenwick and Sage are located. For a short while Streamline was the number-one wader in fly-fishing specialty shops."

Scott was finishing up his season in Alaska when his dad asked him to come to work with him. "I tried repping for awhile, even moved to Islamorada, Florida, for a year and a half. I picked up some good lines, ExOfficio clothes, and Scott rods, in addition to our neoprene waders. I hated it—all the detail, follow-up, and paperwork. I opened a few shops but I realized I would rather be wearing the waders than selling them. I knew right then that I wanted to become a full-time professional fishing guide, and that's what I set out to do."

Actually I've met a lot of great guides like Scott who talk of a similar calling. They are clearly distinguishable from those who are simply dabbling or trying a new pastime to pass time. In *Tales from the Water's Edge*, Tom Quinn defines a "real guide" when he says, "The working life of a ghillie and riverkeeper rests always in the balance between respect for the client who pays his wages and the understandable sense of superiority to almost every client because he, the ghillie, is the master of the river in all its moods."

If Scott Keller's guiding career around the world has been spectacular, his marriage record has been far less successful—but never boring. He met his first wife (from Mexico) at a bar in Sacramento. "She was a beauty," he told me, "and boy, could she cook Mexican food. In hindsight I think I bought her a ring to get her off my back.

"I guess I knew it wouldn't work when she bragged to my dad at our wedding that I'd never go fishing again. Anyway, guiding season came and I went fishing. That was the end of the marriage."

"So you parted as friends?" I asked facetiously.

"Yeah, right," Scott said. "She told me she hoped I'd get sick and die."

His second marriage lasted a little longer. "I was guiding on the Pere Marquette in Michigan. That was the river in the U.S. where they introduced brown trout. They call them German browns, but they were originally stocked there by Brits in 1916. I met my second wife-to-be at Edie's Log Bar in Baldwin, Michigan. She was beautiful. We dated for awhile and she got pregnant and proposed to me." He told me, "The wedding was nice; she wore a white dress and I wore a borrowed tweed jacket. I've always liked tweed. I guess it's because I'm Scottish.

"We got a preacher and headed down the river in a drift boat to find my best man Kelly Gallup, who was guiding that day. After about an hour's float we found him, guiding a husband and wife. He put on a sport jacket and stood up for me while we got married right there on the shore."

"What about the couple?" I asked.

"Who?"

"The husband and wife, fishing with Kelly."

"Oh, them," Scott said. "They kept on fishing and we rowed an hour downstream to Edie's Log Bar for a great party."

"So you found true love?" I asked him.

"Well, yes and no," he said. "We had two great daughters, Skylar and Madison, named after the river my grandfather loved to fish so much, but our marriage just didn't work out."

I asked Scott if guiding got in the way again.

"Kind of, I guess," Scott responded. "She's a type A personality and I'm a natural-born slob. I guess it comes from living most of the year with other guides who are also slobs. The divorce took over a year."

Thinking I should change the subject, I asked him, "Tell me about your world-record brown trout."

"Well," he said, his voice brighter, "it was during my sixth season guiding on the Rio Grande River in Tierra del Fuego in southern Argentina—the greatest brown trout fishing in the world." Scott Keller becomes a walking encyclopedia on fishing when he sets the stage for a good fishing story. "A Brit named John Goodhall was the ranch manager for the Jose Menendez Estancia—the largest private land holding in South America. He brought brown trout over from Britain in 1930 and put them in the river.

"The fish became sea run, which most brown trout will if given the opportunity. Many of them migrate to the ocean and return year after year to spawn in the river, although some others live their whole life in the river and never travel more than fifty miles.

"Anyway, it was the fall of 1998, three years before 9/11. My anglers were Mark and Betsy Gates, two professional people from San Francisco. He's in real estate and she runs a fly-fishing school for women only. It was their first time fishing Tierra del Fuego.

"They arrived in the afternoon and we went out fishing after dinner, just to check out the river. As you know, it stays light there very late. Anyway, Mark and Betsy caught a nice ten-pounder. I always carry an underwater camera, and I got a nice picture of the fish before we released it, not realizing it was my last shot on the roll.

"Tierra del Fuego is known for its winds. It always seems to be blowing at least twenty-five or thirty miles an hour and gives the anglers a real workout. On our next day, there was no wind at all. It was dead calm. There was a light drizzle, not rain but drizzle, which would obscure the view of the angler from the fish. The conditions were, in a word, *perfect*. I knew we were in for a great day and I wasn't wrong.

"We got rolling early and got a one-mile beat that went into Red Francis pool, named after a famous Atlantic salmon fly. I always fish the pool with a girdle-bug fly tied on a size eight hook. I learned how to tie it from my friend Ron Meek—in my mind, the 'king of all guides.' Ron made the flies with black chenille and lead eyes with eight white rubber legs. He fished it by throwing it one-quarter downstream and then swinging it like when you're fishing a stream for Atlantic salmon and steelhead. I now fish it down there exclusively in bright daylight hours and a four-by long streamer hook Woolly Bugger when you start to lose the light."

Once again, Scott the teacher's narrative migrates quickly to instruction, but not in an overbearing way. "Anyway," he continues, "Mark and Betsy went into the pool. It was absolutely percolating with fish. I set Mark up in the middle of the pool and showed him the drill. It's best to use an eight- or nine-weight rod and a nine-foot, ten-pound Maxima leader on a floating head fly line, and throw short, mid-length, and long, take a step, and repeat the process.

"Then I walked upstream with Betsy and got her set up in the neck of the pool. Just then she said, 'Oh, look, Mark's got one!' I walked back to Mark, who was indeed hooked up. His fifteen-foot, eight/nine-weight Sage Spey rod with ten-pound test line was bent over like a half moon. The fish really wasn't doing anything. It was hunkered down deep in the pool, sliding back and forth, ten to twenty feet at a time.

"I knew it wasn't going to be over for awhile, so I walked back to my truck to get my net and a cup of coffee. When I came back it looked like a Mexican standoff. I figured that it was a pretty big fish, probably foul-hooked.

"About twenty minutes into the fight, Betsy hooked up too, and I walked over to net and release her fish. Having done that, Betsy and I walked over to Mark and I got the net ready. It wasn't until five seconds before netting that I got my first look at Mark's fish. It was huge—the biggest brown I'd ever seen in six years on that river. It blew my mind. 'Mark,' I yelled. 'I think you've got a world record there.' He, of course, thinks I'm giving him that typical guide BS.

"Now, Betsy—who's just released a fifteen-pound monster, the largest in her life—starts to get excited too.

"Mark had the fish whipped. I waded into the pool and barely netted the fish in one try. It almost didn't fit into my net. I hauled it ashore for some measurement. The fish weighed sixteen kilos on my Chatillon scale—that's thirty-five-point-two pounds, easily a new world record. We measured him; he was forty-four inches long with a twenty-five-and-a-half-inch girth. He was a freak of nature!

" 'Okay, Mark, I'll hold him while you get your camera,' I said.

" 'I don't have a camera, Scott,' he replied. 'Surely you've got one.'

" 'I do, Mark,' I said, 'but I ran out of film last night.'

"Here we were. What a predicament. You need measurements and a line sample to qualify a fish for a world record to be submitted with a picture. We're literally in the middle of nowhere with no camera.

"I had Mark hold the fish in the net and ran back to my truck to get on the radio and see if there was anyone near us who could help. Happily, one of the Argentine guides, Miguel Carreras, who was fishing ten miles away, heard my call and drove over with his client's camera.

"It took him about ten minutes to get to us, driving like a madman. He shared our excitement and helped us take about a dozen shots of the fish before driving back to his party.

"The rest of the day was magical. We were in fish all day long and caught ten in the fifteen-to-twenty-pound range.

"Now the Argentineans are great hosts, friendly and hospitable. Kevin and Marie Jose Tiermersma, the hosts and managers of Kau

*Scott (right) with Mark Gates and his world record brown trout, "the big one."*

Tapen, had champagne waiting for us when we got back to the lodge, and everybody was real excited. Kevin said he'd get the film processed the next day. I went over to see Miguel's client and get the film. He's English—and rich—a duke or a lord or something. He says, with this English accent, 'Well, actually, I've still got six shots left. I'll shoot them off fishing tonight and give you the film then.'

"So he goes out for the evening fishing, comes back, and says something like, 'Sorry old chap, I haven't used those shots yet, maybe tomorrow.' Well, I grabbed the camera, clicked off six shots, took the film, and handed the camera back to the English angler. He looked shocked. It wasn't very professional of me, but we needed those pictures, and I figured, what would happen if he took an unplanned swim in the river with his camera. And you know what? That's exactly what happened the next day. He fell in the river. Thank God I got that film. Those pictures would have been ruined."

"So you got your world record in Argentina?" I asked Scott.

"Yeah, it was great," he said. "Actually, I got more than that down there. I also found my third wife—the love of my life! She was an Argentinean who was working as a chef at a neighboring camp. Her name is Nadina. I learned Spanish pretty good before leaving to guide for awhile in Mongolia. When I came back the next season, we got married at a beautiful wedding with two hundred people and me, the only gringo. My friend and fellow guide, Sebastian Graciosi, even played the bagpipes.

"We now live in Fairfield, Idaho, with our daughter Lola. I'm happy as a clam. I guess the third time is the charm."

"So what's the draw for you in guiding, Scott?" I asked him as we sat on the porch at Enchanted Lake Lodge, watching the late-evening shadows lengthen on the nearby Alaska range. "Is it about the wilderness, the people—the fish?"

"It's all about the water. New water—that's where the magic is. Like going to the Ponoi River in Russia for the first time in search of Atlantic salmon. New water is really killer. The first time you're looking at new water, water that you've never seen before, you're at your best. Not like being in old reliable water that you know like the back of your hand, but being in new water with clients, trying to work it out, to figure out in your head how everything works. Then you're totally focused. All your senses are working—there's nothing else like it. And you know what? It's like sharing a good secret with friends.

"I don't know if it's sport or art. All I know is that I never get tired of it. New water is like starting over again—like going back to the beginning to get the same feelings you had as a child. For me that's what fishing is always about: searching for those old feelings over and over again."

*Scott finds magic in new water like the Ponoi River in Russia where he caught this nice Atlantic salmon.*

Searching for those old feelings over and over again in new water . . . Scott wasn't making my search any easier, I thought. But what the heck—I decided to just go with the questions and learn from a veteran.

"And how do you choose locations, Scott?" I asked him. "How do you get set up to fish around the world?"

"Networking is really important," he said. "I remember the name of every guide I've ever met, and most of the anglers I've fished with, too. I like to keep up relationships. There are a handful of guides who've been extremely important to me in my career, like Tom Johnson, who owns Johnson's Pere Marquette River Lodge in Michigan with his brother Jim, who also took me in at Islamorada in the Florida Keys.

"Then there were the Vermillion brothers, who I affectionately call the Vermin brothers. They are Alaskan guides—simply awesome—the best of the best, who own the Copper River Lodge in Alaska. They also fish for peacock bass in South America. We met in Russia and they dialed me into guiding for forty-pound taimen on dry fly in Mongolia. My friend Ron Meek then pulled together the Mongolia trips, which I'll never forget.

"You should have seen us the first year. We barged jet boats from Seattle to Korea and then loaded them on trains to Ulan Batar, or UB as it's known, and finally trucks to the center of Mongolia.

*Scott got to Mongolia with "a little help from his friends" and it didn't take him long to capture this hefty taimen.*

"It was like going back in time, driving up and down virgin rivers in jet boats where I'm sure no fisherman had ever been before. We passed farmers chopping crops with machetes and carting them away in ox-drawn wagons. They looked at us like they'd never seen motorboats or Americans before, and I'm sure they hadn't.

"One day this guy came down to the water and insisted we follow him. We walked through the brush for an hour and came to this Buddhist monk standing by a big rock that looked like a cow. He didn't speak English but signaled that we should walk three times counterclockwise around the shrine and then give the cow a gift for good luck."

"What did you do?" I asked, savoring this somewhat long and unexpected story.

"Well, we're fishermen and we wanted the luck," he said, "but we didn't have any money on us. All we had was some candy in bags that we'd been giving the local kids."

"So what did you do?" I asked.

"Well, we walked around the shrine three times and gave the cow some candy," he replied.

"And was the monk disappointed not to get money?" I asked.

"No," Scott said, "he was delighted—must have had a sweet tooth. He gave us all some sacred dirt wrapped in paper for good luck and safe passage, so at least I've got that going for me."

Scott's stories just kind of come in and pull up a chair, like old friends, of which he has many. His international tales delivered in a soft voice all seem to be unique, but yet very believable.

"Tell me, Scott, about your favorite and least-favorite kinds of clients," I asked him.

"Well, to tell you the truth," Scott said, "I've had very few I couldn't get along with. I think the worst are those who think they know it all, who refuse to take any kind of help or instruction. I had a Belgian client who threatened to walk home one day. He was pretty arrogant, but he came around.

"The best are those who appreciate the beauty of the surroundings and the whole experience. Like Yvon Chouinard, the owner of the

Patagonia company, who I fish with a lot. He has a wonderful appreciation of water. I'll take him to a pool and he'll be content to just watch it, look at the fish, and figure out how it works. He'll walk around the pool taking it all in before even fishing it, saying *Wow* over and over. 'Wow, look at that.' He's a guide's ideal client."

"Well, Scott," I asked then, "what's the most frustrating thing about your job?"

"Untangling lines can get a little old," he said, smiling.

"Don't you get angry with the anglers?" I asked.

"No," he said, "they're doing the best they can. It just gets frustrating. Sometimes it's like watching a guy trying to hammer a sixteen-penny nail and hitting his thumb every time, but at the end of the day it's worse for him than me—it's his thumb."

"So wouldn't you love to change places with your angler—to make a bundle of money and be the one on the pointy end of the boat, the guy having his tangles taken out, the person waiting for the shore dinner?" I asked.

"No, not at all. I am a ghillie—a servant to fishermen. That's my profession. I'm very proud of what I do. I love to live vicariously through my anglers' successes, to see a good strategy end in a hookup, and to watch how thrilled they are to catch that big fish of their dreams. I wouldn't change my life with any man."

I believe Scott Keller. His self-contentment is very obvious. He has fishing skills from one side of his family perfectly blended with teaching skills from the other.

"And what's the most important lesson you've learned about fishing to help you in your profession, Scott?" I asked.

Without hesitation he launched into a great story that I'll always remember. The story tripped off his tongue like he'd told it, if not thought about it, many times before.

"I was eighteen years old, fishing for steelhead with my dad, Uncle Wally, and Mike McLucas, the head of the Oregon Guide Association and owner of the Maupin Inn on the Deschutes River. It was my first experience with sea run fish. Mike was a big guy with a salt-and-pepper-colored beard, a great guide who would become an important teacher and good friend.

*A trip to the Deschutes River with (from left) Scott's dad, Scott, Uncle Wally, and Mike McLucas in the background.*

"It was a three-day trip. The first day, my dad caught four, my uncle Wally caught two, and I got shut out. The next day, my dad caught four again and Uncle Wally got four also, and I caught nothing.

"By then I was feeling pretty miserable—sad for myself and embarrassed in front of my dad and uncle.

"The third day, Mike stayed pretty close to me, helping me spot fish and giving me tips. Halfway through the morning, I cast and got this tremendous pull on my line as a monstrously large steelhead hit my fly like a Mack truck and headed off downstream. He ran out over a hundred yards of line, did this great jump, and then he was gone—just gone.

"I was devastated. I turned to look for sympathy from Mike and he started to laugh—this big uncontrollable laugh from his stomach. I'm crushed and he's rocking back and forth laughing like Santa Claus. I couldn't believe it! Then I started laughing too. Here we are like a couple of madmen, standing in the river laughing.

"We finally stopped laughing and sat down next to each other on a log at river's edge and Mike finished teaching me a lesson I've never forgotten.

" 'Look,' he said, 'that was an awesome spectacle and you were lucky enough to be a part of it. It was a most positive event, one of the greatest things a man could ever see, and it was your moment to enjoy and you did. Never, ever forget it.'

"Of course he was right. Catching that fish would have just been an afterthought to that special adventure.

"With the pressure off, I went on to catch three nice steelhead after lunch, but more importantly, my philosophy on fishing and guiding was formed.

"My Uncle Wally died twenty years after that trip, fifty-five years old, of skin cancer. I'm glad we had that trip together."

"Scott you've fished all around the world; what is your favorite place to fish?" I asked him.

"That's impossible to answer," he said. "Like life, every river has its season. I love the rainbow fishing in the wilds of Alaska, the warmth of the bonefish flats in Islamorada, the virgin waters of Mongolia for taimen on dry fly, the sea run browns of Tierra del Fuego, the browns and rainbows in Big Wood near Ketcham, and, of course, there's all that new water out there waiting for me—places I've never tried."

"But if you had just one day to fish, where would it be?" I persisted. "And who would you fish it with?"

"Well," he said again without hesitating, "I'd love to turn back the clock and have one last day of trout fishing on the Henry's Fork with my dad and Uncle Wally."

*Anglers must always face the fish alone, and that is how it should be. But the very best fishing moments will ever be those we spend in the company of a partner and a friend.*

—STEVE RAYMOND, *RIVERS OF THE HEART*

Ted Williams with his passion for excellence, his outrageous almost belligerent intelligence and the sheer force of his unyielding personality, might have become a brilliant brain surgeon.

—David Halberstam

11

# TED WILLIAMS: AN AMERICAN HERO

*I loved Jack Brothers. Don't get me wrong, I'm not gay or any-thing like that. I just loved being with him and fishing together. He was a damn fine captain and a very knowledgeable saltwa-ter angler and great fun to spend time with.*

*I remember one day we went fishing together in Islamorada [in the Florida Keys]. I put him in the bow and I went to the stern to pole him around. Well, don't you know I spotted a nice bonefish for him and he cast to it, hooked him up, and then broke him off, and I started cussin' at him like crazy. Then he hooked another and broke him off too.*

*Boy, did I give it to him. So he says, "You get up here and try it," and I did, and I caught two nice bonefish and I'm givin' him the horse laugh all the time.*

*Then he gets back to the bow and breaks off two more. Then I get up there and catch two more, just like that—and that's how the day ended, with me tellin' Jack over and over again, "Don't forget I'm the greatest cotton-pickin' angler in the world."*

*Jack Brothers never forgot that day 'cause I never let him.*
*Boy, he was a good fisherman, but that was my day.*
—Ted Williams (as told by Jack Brothers's
son Frank, who was Ted Williams's
longtime friend, driver, and confidant)

TED WILLIAMS WAS ONE OF THE MOST talented heroes this country ever worshiped. Whether he focused on baseball, fishing, or flying fighter planes, he was simply the best. While he died on July 5, 2002, at the age of eighty-three, his memory lives on as one of the greatest sports legends in history—a one-of-a-kind Hall of Fame baseball player who twice interrupted his career to serve his country as a wartime fighter pilot. Off the field he appeared to be standoffish and sullen. He was a dedicated sportsman who preferred hunting and fishing to all other pursuits, and was the first living person inducted into the International Game Fishing Association Hall of Fame.

*Ted Williams, Hall of Fame baseball star, decorated war hero, world class angler.*
CREDIT: REDBONE GALLERY.

When President Bush suggested that John Wayne could have played the part of Ted Williams, sportswriter Robert Lipstyte put it in a slightly different perspective. "Ted Williams was what John Wayne would have liked us to think he was—so big, and handsome, and laconic and direct and unafraid in the uniquely American cowboy way. To me he epitomized the sense of the athlete as a gunslinger." Former Red Sox Executive Lou Gorman said of Williams, "He symbolizes all the good things about baseball."

From 1939, when he broke into the Big Leagues as an outfielder for the Boston Red Sox and batted .327 with 31 home runs and 145 runs batted in, until his retirement in 1960 with a home run on his last at bat, Ted Williams rewrote the record books and, to paraphrase the popular Frank Sinatra song, he did it his way. He laid a solid claim to being the greatest hitter in the history of the game by compiling a lifetime average of .344 with 521 homers. In 1941 he became the last major league player to hit over .400 in a season and then sixteen years later, he became the oldest player ever to win a batting title, hitting .388 at age thirty-nine.

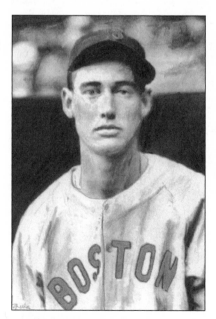

*Legendary Boston Red Sox's Ted Williams.* CREDIT: REDBONE GALLERY.

By the time he retired, Ted Williams had probably picked up more nicknames than any other pro athlete in history. The Splendid Splinter, The Kid, Teddy Ball Game, and Thumper are just a few. Given all these terms of respect and endearment, it's hard to believe that he carried on a nearly lifelong battle with many fans and members of the press corps.

Favorite baseball stories about Ted Williams also abound. I have two: one about his hitting .400, and the other about his last at bat in Boston. Hitting .400 in a major league baseball season is bigger than huge. No one had accomplished it since his idol Bill Terry in 1930, when Williams went to Shibe Park for a doubleheader against Connie Mack's Philadelphia Athletics on the last day of the season in 1941. With an average of .39955, he could have sat out the games, knowing his average would be rounded to .400 at the end of the season. In fact, that's just what his manager Joe Cronin wanted him to do, but Ted would have no part of it. He suited up and banged out six hits against the Athletics to drive a Red Sox sweep, and finished the season hitting .406. No major leaguer has since broken the .400 mark.

Ted Williams's attitude toward "ignorant fans" and an equally ignorant press who he called "Knights of the Keyboard" gained him a reputation as sullen and arrogant that he did little to disprove throughout his career.

Famous American author John Updike chronicled Ted Williams's last game of his career in Boston's Fenway Park in 1960 in his *New Yorker* essay entitled, "Hub Fans Bid Kid Adieu." Boston fans are tough and vocal, and it's not uncommon for them to boo their own team's players. Williams, in spite of his legendary status, was not exempt and was jeered openly by many of the Fenway faithful. Williams never accepted this treatment gracefully and symbolic gestures like spitting toward the spectators perpetuated his running gun battle with them. (Referring to Williams's habit of spitting toward the fans, columnist Red Smith coined the classic phrase "Great Expectorations.")

And then, almost in an instant, his career—which spanned four decades as a Red Sox interrupted by almost five years of military combat service—came down to his last at bat in Fenway. When he drove a home run out of the park, the crowd rose en masse and begged their left fielder to pop out of the dugout and doff his cap for a curtain call, as is the custom in baseball. With a standing ovation in process, Ted Williams refused and stayed planted in the dugout.

His final sullen response earned a great deal of criticism from the national baseball press, but Updike put a wonderful twist on it when he wrote:

*Ted at bat.* PHOTO CREDIT: SPORTING NEWS.

Our noise for some seconds passed beyond excitement, kind of immense open anguish, a wailing, a cry to be saved. But immortality is non-transferable. The papers said that the other players, even the umpires on the field, begged him to come out and acknowledge us in some way, but he never had and did not now. Gods do not answer letters.

While Williams outwardly criticized Boston fans, he privately showed his concern for their community. He was always a generous contributor to the Jimmy Fund, helping sick children in the greater Boston area. Perhaps his concern had its roots in his own childhood memories of growing up in San Diego in a broken family.

To his credit Williams attempted to make public amends with New England fans when he was attending an event at Fenway on May

*Ted always made time for children's causes like the Jimmy Fund and the Redbone's quest to "catch a cure" for cystic fibrosis.* CREDIT: REDBONE GALLERY.

12, 1991, commemorating the fiftieth anniversary of his .400 season when he doffed a Red Sox cap, waving it to the assemblage, and said into a microphone, "Today, I tip my hat to all the fans of New England, the greatest sports fans on earth."

He later re-created that scene at the 1999 Major League All Star Game in Boston, sixty years after his rookie season, when he put many years of ill health behind him, stepped out of the golf cart used to take him to the mound at Fenway, and threw out the ceremonial first pitch surrounded by the admiring and emotional athletes of the National and American League teams.

Later on he was quoted as saying, "Wasn't it great! It didn't surprise me all that much because I know how these fans are in Boston. They love this game as much as any player and Boston's lucky to have the faithful Red Sox fans. They're the best." (Some might say that Williams's second curtain call was diminished by his hat selection. Instead of the classic all-blue wool baseball cap with the familiar stylish *B* for Boston, he donned a cap with the logo of his son John Henry's Internet service—but that's another story.)

Earlier in his life, Ted Williams told a friend, "All I want out of life is that when I walk down the street folks will say, 'There goes the greatest hitter that ever lived.'" He got his wish. Knowledgeable folks like Baseball Hall of Famers Bob Feller, Satchel Page, Frank Howard, and Mickey Mantle acknowledged his unparalleled hitting prowess. Perhaps his chief rival for the title of greatest hitter ever, Joe DiMaggio,

*Ted belting one out at Cooperstown.* PHOTO CREDIT: BOSTON RED SOX.

summed it up to Rod Beaton of *USA Today* when he stated simply, "He was absolutely the best hitter I ever saw."

If this was all Ted Williams wanted, he certainly exceeded his goals when he also became an American hero after winning the Triple Crown in 1942, batting .356 with 36 home runs and 137 RBIs, while enlisting in the Marines and becoming a fighter pilot and the equivalent of a "top gun" flight instructor until WWII ended. He solidified his hero status by serving for three years, missing three seasons (1943–45), making a successful comeback, and then reenlisting and flying combat missions during the war in Korea, missing most of the 1952 and 1953 seasons. During this second stint of military service, he flew thirty-nine combat missions over the Korean mainland and took enemy fire three times.

During one of those missions on February 19, 1953, his F-9 Panther jet took enemy ground fire. Somehow, he managed to follow one of his squadron buddies back to base with no hydraulic systems functioning. He later told *USA Today* "Baseball Weekly" writer Chris Colston that as he was fighting the stick of his crippled bird, he said to himself, "If anybody up there can help me, now's the time to do it." He crash-landed his F-9 in a wheels-up landing at his base, and was barely able to escape before his plane burst into flames.

In Korea, his operations officer, future astronaut John Glenn, chose Williams to be his wingman. When asked how good a pilot Williams was, Glenn said, "Ted was an excellent pilot and not shy about getting in there and mixing it up." As biographer Ed Linn has said about Williams the Warrior, "You don't pick a wingman because he can hit a baseball. You pick him because he can save your life."

In retrospect, it's hard to imagine how he was able to perform on a baseball diamond as he did and how many more records he would have smashed if his baseball career hadn't been interrupted by almost five years in the military service. I asked him that question years later after meeting him for the first time in the Florida Keys in 1974. He merely shrugged his shoulders and said, "I have no regrets. I was just doing my duty."

Nine years after retiring in 1960, Ted Williams came back to the game for four seasons of managing, three with the Washington Senators and one with the Texas Rangers. But I never thought his heart was totally in it. He often shared with me the frustration he felt at not being able to pass along more about the game to his players as a manager and as a coach. His passion was the outdoors, and retirement gave him time for hunting and fishing. (For a list of Ted Williams's many baseball accomplishments, see the Appendix.)

Ted Williams was born in San Diego in 1918. His parents had a strained relationship and he and his younger brother Danny were mainly raised by his mother, May, who worked for the Salvation Army and played the cornet in one of their bands. His first memories of fishing were with his mom, who was known as "the Angel of Tijuana." While he never talked much about his fishing in those days, we know that he'd been "bitten by the bug" from teammates who reported that he used to carry a fishing rod with him on the road. Williams would later admit, "Yes, I firmly believe there's no greater outdoor activity available to human beings than sportfishing. You're never too young or too old to participate, and the excitement, pleasure and challenge are always there. It doesn't matter if the fish you're after is a 2-ounce bluegill or a 200-pound marlin. If the tackle is right for the size of the fish, it's always a sporting proposition, and a damn fine one at that."

*Ted as a child, left, with his mom and younger brother, Danny.* PHOTO CREDIT: SPORTING NEWS.

After baseball, Ted Williams retired to Islamorada in the Florida Keys where I first met him having breakfast in a popular bayside restaurant looking out over the Florida Bay backcountry called The Islamorada Yacht Basin. The name itself was a misnomer. I don't think there was a motorboat in sight that was over sixteen feet long, and not one sailboat, either. Here amidst fishing guides, anglers, waitresses, breakfast cooks, and other early risers, Ted Williams seemed most at home. He flung jokes and fishing stories back and forth in his characteristically colorful language. Far from jeering fans and never-satisfied press pundits, Ted Williams seemed to have surrounded himself with the "just plain good folks" with whom, like the clubbies, doormen, waiters, and working people in the big baseball cities, he had always felt most comfortable. Here's a man who never sought celebrity and was extremely uncomfortable when it found him; a man who literally didn't own a necktie and would turn down accepting an award to spend time by himself on a trout stream.

*Ted, second from right, with his Islamorada fishing guide friends from right, Cecil Keith, Jimmie Albright, and Jack Brothers.* PHOTO CREDIT: REDBONE GALLERY.

And no story about Ted Williams would be complete without mentioning his special ability to argue, whether it was with his favorite Red Sox teammates, Johnny Pesky, Bobby Doerr, and Dom DiMaggio, or his iconoclastic fishing guide pals in the Keys. Writer/historian friend of Ted Williams, David Halberstam, tells it best in his wonderful book *The Teammates: A Portrait of Friendship*: "Ted Williams never lost an argument, in no small part because he was bright and he marshaled the facts and argued well, but also because he shouted all the time and appointed himself judge and jury at the end of each argument to decide who won."

Just as there are a multitude of stories about the talent of Ted Williams the baseball player and Ted Williams the fighter pilot, so too are there many about Ted Williams the angler. And just as some of the best endorsements of his talents in the former two categories come from other baseball and war heroes, so too do some of his greatest fishing testimonials come from famous anglers like Stu Apte, Jack Brothers, and Jimmie Albright. Legendary sports announcer Curt Gowdy was one of Williams's greatest fans. They first met, early in their careers, when Curt was hired as the "Voice of the Red Sox," and they formed an immediate bond around their mutual love of fly fishing. Williams appeared often as a regular guest on Gowdy's *The American Sportsman*, one of the first and most popular outdoor shows on national television, and Curt loved to relate to audiences at his public speaking appearances his favorite Williams fishing story:

"I talked our producers into doing a show on fishing for permit in the Yucatan Peninsula in Mexico with Ted Williams. Now, anyone who knows about permit, a member of the jack family, knows how impossible they are to catch, but we went ahead anyway. We had a great location, a good time of year, and a great angler. If anyone in the world could catch those darn fish, I knew Ted could.

"Well, we're down there on location and when it wasn't raining the sun was blistering and the bugs were terrible. To complete the picture, we'd been down there six days and hadn't seen a fin or a scale.

"By this time, the film crew had had it. They're ready to pack it up and skip our last day, but Ted says, 'C'mon, we're going to catch that fish tomorrow.'

"Well, tomorrow came, and by noon when we took a break for lunch we still hadn't seen or caught a permit. Now the crew really wanted to quit, but again Ted says, no, we're going to catch one. By this time I was agreeing with the film crew, but Ted said, 'Curt, I'll bet you a thousand dollars I'll catch one this afternoon.'

"By then I thought he was nuts, but a thousand bucks is a thousand bucks, so I went along. Don't you know that right after lunch we see this big scythe-shaped permit tail; Williams casts to him, catches him, and we get it all on tape. Then he goes on to catch four more before the afternoon ended. His belief was so infectious, even I caught one. We had our show 'in the can,' and I learned a lesson that day. Never bet against a man with supreme confidence," Curt concluded.

I often fish with a guy in South Florida named Ronny Hueston who is one of the world's top snook fishermen—and cursers. It is not unusual for Cap'n Ron, the son of a Miami policeman, to blend ten swear words into a sentence. "That's nothing," Captain Gary Ellis, my longtime fishing pal from Islamorada, says. "Ted Williams could manage whole paragraphs of expletives with only a few pronouns thrown in for good measure. Teddy Ballgame raised cussin' to an art form!"

He was, for all his skills and success, a man of the people, an athlete and a loyal teammate. His language was coarse but honest. He never put on airs or tried to be anything he wasn't. Like his language, Ted Williams was brutally frank and to the point, even if his critics were often offended.

I have always believed that you are what you do when you think that no one else is watching. If this is true, then the "real" Ted Williams came out in his growing concern for conservation and the environment, in the hunting and fishing that he did, and in the meticulous preparations that he made in anticipation of his trips.

As in baseball, Ted Williams threw himself into his outdoor pursuits. Just as he had meticulously chosen his Louisville Slugger bats and endlessly practiced to perfect his swing, so too did he carefully choose his fishing rods and practice his casting until he could consistently cast a fly, plug, or lure to a handkerchief in his backyard. Just as he loved to talk hitting with young hitters, so too would he talk for hours about fishing tackle with his guide friends. For Ted Williams, technique—or what business gurus now call "process"—was extremely important.

Famous Keys guides like George Hommell, Lee Baker, and Billy Knowles also say that competition was always a key part of Williams's fishing, just as it had been in baseball. There was always a lot of joking and good-natured kidding going on, but as Hommell says, "Ted was always looking for more information to give himself a competitive advantage. Location and habits of fish, how to make the best knot, how to tie the best fly—these were the things he was looking for all the time." He spent a lot of time by himself tying flies and rigging tackle, and while he wasn't a hermit as some have suggested, he certainly was comfortable with his own company.

While fly fishing became his favorite, he also mastered all types of tackle and made a strong case for using the right equipment for the right situation. For example, "When the wind blows strong in your face, that's a great time to pick up a good spinning rod." He also preached against those people who cared only about catching big fish on light tackle. He thought that if you fought a fish too long on light line, it wasn't good for the angler or the fish, which would be exhausted and vulnerable to prey.

Ted's interest in and knowledge of fishing led Sears to hire him as a consultant to develop and market a line of fishing equipment made with his recommendations. In fact, there are still some aluminum bass boats around today that were advertised and sold as "Ted Williams" boats.

As far as geography, he used to rave about fishing in the United States as the best in the world, quickly citing great fishing in Canada as well. He said, "I guess you could call me a Will Rogers fisherman: I've never met a fish I didn't like."

He said, "I've had the good fortune to fish for walleye and muskie in the Midwest, bonefish and tarpon in Florida's saltwater flats, marlin and tuna in the ocean, salmon and trout in streams from Maine to the Flathead River system in Montana, and bluegill and bass in the Arkansas River, near Little Rock and throughout the South. But my point is that whatever kind of fishing you like to do, we've got plenty of it right here in America. I like to fish for all sorts of fish, but it's no secret that I favor hunting what I call 'the big three': bonefish, tarpon, and Atlantic salmon."

Ted Williams was proud that he had caught 1,000 bonefish, 1,000 tarpon, and 1,000 Atlantic salmon. He was also proud of the fact, especially later in his fishing career as he became part of the catch-and-release school of thinking, that he had released "all my bonefish, tarpon, and but a fraction of my Atlantic salmon," which he kept for dinner. "Why?" he added. "Because it's clear to me and to anyone who's been

*Good with all types of tackle, Ted is best known for his mastery of a fly rod.* Photo
CREDIT: BOSTON RED SOX.

fishing for the last few decades, that the size and quantity of gamefish are far below the levels they used to be."

It's apparent that in his later years as an angler, Ted Williams became an engaged environmentalist as well. He thought, spoke, and wrote about the need to protect gamefish and their environments. He ended an article he wrote for *Popular Mechanics* with, "Fishing has given me a lot in life, and the reason I've made such strong statements regarding its future is that I'd like to give something back. We've got the best country in the world for fishing right here in America. Let's do everything we can to keep it that way."

He hunted his favorite of "the big three"—Atlantic salmon—from his cottage in New Brunswick, Canada, on the Miramichi River, while his home in Islamorada was headquarters for his pursuit of bonefish and tarpon. Both communities consider him a hometown boy and bore great grief on his passing, even though he pulled up stakes and left the Keys in the 1980s and was forced soon after to give up wading in northern rivers.

Williams's sad move from Islamorada to Northern Florida was no doubt due in part to his failing eyesight and his concern about overpopulation in the Keys. He was also plagued by a variety of health problems, including a series of strokes and congestive heart failure.

Ted Williams's move north also left behind three failed marriages, one of which had produced a daughter, and another, a son and daughter. His life in the 1980s and 1990s was not without its comforts as he took advantage of the lucrative trade of signing autographs and baseball memorabilia. This must have been especially comforting in his old age when you consider he played baseball long before the age of bonus signings and multimillion-dollar salaries. (He made $98,000 playing for the Red Sox in 1955, compared to some players in 2005 who are signing multi-year deals for more than $98 million.) He also started the Hitters Hall of Fame in Hernando, Florida, and received several prestigious awards, including the Presidential Medal of Freedom from George Bush, as well as his induction into the IGFA Hall of Fame.

As Williams's health declined, his visits to the Keys became fewer and farther between, and more poignant. During his last trip to

Islamorada for the opening of Johnny Morris's Worldwide Sportsman store, he talked emotionally with close friends about long home runs and big tarpon. He took special interest in the Gary Ellis family and their fight to find a cure for cystic fibrosis, and he talked about his wish, after his death, to be cremated and have his ashes "scattered off the deep water of Islamorada."

*Curt Gowdy with Ted at the opening of Johnny Morris' Worldwide Sportsman in Islamorada.* PHOTO CREDIT: RED-BONE GALLERY.

Soon after his last visit to the Keys, word spread that Ted Williams had passed away—pronounced dead of cardiac arrest in a hospital in Inverness, Florida. As F. Scott Fitzgerald once said, "Show me a hero and I'll write you a tragedy." When word got out, grief spread quickly through this island home of 2,500 people, a community that had accepted Ted Williams as a friend and member of the family and ultimately considered him its favorite son. Several members of the fishing community came together informally to discuss how they could help Ted's family carry out his last wishes for cremation and an "at sea" memorial, but that wasn't to be. Ted Williams's family decided, and a judge affirmed, that his body would be frozen and stored in a suspended state until a cure for heart disease was discovered and he could be brought back to life. It was a bizarre ending to an incredible life, and a decision which still spawns controversy. Suffice it to say that the Florida Keys miss their "first son," old-timers still talk often about Ted Williams, the games will go on as they always have, and the stories will continue to be embellished and shared.

One of my favorites about The Kid was told by Floridian Ted Lund in the 2002 fall issue of *The Redbone Journal.* While still playing for the Red Sox, Ted Williams was getting a massage in the clubhouse. During the rubdown, he struck up a conversation with the trainer. "I've caught thousand-pound marlin, thousands of tarpon on fly rod, hundreds of bonefish, and Atlantic salmon." Williams said. "In fact, I bet I am the greatest fisherman in the world."

Then he asked the trainer, "Can you think of a better fisherman than me?"

The man continued with the rubdown, grinned, and replied without hesitation: "Yes, sir, Mr. Williams, I can."

Caught off guard, Williams asked, "Who can there possibly be that is a better fisherman?"

The trainer said, "The good Lord," and it was Williams's turn to pause.

"All right," he conceded. "I'll give you that one."

*Baseball legends, Ted Williams and Babe Ruth.* PHOTO CREDIT: BOSTON RED SOX.

*Time is but the stream I go a-fishing in*
*I drink at it; but while I drink I see the sandy bottom and*
*detect how shallow it is. Its thin current slides away, but*
*eternity remains. I would drink deeper; fish in the sky,*
*where the bottom is pebbly with stars.*

—HENRY DAVID THOREAU, *WALDEN* (1854)

# 12

# TOBY COSGROVE: DOCTOR OF THE HEART

———◆◆◆———

*My wife and I went out on our boat for a Sunday of fishing off the shores of Nantucket. We left the harbor at 10:00 A.M. and drove to Madaket to pick up her sister and husband and then headed out toward Tuckernuck Island, about five miles away. It was a beautiful summer day with a prevailing southwest wind blowing about five knots.*

*As we approached this small sandy island, we saw hundreds of seabirds diving on the water. We drove straight to the spot and could see that a large school of medium-sized bluefish had herded up a school of sardines in the four-foot waters inside the sandbars surrounding Tuckernuck.*

*The bluefish were crashing the surface everywhere as they cut through the clear water, ferociously attacking their prey. We idled into the middle of a bait shower and turned off the engine. You could see the fish in the water, on the surface, and even skyrocketing into the air, five and ten feet high as their momentum pushed them out of the water. The screeching of the diving birds was piercing as they dove on the panicked bait, driven to the surface by the bluefish.*

*Any plug, lure, or fly thrown into the melee was sure to be struck as this feeding frenzy continued. My companions asked me if I was going to grab a rod. I said no, totally content to watch this ritual of nature played out so often in these coastal New England waters. Never had I seen so many fish in one place. They were busting the surface in all directions as far as the eye could see. For me, I was just happy to watch the spectacle, feeling totally connected to the environment, believing that on this occasion, even a single cast would be a potential interruption—an invasion of nature's special drama.*

*In these pristine shallow waters, the baitfish were trapped, and they hung together with nowhere to go. We floated for half an hour in the midst of this bait shower, watching these magnificent bluefish knife through the water in pursuit of their prey. Then, just like that, the sardines were gone, the bluefish disappeared, and the birds flew away. As in a dream, it was over, and a calm returned to the seas. Without ever touching a rod, we started the engine, powered up, and drove to the beach for a picnic lunch.*

—Dr. Toby Cosgrove

IF MY FATHER AND MOST OTHER OLD-TIMERS fail to believe that anyone would catch and release "a perfectly good fish," they would certainly never believe that there are people who actually fish without hooks, or even someone like Toby Cosgrove who is so satisfied, even thrilled, to watch fish without trying to capture them or even disturb their habitat that many times he doesn't even put a line in the water! For Cosgrove, the fishing grounds themselves are part of a larger stage, nature itself stretching from horizon to horizon, an ever-changing sanctuary far from the setting he is most used to—an operating room at The Cleveland Clinic, where he performs his duties as head of cardiac surgery. Dr. Cosgrove is arguably the premier heart surgeon in the world and also one of the kindest, most self-effacing people who has ever sought and found refuge from his daily routine in the mystical world of water.

*Dr. Toby Cosgrove, head of cardiac sur-gery at the Cleveland Clinic.* PHOTO CREDIT: THE CLEVELAND CLINIC FOUNDATION.

For a few summers now, he has tried to arrange his schedule so that he can leave Cleveland (when possible) on Friday after-noons, flying to his vacation home on the old whaling island of Nan-tucket. It is here that he keeps his twenty-foot outboard that launches him on his weekend fishing trips. His boat is a center-console Mako with a 125-horse-power Evinrude. I think *The Great Escape* would be a perfect name for his vessel, which he has instead named *Good Thing*—an under-stated handle from a guy perform-ing at the top of his game in a pressure-packed profession, always with quiet, understated self-confidence.

At The Cleveland Clinic, Dr. Cosgrove and his team of twenty surgeons perform more than five thousand open heart surgeries every year, earning their hospital the *U.S. News & World Report* number-one rating in the country for cardiac surgery for the past eleven years in a row. In addition to bypass surgery, Cosgrove and his team are pio-neering new surgical procedures for dealing with a variety of medical problems including valve disease, arterial fibrillation, and congestive heart failure.

Not only has Toby kept up his surgical practice, but he has also built a world-class team for the clinic and mentored them along the way. He is credited with pioneering many new procedures and developing modifications to a number of tools, like clamps that are more ergonom-ically designed to help surgeons perform intricate life-saving proce-dures. These devices are now patented and known as "Cosgroves." As if he weren't busy enough, he is now traveling around the world helping The Cleveland Clinic raise $350 million to fund the creation of their

*Toby flanked by his dream team of cardiac surgeons at the Cleveland Cinic.*
PHOTO CREDIT: THE CLEVELAND CLINIC FOUNDATION.

new Heart Center, which will be one of the most outstanding medical centers in the world. On his desk sits a small plaque with his favorite saying: WHAT CAN BE CONCEIVED, CAN BE CREATED.

Ask any of his patients about Dr. Cosgrove and two recurrent themes will emerge: caring and confidence. Everyone I spoke with knew how incredibly busy he was, but spoke at length about how he made them feel special, and how his quiet self-confidence gave them the assurance they needed to make it through and be okay.

If what Dr. Toby Cosgrove does in such a matter-of-fact way is incredible, how he arrived at this pinnacle of his profession is absolutely unbelievable. Not knowing he was dyslexic until he was thirty-one years old, Toby fought hard not to excel but just to graduate from college. Twelve out of the thirteen medical schools he applied to subsequently rejected him. He risked his life in ocean racing and again in Vietnam, and fell in love with and married a woman whose twin sister had refused to go out with him. When asked about these events, Toby just shrugs his shoulders, smiles, and says that his character was forged by adversity and rejection.

It's clear that his future was also founded on a special kind of love. Toby grew up in a small city in upstate New York called Watertown. Born in 1940, he was nicknamed Toby after an uncle, although his official name was Delos Marshall Cosgrove III. He was named after his father, a local attorney, and his grandfather, the son of Irish immigrants who taught himself the law and became one of the most famous trial lawyers in New York City, and also ran for governor. While Toby doesn't know why his grandfather was first named Delos, he is quick to point out that Delos is a beautiful island in Greece, reputed to be the birthplace of Apollo—the god of music and the arts.

Mr. and Mrs. Cosgrove had one other child, a daughter two years younger than Toby named Jody. The Cosgroves were a very close, supportive family and always cheered each other on in their various sporting events, from sailboat racing to basketball.

The family lived on Lake Ontario at the mouth of the St. Lawrence River. Toby says it was here that he developed a special fascination and attachment to water. In fact, one of his neighbor's docks would play a huge role in his choice of professions and hobbies as well. As he tells it, this dock was owned by one Dr. Daniel Borden, a close family friend who served as chief of surgery at George Washington Hospital. His first memories of fishing were of times spent on Dr. Borden's

*Toby and his dad sailing together on Lake Ontario.* PHOTO CREDIT: DR. TOBY COSGROVE.

dock when he was eight years old. Not only does he remember fishing there with his maternal granddad, who taught him how to cast, but he also says that it was that same year on the same dock that he made the decision to become a surgeon.

At the end of the dock was a boathouse with a single, second-floor recreation room, the walls of which were covered with professional pictures of Dr. Borden. The doctor was pictured operating on patients, surrounded by his surgical team, talking with patients, giving presentations, and receiving honors. The eight-year-old was hooked. "It looked so dramatic and important," Toby reflects today. "I knew at once that this was what I wanted to do. Not just be any kind of doctor. I knew right away, I wanted to be a surgeon."

Nothing in his career at Watertown High School offered any kind of sign that these lofty goals would be out of reach for this gangly, brown-haired, blue-eyed, basketball-playing teenager from the shores of Lake Ontario. He fished and sailed in the summers, worked hard in school, and graduated with honors, becoming one of only 13 percent of his graduating class of 275 to go to college with no clue of what was about to hit him when he got there.

"I never realized until I went to Williams College that I had really only been a big fish in a small pond. I was a big man on campus in high school and skated through without anyone knowing that I had a severe reading disorder known as dyslexia. In those days afflictions like dyslexia, and attention deficit disorder, were not understood let alone diagnosed. In fact, I don't even know if attention deficit disorder had been named. Anyway, it was not until I was thirty-one years old that my learning problem was identified by a girl I was dating at the time. I was in a car with this friend who was a teacher. She was driving, and I was trying to read her selected stories from *The New York Times* and struggling with phrases. She said to me, 'Toby, you're dyslexic.' I didn't even know what that meant. She explained how dyslexia is an umbrella term for a variety of learning problems such as letter reversal. All of the sudden a light went on, and I realized why I had so much trouble in college."

A July 28, 2003, *Time* magazine article sheds a great deal of light on this learning disability, and lists several other famous and accomplished dyslexics, including Thomas Edison, Tom Cruise, Jay Leno, Agatha Christie, Walt Disney, and even Whoopi Goldberg. Best-selling writer John Irving, Pulitzer Prize–winning playwright Wendy Wasserstein, and revolutionary discount stock broker Charles Schwab also battle dyslexia.

One of the most charming and disarming qualities of Toby Cosgrove is his self-effacing candor. He has the self-confidence not to rewrite his own history but to tell it like it was, all the while poking fun at himself. When he says he struggled in college, he is being totally honest. Believe me, I know. I was a year behind him in school, and roomed a few doors down from him at the Kappa Alpha fraternity house at Williams College. He struggled.

Toby, the high school honor student, finished his first semester with three Ds and two C minuses. "All my courses were tough," he says, "but French nearly killed me. Here I am full of myself, an honor student throughout high school, scared to death I was going to flunk out. I've never met so many talented guys. They never seemed to study and the workload was incredible. It seemed like I never did anything *but* study.

"I struggled through the fall, looking forward to winter and basketball season," Toby recalls. "I knew this was a place where I could shine and get my mind off of class for awhile. Man, you should have seen our teams," he says, forgetting I was there. "We were loaded with superstars, even a small college All American named Bobby Mahland. We only lost a couple of games each year and even went to the Small College NCAA tournament one year where we lost in the finals. I never got off the bench."

"Wait a minute Toby," I consoled him. "I remember you as the 'go-to' guy, the first off the bench, the ultimate sixth man."

"Forget about it," he said. "I rode the pines my entire career, always six men away from the coach. By the way, I'll never forget him: Al Shaw, a real holler guy always yelling at everyone, except me. That is until that

NCAA championship game when we were playing lousy. We went into the dressing room at halftime and he yelled at everyone who was playing. That, of course, left me out. He then caught his breath and shouted at me too: 'That goes for you too, Cosgrove—you're not cheering loud enough!' "

Toby's folks are gone now, but how proud the Cosgroves would have been to see their son—who struggled so mightily at Williams to overcome a learning disorder he never knew he had—invited many years later to give the 1997 commencement address at his alma mater, and subsequently elected to the school's board of trustees. During his commencement speech, Toby spoke about a lesson he'd learned from one of his favorite professors at Williams, an historian named Charlie Keller whom he met with his parents when he was applying for admission. Keller said, "Don't tell me his IQ. What is his GQ? Tell me about his Guts Quotient." He went on to explain that the SATs, which he helped originate, were not the only predictor of college success. Ancient Greek philosophers arrived at a similar conclusion and wrote, "Character is destiny."

How prophetic those words were in his own life. Toby proved that his guts quotient was as high as anyone's could be.

*Toby and Williams College President Hank Payne in the college's 1996 commencement procession.*

Imagine what must have been going through his mind as a second-semester senior who worked so hard and was turned down by the first twelve medical schools to which he applied, especially when all he ever wanted to do was become a surgeon. But then success came in his acceptance from the thirteenth, the University of Virginia. If, as it appears from my discussions with friends, perseverance is the first ingredient in making a fisherman, Toby Cosgrove certainly has it! In his commencement address to the Williams College Class of 1997, he would later advise:

> The subject is the nasty F word—FAILURE. Many of you may assume failure is something you'll avoid. I have good news and bad news. The good news is that failure can be avoided: by saying nothing, doing nothing, and being nothing. The bad news is that if you are to achieve anything, you must accept risk, and with risk comes the possibility for disappointment and failure. Failure is a great teacher . . . an opportunity to learn . . . Failure will teach you, if you let it.

Williams College could not have chosen a better commencement speaker than Dr. Toby Cosgrove, whose life has been an embodiment of Mark Hopkins' words of advice inscribed on Hopkins Gate at the college, "Climb high, climb far. Your aim the sky; your goal the star."

Back in 1962, the year Toby graduated, Hopkins' advice to students may have sounded somewhat simplistic considering the times and what lay ahead. While the United States was at peace, we still had a draft and the war in Vietnam had not yet broken out. Toby enlisted in the Air Force and then got a deferment so that he could continue his education in medicine. "I sold my soul to Uncle Sam," he says, "knowing that I would owe two years to the military after completing medical school and [my] internship."

Toby relates that medical school came relatively easy to him. "The courses were more relevant to my goal of becoming a surgeon, and I had a lot of chemistry courses out of the way. Thank God I didn't have to take French! Hey," he told me, flashing a proud grin, "I even got my first A!"

He also found time to escape the academic world and pursue his love of sailing. He recalls some harrowing ocean-racing experiences, especially in a Bermuda race where he thought he was going to die. The highlight of Toby's sailing career came when he raced on Ted Hood's boat in the America's Cup. Hood was an authority on building sails and sailboats, and Toby remembers him as a focused taskmaster and patient mentor. Unfortunately, Hood lost to Bus Mosbacher on the boat *Weatherly*, but Toby's love of the ocean continued to grow.

*Toby was a passionate offshore racer who sailed twice in the America's Cup races.* PHOTO CREDIT: DR. TOBY COSGROVE.

Then, after two years of internship at Strong Memorial Hospital in Rochester, New York, it was time for the young doc to pay his dues to Uncle Sam. The war in Vietnam was in full bloom, and he was contacted by the Air Force and told that he would be going there in six months.

"I knew nothing about the military," Toby told me. "I didn't even know what my captain's bars were or how to wear them. I'll never forget the military flight from San Francisco to Saigon. It seemed like everyone was either drunk or hungover. When we landed in Vietnam, it was like walking into an oven. It must have been over a hundred degrees Fahrenheit.

"My first real taste of the war came while I was in Da Nang waiting for assignment. It was right after the Thet Offensive. Everyone called the place Bang Bang Da Nang. A buddy of mine asked me if I wanted to go for a helicopter ride. I had nothing to do and said, 'Why not?' We climbed aboard this helicopter gunship and flew out over the countryside. The beauty of the place with its farms and rice paddies made it easy to forget that there was a war going on. I was so naive, I didn't even know the helicopter was on a mission.

*Toby in his Air Force uniform in Da Nang, Vietnam.* PHOTO CREDIT: DR. TOBY COSGROVE.

"The next thing I knew, we were in a dive and the captain was shooting off rockets. *Whoosh, whoosh* just like that. Then he'd climb and dive again and the helicopter would shake every time he fired a rocket. All of the sudden in the midst of a steep dive, we started taking enemy small-arms fire. You could hear bullets bouncing off the helicopter. Then, we pulled out of the dive, just over the treetops; the pilot banked right and our machine gunners opened up on the enemy below. It was a ride I'll never forget. When we landed, I said to the pilot, 'Boy, that was pretty exciting.' 'That was routine, Doc,' he said. 'I've had five helicopters shot out from under me since I got here!' I often wonder if he made it back home alive."

Hearing this story, I asked him whether after a mission like that one, catching a big fish on a rough day didn't seem a bit tame.

"Well," he said, smiling, "it certainly put things in perspective. But there is still a great thrill in catching any size fish—or even just seeing them."

About a month after arriving in Vietnam, Toby finally got his assignment to run the Air Force's Casualty Staging Flight, an evacuation hospital at an airport on the perimeter of Da Nang. "We were absolutely swamped," he told me, "and a lot of those wounds were extremely severe. In five and a half months we shipped over twenty-two thousand wounded personnel back to the United States. And you know what, to the best of my knowledge, one hundred percent of those we treated did survive the flight home. I'm really proud of that.

"We were on the outskirts of a town separated from the jungle only by our airstrip and a couple of rice paddies. One day I remember taking a break on our back porch and watching our guys engage in a firefight with the Vietcong, right in our own rice paddy! The spectating stopped real fast when the Cong shot a few rounds at the hospital and we all headed inside.

"In spite of our overloaded schedules, a bunch of us took time to adopt a Vietnamese obstetrics hospital. We got a water line to them, did some carpentry, and even painted the place. We'd also go over there and treat civilian patients and help deliver babies on any time off we had," Toby said.

*Some of the doctors including Toby found time to help out in a Vietnamese civilian clinic that they "adopted."* PHOTO CREDIT: DR. TOBY COSGROVE.

"Toby, so many Americans got so depressed and psychologically messed up in Vietnam that they couldn't even carry on with their lives when they came home. How did you handle it?" I asked him.

"You know, I've never talked about Vietnam before with anyone. It was tough on doctors just like soldiers. When we were trying to work and were being shelled by artillery, I watched some of them crumble, and a few who left the operating room got into their beds and pulled their sheets over their heads, totally unable to function." A sad look came over his face and he thought for a minute before he said, "It was so horrible and so sad and so depressing and so tough that it had a very different effect on me. In the midst of the hardest times trying to treat thousands of injured troops, I thought to myself, *If I can do this—if I can lead in crisis, if I can do this—then I can do anything when I get home.*"

"Toby, what about post-traumatic stress disorder?" I asked him. "Is it a real condition, and did you ever suffer from it?"

"Yeah, it's real," he said. "You know, not a day goes by that I don't think of Vietnam," he said. "Many things bring it back, like when I hear a helicopter fly by or a loud noise. It changed all of us," he shared, as a sadness came over his eyes. "I've never been able to watch any of those Vietnam War movies, and it took me ten years to visit the Veterans Wall. I think I've also become more of a pacifist. War is so horrible; we have to make sure it is well justified and a last resort. A lot of the professional soldiers were great, but many of the draftees weren't emotionally equipped. War warps people.

"And they were protesting when I came home. It was tough to come back and see it. I'd been away, doing my job for my country, seeing death every day, and the antiwar people made me feel like a villain. And do you know what the hardest part is to this day? No one has ever said thank you."

Toby was awarded a Bronze Star, but it's clear to me that it's not an award he brags about, or even discusses.

When Toby came home, he spent two years in a surgical residency at Massachusetts General before going to England for a year, where he did chest surgery before returning to Mass General.

"At that time," he said, "they were the best in training cardiac surgeons." In fact, that's where he met the guy who would become his

*After Vietnam, Toby signed on at prestigious Massachusetts General Hospital.*
PHOTO CREDIT: DR. TOBY COSGROVE.

brother-in-law, Cary Akins, a fellow resident who went on to become one of Mass General's preeminent cardiac surgeons. What are the chances of two cardiac surgeons marrying two nurses who are sisters? That's exactly what happened.

On a beautiful bluefish fishing day, Cary joined my wife and I along with Toby for a picnic lunch on a beach at Tuckernuck Island, and we heard the whole tale. Toby was a little laconic, so it was lucky that we had Cary along to provide some of the more interesting details.

Cary married a nurse by the name of Barbara Desiderio, whose dad was an Italian produce distributor. She also had twin sisters working as nurses at Mass General. Toby fell in love with one of the sisters, Anita, and they were married several years later after he had completed his residency and taken a job at The Cleveland Clinic. Theirs was a wedding Toby says he'll never forget.

"Anita comes from a big Italian family," he told me, "so of course it was a large and festive affair with great food and dancing. It was held in Buffalo where she grew up, and I met a lot of aunts, uncles, and cousins. There were a lot of nice toasts and a lot of hugging and kissing, and about halfway through dinner, her father came up to me, put his arm around my shoulder, and said, 'If you hurt my daughter, I'll kill you.'"

"He must have been kidding," my wife said to Toby.

"I don't think so," Toby's brother-in-law, Cary Akins, chimed in. "He said the same thing to me after giving me his blessing to marry Barbara."

I got to know Toby's wife when they visited us in Islamorada in the Florida Keys. She's very attractive and fun to be with, and we had one of the most awesome offshore fishing days ever, catching fourteen species of fish in one day. We kicked it off with a large sailfish, followed by six blackfin tunas, three sharks, two cobias, a kingfish, and too many dorado to count. Anita handled the rod on a majority of the catches and never quit, although I know her muscles were aching.

Anita went on from nursing to become a lawyer working in the health care industry. Even while working in Boston, Anita has been a huge help to her husband in his stressful career. Serving as best friend, counselor and confidante, she has helped Toby advance his goals for the Clinic to become one of the top medical facilities in the world.

The Cleveland Clinic turned out to be a wonderful fit for Toby Cosgrove. Even when he started there, the Clinic doctors were celebrated as pioneers who had been working on revolutionary procedures in cardiac surgery since the fifties. Then in 1967, a surgeon named Rene Favaloro performed the first bypass surgery, and a new era in cardiac care was launched. By 1975, The Cleveland Clinic was doing three thousand operations a year, and Toby was thrilled to be invited to join their staff. During his first year, he performed five hundred surgeries.

And good things continued to happen for Toby. He and his wife have two grown daughters and are able to carve out some good fishing time off the shores of his island getaway, Nantucket. Then in June of 2004 Toby was chosen to become the new president and CEO of The

Cleveland Clinic, capping quite a journey for the "shadow reader from Watertown."

There is something special about sharing a friendship with someone that goes back so many years to such a different time and place. It's fascinating to watch a friend grow and change, get married and raise kids, and develop his beliefs and philosophies. It gives you a chance to reflect on your own life's journey in relationship to his, and makes it even more meaningful to later reconnect on a fishing boat to enjoy a pastime that you both love.

So many people achieve status and success and turn into other people, forgetting their roots and what got them to wherever they are. Toby has never been one of them. Though tempered by life, he remains unfazed by his incredible success and the fame that has followed. In his heart, I believe that he is still that gangly, hardworking, self-effacing kid from Watertown High who has found his special calling and the love of a wonderful woman, while developing the self-confidence to remain constant with himself and his values.

In a day of fishing with Dr. Cosgrove in Nantucket, the conversation may go anywhere and everywhere. On our first outing, I asked Toby about his love of fishing.

"Well," he said, "I still remember fishing at home when I was a small boy with my dad. I learned how to fish these waters from a guy named Tom Mlesko. He used to teach school and coach in Connecticut before moving here and becoming a full-time fishing guide. He's one of the most avid, hardworking fishermen I know. During the season he targets albacore, blues, and stripers—fishes three charters a day. I remember my first fishing trip with him to a place called Old Man Shoals. We caught a fish every cast. Sometimes I make him nuts when I want to just go to the rips and hang out."

Then I asked him about his success rate in fishing and cardiac surgery.

"I guess our success rate in fishing has improved with practice," he said smiling, "and when I started doing cardiac surgery," he recalls, "the mortality rate was over twenty percent. Now it's down to less than one percent. I feel that my colleagues and I have met a challenge to make it better and do it now. It's hard work, but it's also very rewarding."

"Does it take a lot of courage to do heart surgery?" I asked him.

"No," he said. "I believe it takes a lot of training and tenacity. It takes a lot of courage for the patients."

"So, pal," I asked him when we were pulling up anchor during a great fishing day in Nantucket, "you've got a big birthday coming up on Saturday. What have you learned? What's it all about?"

Toby paused before starting the engine. I could see him thinking, and then he spoke. "Like my brother-in-law, I consider myself privileged to be able to do what I do. I've enjoyed building and being part of a great team in Cleveland, operating in a wonderfully professional, caring environment. I have been blessed with a loving family and good old friends, and I've enjoyed helping a lot of patients, many of whom have become new friends. I've also loved staying in touch with the ocean where I feel that I am constantly reborn and in whose vastness and majesty I am able to keep all things in perspective." He paused again, smiled, and added, "And who knows—I may even catch a few more fish before I'm done."

*Dr. Toby Cosgrove relaxes on the ocean.*

Even though he joked about catching a few more fish "before he's done," for some reason, I think he couldn't care less. I'd found a fisherman who went out there with the sole purpose of relaxing and finding a refuge from a pressure-cooker world that few of us can even imagine.

I thought a lot about his words that evening. Clearly, Toby's tenacity, persistence, and nerve are great personality traits. Being thoughtful and articulate serve him well not only in his profession, but also in his ability to identify, re-late, and describe his feelings about the ocean, where he, like so many of my other friends, have found solace and even rebirth.

*Virtue is bold and goodness never fearful.*

—WILLIAM SHAKESPEARE, *MEASURE FOR MEASURE*

Time is probably more generous to an angler than to any other individual. The wind, the sun, the open air, the colors and smells, the loneliness of the sea or the solitude of the stream, work some kind of magic.

—Zane Grey, "The First Thousand-Pounder"

———————— ✦✦✦ ————————

# CONCLUSION

WHEN I FIRST STARTED WRITING THIS BOOK, I firmly believed that optimism and patience were the two most important prerequisites for anglers—optimism to go out there and patience to stay the course until you succeed and catch "old fighter." The more I spoke with my friends, the book's subjects, the more I felt that one of these qualities took precedence: optimism. Like all other anglers I've known, everyone here certainly qualifies as an optimist.

Patience was a far more controversial subject. Fishing literature dating back to the 1600s, along with Izaak Walton ("Angling is an art worthy of the knowledge and patience of a wise man") instructs us that patience is the most important attribute for an angler to possess. I believed it too, but many of my friends disagreed, some of them violently.

"I'm not patient," Sandy Moret said. "I'll move around the whole Florida Bay to find a tarpon."

"If the blue marlin aren't in, we'll pick up and leave," said Don Tyson.

"I'll make a thousand moves on a river if I have to, to find the right fish," Scott Keller told me.

These attitudes were obviously in great contrast to William Bradley, my friend in Buffalo, who is more than content to patiently wait for the fish to come to him.

Perhaps Thomas McGuane, the prolific and articulate author of so many great books including *The Sporting Club*, *Nothing But Blue*

*Skies*, and *92 in the Shade*, put it best in *The Longest Silence* when he wrote, "Persistence for the fisherman is a virtue that transcends patience." But persistence, I thought, is only 90 percent of it. I was looking for a word that better implied the ultimate attainment of a goal. Then it hit me: Perseverance is the ability to continue doing something in spite of serious difficulty, and even opposition, with singleness of purpose. The Calvinists talked about perseverance as "the continuance in grace of people elected to external salvation." I like that definition; it almost suggests a common bond and blessing on anglers. I bounced my idea off some of my pals and they liked it too, so I've modified my model to say that optimism and perseverance are the most crucial attributes for an angler. Patience is optional.

Having reached this conclusion, I turned my attention to the seminal question that I set out to answer at the beginning of the process: Was there a common interest that drew them to the water and the pursuit of fish?

Throughout my conversations, I asked my friends repeatedly, "*Why* do you fish?" and compiled their responses. Here is a compilation of what they said—the reasons for fishing from my baker's dozen plus one.

*It's . . .*
*the hunt, the strike, the bite, the fight, the catch,*
*the release, the challenge, the kill, the food,*
*the outdoors, the camaraderie, the solitude,*
*the wildlife, the birds, the escape, the adventure,*
*the thrill, the getaway, the exercise, the rest, the magic,*
*the science, the mystery, the beauty, the water, the river,*
*the stream, the ocean, the lake, the pond, the planning,*
*the anticipation, the unknown, the familiar, the fulfillment,*
*the colors, the smells, the sights, the sounds, the traveling,*
*the stories, the traditions, the spirituality, the rebirth,*
*the satisfaction.*

Forty-five answers gleaned from fourteen anglers on why they fish; many reasons repeated by others, many in total contradiction with each other, and none agreed upon by all.

Where was the bond, then, the common reason why everyone fishes? Challenge worked for many but not all, especially the older anglers. Adventure also attracted some but not others. Time with family and friends looked good but seemed to be tempered by the search for solitude. Maybe the common driver doesn't exist. After all, it seemed that fourteen of my friends, avid anglers all, couldn't deliver a consensus on the subject.

I sat down late one night in my library to reread their stories in an effort to put it all in perspective. While rereading Andy Mill's comments, it hit me. Andy had said, "Fishing for me is a sense of adventure where the elements of the unknown combine with *hope*." That made me think of a quote I'd read a long time ago by a popular Brit named John Buchan, the Earl of Tweedsmuir (1875–1940), who was recently profiled by Andrew Lownie in *The Presbyterian Cavalier*. Buchan, a true renaissance man who wrote spy thrillers in his spare time, was a lawyer, war correspondent, intelligence officer, chairman of a news agency, Tory Member of Parliament, and governor general of Canada. Buchan wrote:

> The charm of fishing is that it is the pursuit of what is elusive
> but attainable, a perpetual series of occasions for hope.

*That's it*, I thought. *That's the key*. It's all about *hope*. Hope, the motivator, the driver that pushes us on to the water to fish. But maybe it wouldn't stand up, in light of something once said by Benedict Spinoza: "Fear cannot be without hope nor hope without fear." No, I thought, fear goes along with hope, and fishing as well. The fear of getting skunked, the fear of a grizzly in the woods, the fear of a storm at sea. I believe that in fishing, fear seems to heighten hope.

I thought about all of my angling friends, their similarities and their differences. On salt water or fresh-, with plug or fly rod, killing or releasing, they all seemed to share in the *hope* that they would convert the unknown possibility into the known reality of a fish, and then repeat the process. I have a local fishing pal who even after a long day of catching no fish always says, "I have high hopes that this next cast will be the cast of a lifetime."

*Hope!* I was dying to call a bunch of them to get their reactions, but it was after midnight. What about the bigger audience, I wondered? Does hope drive all people who fish? I decided to do some research on hope as found in literature in general, and fishing specifically. Here are some of the quotes I found to support my premise, from a variety of sources in chronological order, beginning with the Bible.

> *But if we hope for that we see not, then do we with patience wait for it!*
>
> —ROMANS 8:25

Who could read this passage and not think of Mr. Bradley sitting on a pier on the Great Lakes with his friends waiting for a bite, or Dr. Toby Cosgrove motoring around Tuckernuck Island off Nantucket, hoping that the bluefish would show?

> From *The Compleat Angler:*
> "... he that hopes to be good angler must not only bring an inquiring, searching, observing wit, but he must bring a large measure of hope and patience, and a love and propensity to the art itself; but having once got and practised it, then doubt not but Angling will prove to be so pleasant, that it will prove to be like virtue, a reward to itself.
>
> —IZAAK WALTON

In England, John Bailey has not only employed an "inquiring, searching, and observing wit" as a boy to figure out how water works, but also later as an adult to bring stories to his readers of incredible fishing tales from around the world.

From *Moby-Dick:*

*And hence not only at substantiated times, upon well known separate feeding grounds, could Ahab hope to encounter his prey; but in crossing the widest expanses of water between these grounds he could by his art, so place and time himself on his way, as even then not to be wholly without prospect of a meeting.*

and

*But in the cautious comprehensiveness and unloitering vigilance with which Ahab threw his brooding soul into this unfaltering hunt, he would not permit himself to rest all his hopes upon the one crowning fact above mentioned, however flattering it might be to those hopes; nor in the sleeplessness of his vow could he so tranquillize his unquiet heart as to postpone all intervening quest.*

—HERMAN MELVILLE

Like Ahab, Don Tyson has pursued his own Moby-Dick in the form of 1,000-pound marlins across the "widest expanses of water around the world." So too have Ken Longaker and Karl Bratvold put their lives on the line in the treacherous Bering Sea in the hopes of filling their holds with fish.

From *Byme-by-Tarpon:*

*Here was a day to warm the heart of any fisherman; here was a beautiful river, celebrated in many a story; here was the famous guide, skilled with oar and gaff, rich in experience. What sport I would have; what pleasure of keen sensation would I store; what flavor of life would I taste this day! Hope burns in the heart of a fisherman.*

—ZANE GREY

Andy Mill joins ranks with Ted Williams and Sandy and Sue Moret, who have known the excitement of seeing giant 150-pound tarpon and hoped to repeat the thrill of watching them eat a fly and jump to free themselves so close to the skiff that they themselves were splashed.

From *The Old Man and the Sea:*

    *The breeze was fresh now and he sailed on well. He watched only the forward part of the fish and some of the hope returned. It is silly not to hope, he thought. Besides I believe it is a sin.*

                              —ERNEST HEMINGWAY

Like Santiago and his generational affection for "the boy," grandfathers George Bush, William Bradley, and Bill Dance talk lovingly about learning to fish from their grandfathers and their hopes of passing this torch to their grandchildren.

From *A River Runs Through It:*

    *Then in the Arctic half-light of the canyon, all existence fades to a being with my soul and memories and the sounds of the Big Blackfoot River and a four count rhythm and the hope that a fish will rise.*

                              —NORMAN MACLEAN

Out west Scott Keller's "hope that a fish will rise" has led him from his beloved western rivers to watery venues around the world, while on the East Coast, Jane Cooke celebrates hope of a new fishing season with a champagne toast on the shores of her beloved Beaverkill River.

The sun was coming up, but I felt wide awake and invigorated by my discovery, its literary validation, and the successful cross-referencing of my late-night research. I started making some calls, wanting to share my findings with my pals. To the angler, they agreed with kind of a consensual response: "Yeah, you're right. I've never thought about it before, but hope is the important reason why I fish."

The only modification on that response came from my longtime friend and fishing companion, Sandy Moret, long considered to be somewhat of a fishing philosopher and mentor to many anglers. The phone conversation went something like this:

"Good morning, Florida Keys Outfitters."

"Sandy Man, I've got it! The driving force for all anglers, the motivator, the reason we do what we do, the thread that holds us all together . . ."

"Yeah," Sandy said, sounding almost bored, "what is it?"

"It's *hope!*" I nearly shouted through the receiver.

"You're right," the laconic Sandy said after a pause, and sounding something like a philosophy professor talking to a student.

"Sandy, I've just had an epiphany and all you can say is 'You're right?' That's how you treat my news? If you knew all along, why didn't you tell me?"

Still enjoying playing the role of professor, Sandy answered, "Bubba, I just *hoped* you'd find it out for yourself."

Sandy's comment made me laugh. I walked to the kitchen and made myself a mug of coffee and took it out on our porch to watch a flock of pelicans diving on small baits as the rising sun began to warm the ocean shallows. I was excited that the members of my "fishing club" had confirmed the role of hope in their pursuits.

Maybe, I thought, in a larger context, fishing is a metaphor for life, and hope is a key driver for all of us. Had I actually discovered through my fishing friends a larger life lesson about happiness and fulfillment? Could I distill what I had learned into a sentence that would be so simple that even my seven grandchildren would understand it? A quote drifted in and out of my mind, something I'd heard long ago that now seemed so relevant and yet hard to remember. I grabbed a paper and pencil and then it came back to me. "The grand essentials of happiness are something to do, something to love, and something to hope for."

All of a sudden I missed those seven grandkids more than ever, so I called them up to say hi and ask them if they wanted to go fishing with their grandpa.

Wild water—how it draws us back to itself from our boyhood to our oldest age, and lures us on and on, down and down, as though just beyond each bend lay the answers to all our questionings and the goal of all our hopes.

—Odell Sheppard, "Thy Rod and Thy Creel" (1930)

# EPILOGUE

IN ADDITION TO BEING INTERESTING PEOPLE and avid anglers, all of those I wrote about here have been actively involved in helping others through favorite charities. Just as I am blessed with good friends, so too am I fortunate to be gainfully employed with a good day job, so that I don't have to depend on writing for a living. I can, therefore, donate the proceeds from this book to my friends' charities, as well as one of my own, Students in Free Enterprise (SIFE). All of these fine organizations depend on hope to build a better world. The benefactors of my book are as follows:

**American Cancer Society**
www.cancer.org
*(Scott Keller)*

**Anglers' Conservation Association**
www.a-c-a.org
*(John Bailey)*

**Bonefish and Tarpon Unlimited**
www.tarbone.org
*(Sandy and Sue Moret)*

**The Cleveland Clinic Heart Center**
www.clevelandclinic.org/heartcenter
*(Toby Cosgrove)*

**The Cystic Fibrosis Foundation**
www.cff.org
*(Andy Mill)*

**The George Bush Presidential Library**
http://bushlibrary.tamu.edu/
*(George Herbert Walker Bush)*

**International Game Fish Association (IGFA)**
www.igfa.org
*(Don Tyson)*

**The Jimmy Fund**
www.jimmyfund.org
*(Ted Williams)*

**St. Jude's Hospital**
www.stjude.org
*(Bill Dance)*

**Seattle Fishermen's Memorial Fund**
www.seattlefishermensmemorial.org
*(Kenny Longaker and Karl Bratvold)*

**Students in Free Enterprise (SIFE)**
www.sife.org
*(Bob Rich, author)*

**Trickle Up**
www.trickleup.org
*(Jane Cooke)*

**Young Men's Christian Association (YMCA)**
www.ymca.net
*(William Bradley)*

# APPENDIX

## Books by John Bailey

*Carp Challenge*, 1994

*Carp: The Quest for the Queen*, 1986

*Casting Far & Wide: Great Angling Adventures of the World*, 1993

*Casting for Gold*, 1991

*Chub & Dace*, 1990

*Fisherman's Valley: Seasonal Tips for Coarse Anglers*, 1992

*Fishing Detective, The*, 1994

*Fish of the Summer Stillwaters*, 1991

*From Water to Net: An Angler's Album*, 1991

*The Great Anglers*, 1990

*In Wild Waters*, 1985

*In Visible Waters*, 1984

*John Bailey's Complete Guide to Fly Fishing*, 2004

*John Bailey's Freshwater Fishing Album*, 1998

*The Master Angler-Coarse Fishing Season by Season*, 1997

*New Encyclopedia of Fishing: The Complete Guide to the Fish, Tackle and Techniques of Fresh and Saltwater Angling*, 2002

*Perch: Contemporary Days and Ways* (with Roger Miller), 1989

*Perfect Your Baits*, 1993

*Perfect Your Float Fishing*, 1994

*Perfect Your Tackle*, 1994

# Excerpts from International Game Fish Association Web Site, www.igfa.org

*Sword Dance—A jumping bronze blue marlin forms the centerpiece of the beautiful fountain at the entrance of the IGFA headquarters and museum.* PHOTO CREDIT: INTERNATIONAL GAME FISH ASSOCIATION.

## What is IGFA?

Sixty-one years ago when IGFA was founded, its main purpose was to maintain records for a few large saltwater gamefish, and create and maintain the ethical fishing rules that would be accepted throughout most of the world. Today, that is just a small part of what we do, but we think our founding fathers would approve of what we have become.

Conservation, education, encouraging youngsters to enter the sport, and maintaining huge databases on the subject of fishing are now part of our mission. Acting as representative for recreational fishing interests in both salt- and freshwater is also an important part of what we do.

We still take our responsibility as the world's record keeper for all species of fish very seriously, and nobody does it better than IGFA. However, if our gamefish species are depleted, there is no need for record keeping. This is why conservation has now become such an important priority for IGFA. More time, more money, more fishery management hearings, more meetings with other organizations to network our conservation efforts are all part of what we are doing to represent your interests.

The average angler can't begin to understand the complicated system of fishery management in the United States or other countries, let alone the international fishery management systems, nor do they want to. They just want to go fishing and catch a few fish. That's why it's important to support IGFA and other conservation groups who represent your interests in this wonderful sport.

Even IGFA couldn't keep up with all that's going on in fishery management, or lack thereof, without our network of well over 300 representatives around the world. Often, these are the conservation leaders in their communities. They are the eyes and ears of IGFA, and this network grows larger and stronger each year.

Worldwide, most species of our important gamefish are in serious decline. Not just billfish, swordfish, tuna, and sharks, but also red drum, bluefish, and even rockfish have fallen victim to commercial overfishing. Landings in both the Atlantic and Pacific Oceans peaked many years ago and are in serious decline. The Indian Ocean may also be beyond sustainable yield. Freshwater stocks are suffering from loss of habitat, pollution, and overfishing.

There is much work to be done, but who is going to do it? Certainly not the 95 percent of all anglers who don't support any conservation organization or even belong to a local fishing club. That leaves the 5 percent, along with the thin line of conservation and involved sportfishing organizations that are fighting to improve our sport, and the gamefish species on which our sport depends. IGFA needs your support to continue the fight. Financial support, letter writing support, attendance at fishery management hearings support, and asking your fishing friends to get involved with the conservation organization(s) of their choice. The future of our sport depends on it.

—Michael Leech, Past President

## Philosophy

IGFA's objectives are founded on the beliefs that gamefish species, related food fish, and their habitats are economic, social, recreational, and aesthetic assets which must be maintained, wisely used, and perpetuated; and that the sport of angling is an important recreational, economic, and social activity which the public must be educated to pursue in a manner consistent with sound sporting and conservation practices.

## Organization and Structure

The International Game Fish Association is a nonprofit, tax-exempt organization, supported by its membership and governed by an executive committee and board of trustees. An elected International Committee of more than 300 sportfishermen represents the IGFA in fishing areas throughout the world. International Committee members act as liaisons between recreational fishermen, fishing clubs, and fishery agencies in their areas and IGFA headquarters.

## Objectives, Projects, and Services

The purpose of IGFA, as set forth in the early bylaws, is: "to encourage the study of gamefishes for the sake of whatever pleasure, information, or benefit it may provide; to keep the sport of game fishing ethical, and to make its rules acceptable to the majority of anglers; to encourage this sport both as recreation and as a potential source of scientific data; to place such data at the disposal of as many human beings as possible; and to keep an attested and up-to-date chart of world record catches." The founding fathers of IGFA—including such sportfishing greats as Michael Lerner, Van Campen Heilner, Clive Firth, and Ernest Hemingway—obviously had foresight; the basic purposes they set forth have increased in importance through the years. Today's IGFA has not changed these goals; rather, it has brought them to the attention of the angling public, enlarged upon them, added to them, and adapted them to the current and increasing needs of the sport-fishing community.

## World Record Keeping

IGFA maintains and publishes world records for saltwater, freshwater, fly fishing catches, U.S. state freshwater records, and junior angler records, awarding certificates of recognition to each record holder. Recognized as the official keeper of world saltwater fishing records since 1939, IGFA entered the field of freshwater record keeping when *Field & Stream* transferred its sixty-eight years of records to the association in 1978.

## International Angling Regulations

The equipment and fishing regulations adopted worldwide are formulated, updated, and published by IGFA to promote sporting angling practices, to establish uniform rules for world-record catches, and to provide angling guidelines for use in tournaments and other group fishing activities.

## Fishing Hall of Fame and Museum

Provides the world's most comprehensive assemblage of sport-fishing information, exhibits, educational classes, fishing demonstrations, interactive displays, and virtual reality fishing. Walk in to the 60,000-square-foot museum's main entrance and you are seemingly immersed in an underwater world filled with fish. There are 170 species of gamefish that earned world-record status suspended overhead with informational plates on date of catch, angler, place, etc., displayed on the floor under each fish. The largest mount is Alfred Dean's 2,664-pound great white shark caught in Australia in 1959.

*The great hall of the IGFA museum.* PHOTO CREDIT: INTER-
NATIONAL GAME FISH ASSOCIATION.

### E. K. Harry Library of Fishes

Established in 1973 in response to the need for a permanent
repository for angling literature, history, films, art, photographs, and ar-
tifacts, this library houses the most comprehensive collection in the
world on gamefish, angling, and related subjects.

### Aiding Fishery Research

IGFA has continuously supported scientific tagging and other
data collection programs, and works closely with fishery biologists in
order to exchange information and relay to anglers the particular needs
and results of research and conservation efforts.

### Fishery Legislation

IGFA serves as consultant to administrative and legislative bodies in order to ensure that the angler is fairly represented in decisions
concerning the management of gamefish populations and other issues
which affect the future of recreational fishing.

## General Information

IGFA

300 Gulf Stream Way

Dania Beach, Florida 33004

(located next to Bass Pro Shops Outdoor World)

Phone: (954) 927-2628

Fax: (954) 924-4299

E-mail: hq@igfa.org

# Ted Williams's Career Highlights

## Career Statistics

1939:       As a rookie, hit .327 with 31 homers and 145 RBI.

1941:       Hit .406, a milestone not reached since, and also led AL with 37 homers, 145 bases on balls, and .735 slugging mark.

1942:       Won Triple Crown at .356 with 36 homers and 137 RBI.

1942–45:  Served in World War II.

1946:       Led Red Sox to the AL pennant, hitting .342 and winning the Most Valuable Player award.

1947:       Won second Triple Crown (.343-32-114)

1948:       Led the league in hitting, .369.

1949:       Won second MVP award; hitting .343 with 43 HRs, 159 RBIs.

1952–53: Served in Korean War as Marine fighter pilot.

1957:       Led the league in hitting at .388.

1958:       At age forty, hit .328 to become oldest batting champion ever.

1960:       Retired after hitting a home run in his final at bat.

1966:       Elected to Hall of Fame.

1969–71: Managed Washington Senators.

1972:       Managed Texas Rangers.

## Ted Williams Career Statistics

### REGULAR SEASON

| Year, | Team | G | AB | R | H | 2B | 3B | HR | RBI | Avg |
|-------|------|---|----|---|---|----|----|----|-----|-----|
| 1939, | Bos | 149 | 565 | 131 | 185 | 44 | 11 | 31 | 145 | .327 |
| 1940, | Bos | 144 | 561 | 134 | 193 | 43 | 14 | 23 | 113 | .344 |
| 1941, | Bos | 143 | 456 | 135 | 185 | 33 | 3 | 37 | 120 | .406 |
| 1942, | Bos | 150 | 522 | 141 | 186 | 34 | 5 | 36 | 137 | .356 |
| 1946, | Bos | 150 | 514 | 142 | 176 | 37 | 8 | 38 | 123 | .342 |
| 1947, | Bos | 156 | 528 | 125 | 181 | 40 | 9 | 32 | 114 | .343 |
| 1948, | Bos | 137 | 509 | 124 | 188 | 44 | 3 | 25 | 127 | .369 |
| 1949, | Bos | 155 | 566 | 150 | 194 | 39 | 3 | 43 | 159 | .343 |
| 1950, | Bos | 89 | 334 | 82 | 106 | 24 | 1 | 28 | 97 | .317 |
| 1951, | Bos | 148 | 531 | 109 | 169 | 28 | 4 | 30 | 126 | .318 |
| 1952, | Bos | 6 | 10 | 2 | 4 | 0 | 1 | 1 | 3 | .400 |
| 1953, | Bos | 37 | 91 | 17 | 37 | 6 | 0 | 13 | 34 | .407 |
| 1954, | Bos | 117 | 386 | 93 | 133 | 23 | 1 | 29 | 89 | .345 |
| 1955, | Bos | 98 | 320 | 77 | 114 | 21 | 3 | 28 | 83 | .356 |
| 1956, | Bos | 136 | 400 | 71 | 138 | 28 | 2 | 24 | 82 | .345 |
| 1957, | Bos | 132 | 420 | 96 | 163 | 28 | 1 | 38 | 87 | .388 |
| 1958, | Bos | 129 | 411 | 81 | 135 | 23 | 2 | 26 | 85 | .328 |
| 1959, | Bos | 103 | 272 | 32 | 69 | 15 | 0 | 10 | 43 | .254 |
| 1960, | Bos | 113 | 310 | 56 | 98 | 15 | 0 | 29 | 72 | .316 |
| **Totals** | | **2,292** | **7,706** | **1,798** | **2,654** | **525** | **71** | **521** | **1,839** | **.344** |

### WORLD SERIES

| Year, | Opp | G | AB | R | H | 2B | 3B | HR | RBI | Avg |
|-------|-----|---|----|---|---|----|----|----|-----|-----|
| 1946, | StL | 7 | 25 | 2 | 5 | 0 | 0 | 0 | 1 | .200 |

### MANAGERIAL RECORD

| Year, Team | G | W | L | Pct. | Stand |
|------------|---|---|---|------|-------|
| 1969, Was | 162 | 86 | 76 | .551 | 4 |
| 1970, Was | 162 | 70 | 92 | .432 | 6 |
| 1971, Was | 159 | 63 | 96 | .396 | 5 |
| 1972, Tex | 154 | 54 | 100 | .351 | 6 |
| **Totals** | **637** | **273** | **364** | **.429** | |

**Source:** *USA Today* (July 15, 2002)

# BIBLIOGRAPHY

## Chapter 1

Bailey, John. *Tales from the Riverbank*. London: BBC Books, 1997.

Bailey, John. *Trout at Ten Thousand Feet*. London: New Holland Publishers, 2001.

Kipling, Rudyard. "On Dry-Cow Fishing as a Fine Art" from *Classic Fishing Stories* by Nick Lyons. New York: Lyons Press, 2002.

## Chapter 2

Brown, Wesley. "Don Tyson Retires," *The Morning News*, October, 2001.

"Don Tyson," Arkansas Business.com, 2003.

"Don Tyson Retires as Senior Chairman of Tyson Foods." *The Morning News*: Business, October 23, 2001.

Quinn, Minrose. "Tyson Marketing the Ozarks Farm," Ozarks Watch, 1993.

Schaffner, Herbert A. *Saltwater Game Fish of North America*. New York: Michael Friedman Publishing, 1995.

Schwartz, Marvin. *Tyson: From Farm to Market* (University of Arkansas Press Series in Business History, Vol. 2). Fayetteville: The University of Arkansas Press, 1991. "The 2003 Top 10 World's Leading Food and Beverage Companies."

## Chapter 3

Boyle, Robert H. *Bass Boss*. Pintlala, Alabama: White Tail Press, 1999.

Circle, Homer. *Circle on Bass*. New York: Lyons & Burford, 1996.

Hiaasen, Carl. *Double Whammy*. New York: Warner Books, 1987.

Raines, Howell. *Fly Fishing Through the Midlife Crisis*. New York: William Morrow, 1993.

Rich, Bob. *Fish Fights: A Hall of Fame Quest*. New York: The Lyons Press, 2001.

Walton, Izaak. *The Compleat Angler*. New York: The Modern Library, 1998.

## Chapter 4

Berners, Dame Juliana. "Treatyse of Fysshynge wyth an Angle" from *The Booke of St. Albans*. New York: Charles Scribner's Sons, 1903.

Burton, Mallory. *Green River Virgins*. New York: The Lyons Press, 2000.

Dickens, Charles. *A Tale of Two Cities*. New York: Penguin, 2003.

Foggia, Lyla. *Reel Women*. New York: Three Rivers Press, 1995.

Louv, Richard. *Fly-Fishing for Sharks*. New York: Simon & Schuster, 2000.

## Chapter 5

Barrie, J. M. *Peter Pan*. London: Puffin Books, 1911.

## Chapter 6

Dillon, Patrick. *Lost at Sea*. New York: Touchstone, 1998.

Gay, Joel with Daryl Binney. "Commercial Fishing in Alaska," Vol. 24, No. 3 of *Alaska Geographic*. Anchorage: Alaska Geographic Society, 1997.

McCloskey, William. *Highliners*. Guilford, Connecticut: The Lyons Press, 1979.

Walker, Spike. *Working on the Edge*. New York: St. Martins Press, 1991.

Wylie, Philip. *Crunch and Des: Classic Stories of Saltwater Fishing*. Guilford, Connecticut: The Lyons Press, 1990.

## Chapter 7

Bush, George. *All the Best, George Bush: My Life and Other Writings.* New York: Touchstone, 1999.

## Chapter 10

*The American Heritage Dictionary.* William Morris, editor. New York: Houghton Mifflin Company, 1969, 1970, 1971, 1973.

Davy, Alfred G. *The Gilly: A Fly Fisher's Guide.* British Columbia Fly-fishers, 1985.

Fobes, Natalie. *Reaching Home: Pacific Salmon, Pacific People.* Anchorage, Alaska: Alaska Northwest Books, 1994.

Raymond, Steve. *Rivers of the Heart: A Fly Fishing Memoir.* Guilford, Connecticut: The Lyons Press, 1998.

## Chapter 11

Beaton, Red. "Baseball Great Ted Williams Dies," *USA Today,* July 22, 2002.

Colston, Chris. "A Living Legend but a Kid at Heart," *USA Today* Baseball Weekly, December 5, 2000.

Ellsworth, Tim (Baptist Press News Service). "Ted Williams Remains Who He Was," Crosswalk.com News Channel, September 1, 2002.

"Fishing World Mourns the Passing of a Legend," *International Angler,* September–October, 2002.

Halberstam, David. *The Teammates: A Portrait of Friendship.* New York: Hyperion, 2003.

Koenig, Bill. "From Hit Machine to War Hero, Williams Left Mark," *USA Today* Baseball Weekly, July 11, 2002.

Lear, Captain Dave. "Farewell to a Legend," *Sport Fishing,* November 2002.

Lund, Ted. "Ted Williams: A Fishing Hall of Famer," *The Redbone Journal,* Fall Edition, 2002.

Mererole, Mike. "There Goes The Greatest Hitter Who Ever Lived," ESPN.com, July 8, 2002.

Sandomir, Richard. "Williams Children Agree to Keep Father Frozen," *The New York Times*, September 21, 2002.

Smith, Brad. "Hall of Famer, Children Signed Cryogenic Pact," *The Tampa Tribune*, July 26, 2002.

Steinback, Robert L. "Ted Williams's Daughter Ends Fight over Will," *Miami Herald*, December 21, 2002.

Underwood, John and Ted Williams. *Ted Williams: Fishing the Big Three*. New York: Simon & Schuster, 1982.

Verducci, Tom. "What Really Happened to Ted Williams," *Sports Illustrated*, August 18, 2003.

Williams, Ted. "Fishing Holes USA," *Popular Mechanics*, September 1, 2002.